The Failure of the
Central European Bourgeoisie

The Failure of the Central European Bourgeoisie

New Perspectives on Hungarian History

Balázs A. Szelényi

palgrave
macmillan

THE FAILURE OF THE CENTRAL EUROPEAN BOURGEOISIE
© Balázs A. Szelényi, 2006.

First published in 2006 by
PALGRAVE MACMILLAN™
175 Fifth Avenue, New York, N.Y. 10010 and
Houndmills, Basingstoke, Hampshire, England RG21 6XS
Companies and representatives throughout the world.

PALGRAVE MACMILLAN is the global academic imprint of the Palgrave Macmillan division of St. Martin's Press, LLC and of Palgrave Macmillan Ltd. Macmillan® is a registered trademark in the United States, United Kingdom and other countries. Palgrave is a registered trademark in the European Union and other countries.

ISBN-13: 978–1–4039–7469–3
ISBN-10: 1–4039–7469–1

Library of Congress Cataloging-in-Publication Data

Szelényi, Balázs A.
    The failure of the Central European bourgeoisie: new perspectives on Hungarian History / Balázs A. Szelényi.
        p. cm.
    Includes bibliographical references and index.
    ISBN 1–4039–7469–1
    1. Cities and towns—Hungary—History. 2. Hungary—Economic conditions—History. 3. Middle class—Hungary—History.
    4. Feudalism—Hungary—History. I. Title

HT145.H8S964 2006
307.7609439—dc22   2006043172

A catalogue record for this book is available from the British Library.

Design by Newgen Imaging Systems (P) Ltd., Chennai, India.

First edition: October 2006

10 9 8 7 6 5 4 3 2 1

Printed in the United States of America.

To Kati

Contents

List of Figures

List of Maps

Acknowledgments

I would like to thank Perry Anderson, Éva H. Balázs, Ivan T. Berend, Robert Brenner, Ivan Chalupecký, Daniel Chirot, Péter Hanák, Gail Kligman, Zsigmond Pál Pach, Michael Mann, Iván Szelényi, and Gábor Vermes for their invaluable comments and suggestions. I am also very grateful to Katalin Szelényi, who contributed countless substantive comments and Lázár Fóti, who assisted in preparing the maps. Research for this text was conducted in the Hungarian National Archive, the Hungarian National Statistics Bureau, the Hungarian National Library, the Slovak National Archive, the Municipal and District Archive of Levoča (Slovakia), the Lyceum Library in Kežmarok (Slovakia), the Sibiu Branch of the National Archive of Romania, and the Brukenthal Library in Sibiu (Romania). Parts of the book have appeared in the *American Historical Review* and the *Austrian History Yearbook*, and I want to thank the American Historical Association and the Center for Austrian Studies for their permission to reprint parts of those articles here. I am also very grateful to the Hungarian National Museum for allowing me to include prints from their collection in this book.

I

Introduction

The classic textbook understanding of European Civilization emphasized the division of Europe into a progressive bourgeois West versus a stagnant noble-dominated East. According to this view, while from the sixteenth century onward the bourgeoisie in Western Europe could boast of one great victory after another, in the East, they experienced setback after setback. While in the West, the occidental city conquered the feudal countryside, bringing three-storied buildings, gas-lit cobblestone streets, tinkerers, shopkeepers, entrepreneurs, enterprises, coffee houses, banks, and newspapers, east of the Elbe the countryside defeated the cities and crushed the bourgeoisie. There were peasants, lords, grain, forests, bears, plenty of wine, and hoards of cattle, but few towns. In Western Europe towns remained strong and multiplied, contributing on the way to the expansion of capitalism and democracy. East of the Elbe, they lost their autonomy, leading to a stunted civil society. This macro-historical view of Eastern European urban development has undergone little modification since Francis L. Carsten's famous summation in the *English Historical Review* in 1947:

> The towns to the east of the Elbe, having been founded considerably later than those of western Europe, never equaled their strength and power; after a short and rapid rise, they were easily subjugated by the combined forces of nobles and princes. In none of the countries concerned, was there any longer a force which could have prevented the nobility from becoming the ruling order of society.[1]

Carsten understood the moment of the town's defeat during the fifteenth and sixteenth centuries as the decisive victory of autocracy and aristocracy over the bourgeoisie. "Medieval democracy had lost its battle, and the burghers of the towns did not raise their heads again until the nineteenth century, when once more they were defeated by the forces which had vanquished them four hundred years earlier."[2] In 1954, he further argued in his famous work *The Origins of Prussia*: "The decay of the eastern towns was a fact of fundamental importance for the course of German and of European history. It opened the way for the rise of the nobility, and it separated events in the east from those of the west: there the renewed rise of the towns and of the urban middle classes transformed state and society, but the east no longer participated in this development."[3] Jerome Blum concurred, noting in the *American Historical Review* in 1957: "The experience of Western Europe suggests that the enserfment of the peasantry and its corollary, the economic and political supremacy of the landed nobility, might have been avoided if the burghers of the East had been as powerful as their opposite numbers in Western Europe."[4]

Challenging Carsten's thesis of noble hegemony east of the Elbe, over the past two decades new scholarship on the micro-historical sociology of seventeenth century Brandenburg, Pomerania, and Mecklenburg, has seriously questioned the thesis that in the seventeenth century West European peasants became freer and those of the East less free. William Hagen, Edgar Melton, Jan Peters, and Heidi Wunder have significantly reformulated the historical understanding of peasant-lord relations and have raised formidable points as to whether the term "second serfdom" is appropriate at all in describing the socioeconomic system of seventeenth century East Central Europe.[5] As its most significant contribution, this new approach evidences less noble hegemony, and significantly more peasant autonomy than previously thought. As Hagen put it, "The villages were not suffocating under the weight of feudal rents and princely taxation."[6] Or as Edgar Melton noted, "In Brandenburg and East Prussia, it was neither the golden age for the Junkers nor a dark age for the peasants."[7]

Interestingly, however, despite the progress made in clarifying serf-lord relations under second serfdom, the place of towns during the manorial reaction has eluded theorists. Carsten's proposition—that towns east of the Elbe were crushed, the bourgeoisie beaten, and the nobles victorious—continues to be the conventional wisdom. A good illustration of this is William Hagen who, on one page resuscitates the life of peasants and writes of sixteenth-century Brandenburg that, "seigniorial authority collapsed over wide regions, if not everywhere," but on a previous page also noted: "The long sixteenth century did not smile on the towns of Brandenburg. The Junkers dealt them hard blows by setting up rival breweries in the countryside and bypassing their wholesalers in favor of merchants abroad, especially in Hamburg."[8] Or as R. J. W. Evans, a leading early modern historian of the Habsburg Monarchy wrote in his classic *The Making of the Habsburg Monarchy 1550–1700* (1979), as "external markets disappeared," and "purchasing power ebbed away . . . the boroughs sank behind their picturesque mouldering walls into a slumber . . . [and] the towns of Central Europe ceased to be bourgeois." With the exception of Prague, Vienna, and Breslau (today's Wrocław), Evans noted that towns were devoid of intellectual vitality, and "[t]he average towndweller became more or less a peasant tending his smallholding as well as plying his trade, unable to raise credit, and dreading the descent of the next imperial garrison."[9]

This work aims to make a contribution to the understanding of urban development during the transition from feudalism to capitalism by revising the notion that towns declined following the establishment of second serfdom. The argument proposed is that the struggle between towns and lords in early modern Europe was not about capitalism versus feudalism, progress versus stagnation, or the future versus the past. Instead, towns and lords coexisted within a system of shared values and norms. A careful look at urban evolution in Hungary during the sixteenth and seventeenth centuries does indicate that some towns were subjugated to noble rule in the sixteenth century, but that fact did not signify urban decline. Moreover, many towns evidence maturation when they should be failing. There were, of course, foolish self-destructive lords who, in fits of ill-tempered rage, acted irrationally. But in general, second serfdom fostered cooperation rather than antagonism. Naturally, some towns declined after they were subordinated, but interestingly that decline was the result of local conditions, such as a devastating fire, pestilence, or simply an invasion followed by decimation, and rarely a consequence of a feudal lord laboring to reduce them to poverty. Equally significant was that many towns remained free of noble control in the sixteenth and seventeenth centuries, yet these independent towns were not islands of "capitalism and modernity" surrounded by a backward feudal countryside. In brief, the occidental city existed in a symbiotic relationship with feudal lords in the West as well as the East, and the origins of the divergence between Eastern and Western Europe cannot be reduced to the noble subjugation of towns following the manorial reaction.

By evidencing urban development under second serfdom, the work will also reexamine Carsten's broader and more controversial claim that the rise of authoritarian regimes in nineteenth-twentieth century

Central Europe can be reduced to the failure of the bourgeoisie to maintain their autonomy in the late medieval period. Carsten, similar to many of his contemporaries, was convinced that the rise of Prussia, as well as the victory of National Socialism in 1933, was intricately tied to the unique road (Sonderweg) followed by Central European society. In developing a new model of the bourgeoisie in East Central Europe, the book focuses on the history of towns in the Hungarian Kingdom from their foundations in the early medieval period to the establishment of the Austro-Hungarian Monarchy in 1867. It is in agreement with the idea that the Central European bourgeoisie followed a different path, but not in the way Carsten had theorized. The work, accordingly, builds on the contributions of David Blackbourn, Geoff Eley, and Jürgen Kocka, whose critical revision of the Sonderweg thesis has thrown new light on the role and contribution of the bourgeoisie in modern Central European history.

The specific case of Hungary, most importantly, illustrates strong contradictions within the macro-historical understanding of urban and bourgeois development, and highlights the need to reexamine what happened to towns and urban dwellers from the onset of second serfdom to the end of the nineteenth century across Eastern Europe. At the moment, historians constructing meta-narratives on Eastern Europe and Hungary do not typically conduct research in municipal archives, while micro-historians do not engage in debates at the national or international comparative level. Macro-historians are often accused of teleology and working with false presumptions while micro-historians are weighed down by infinite details and rarely risk commenting on what is happening outside their small locale. This work does not aim, however, to dismiss either the macro or micro approaches. Instead, its goal is to realign the micro- and macro-perspectives, thereby creating a new narrative and expanding our knowledge and understanding of the transition from feudalism to capitalism in both Eastern and Western Europe.

The Traditional View of Urban Development East and West

In the West there is a long tradition of contrasting the "progressive" city with the "backward" countryside. As John Merrington wrote:

> The centrality of the town-country relation in the transition to capitalism in the West and more basically the equation of urbanism with capitalism and progress were already explicitly formulated in the earliest theories

of the origin of capitalism—those of 18th-century political economy. For the proponents of the new and revolutionary "conjectural" history of "civil society"—Smith, Steuart, Ferguson, Millar—the origins of the division of labour and the market in the "commercial stage" of civilization were to be sought in the separation of town and country. (The highland-lowland division in Scotland provided first-hand evidence).[10]

It was, however, only in the late nineteenth century that the famous Belgian urban historian Henri Pirenne (1862–1935) expanded upon the classic urban-country dichotomy as used by Adam Smith, and drew a direct line between urban growth in Western Europe and urban decline in Eastern Europe. Jerome Blum, Francis Carsten, Hans Rosenberg, Immanuel Wallerstein, and Max Weber were all deeply influenced by Pirenne's model. According to Pirenne's interpretation, in the early medieval period a life-death struggle unfolded between towns and feudalism in Western Europe. Towns promoted the division of labor, trade, and manufacturing; they were home to *homo-oeconomicus*, the agent of progress and the source of civil virtues like liberty, meritocracy, and democracy. Feudalism, diametrically opposed to the values of the occidental city, was a rural-based regime, closed, hierarchical, paternalistic, and oppressive. Instead of promoting development, it was a self-contained political economic system hostile to trade, commerce, and innovation. Pirenne maintained that between the ninth and tenth centuries feudalism strengthened in Western Europe, and civilization declined.[11] Europe's rise to world supremacy, therefore, began when the occidental city triumphed over feudalism. Towns contributed to the decline of feudalism because they were spaces of "free air"—*stadtluft macht frei*—where serfs escaped from overdemanding lords to win their liberty. Feudal lords, deprived of their laborers, were thereafter forced to make compromises, contributing, in turn, to the transformation of serfs into a class of free peasants. For Pirenne and those inspired by his view of history, the victory of the occidental city was the necessary prerequisite for the expansion of European trade in the sixteenth century. Modern capitalism, liberalism, republicanism, and constitutionalism would not have emerged if not introduced by the occidental city. The rise of Western Civilization could not have been possible if the city had not vanquished the feudal countryside in the late medieval period.[12] Oswald Spengler, following an exaggerated Pirennian position, claimed in his famous *Decline of the West*:

"It follows, however—and this is the most essential point of any—that we cannot comprehend political and economic history at all unless we realize that the city, with its gradual detachment and final bankrupting of the country, is the determining form to which the course of the higher sense of history generally conforms. World history is city history".[13]

Ironically, Pirenne further noted that while the victory of the occidental city in Western Europe led to the rise of individual liberties and progress, it was simultaneously responsible for the subjugation of towns by nobles and the decline of freedom in Eastern Europe. Accordingly, the causes of the seigniorial reaction were identical to the rise of the trans-Atlantic slave trade. Namely, as the occidental city grew, demand for raw materials and vital consumption goods escalated. Sugar was imported from the Caribbean, but grain and meat from Eastern Europe. To meet the demand for agricultural produce in the West, landlords in Eastern Europe consolidated their control over markets and labor, subjugating towns, enserfing free peasants, and emerging as the uncontested ruling estate. For Pirenne, landlords in Eastern Europe acted similar to plantation owners in the Americas. Both were agents ready to destroy human liberty for the profits of exporting in bulk to Western Europe. For these reasons Pirenne referred to the burghers and peasants of Eastern Europe as "white slaves," victims of the same world capitalist order that led to the mass enslavement of Blacks in Africa. Pirenne wrote:

> The descendants of the free colonists [German immigrants east] of the thirteenth century were systematically deprived of their land and reduced to the position of personal serfs (*Leibeigene*). The wholesale exploitation of estates absorbed their holdings and reduced them to a servile condition, which so closely approximated to that of slavery that it was permissible to sell the person of the serf independently of the soil. From the middle of the sixteenth century the whole of the region to the east of the Elbe and the Sudeten mountains became covered with *Rittergüter* exploited by *Junkers*, who may be compared, as regards the degree of humanity displayed in their treatment of their white slaves, with the planters of the West Indies. The negro in the New World, and the German peasant in the Old World, were the most typical victims of modern capitalism, and they both had to wait until the nineteenth century for their enfranchisement. This is a fact which must never be forgotten when considering the modern history of Germany and Austria. The enslavement of the peasantry to his noble master explains many things.[14]

In Hungarian historiography the Pirennian explanation of the seigniorial reaction has been widely accepted.[15] It's most famous and influential proponent was Zsigmond Pál Pach. Yet while agreeing with Pirenne that the prime mover of modern history was the development and expansion of international trade, Pach developed a more nuanced explanation of the Hungarian experience. Pach maintained that Hungarian urban development accelerated in the thirteenth and fourteenth centuries, when trade with the Levant was especially vibrant and strong. Like Carsten, Pach argued that up to the mid-fifteenth century, Hungary and the rest of East Central Europe were catching up with the West. From the fourteenth to the mid-fifteenth century, towns with charters were multiplying, peasants were winning their freedom, and seigniorial control over land and labor was waning. Furthermore, peasants were taking their produce directly to the market with increasing frequency, and in the small market towns a layer of enterprising small farmers was emerging, contributing to growing rural social stratification. However, Pach argues that from the second half of the fifteenth century, a new trend set in that counteracted the transformation of peasant entrepreneurs into a class of agricultural capitalists, and instead noble rule was reasserted. The essence of the new trend was summarized by Pach in economic terms as "the growing participation of the nobility in commerce and, subsequently, in the actual production of commercial goods."[16] For Pach, therefore, the second half of the fifteenth century is the genesis of the break between East and West, because "while the disintegration of the medieval order, the rise of capitalist relations, began and proceeded in several Western European countries . . . the feudal system survived, and even consolidated in several respects, in the countries of mid-Eastern Europe, and the rule of late feudalism was prolonged for centuries."[17]

Pirenne and Pach share the belief that larger historical trends are intricately tied to international trade routes. In the fourteenth century, for instance, Pach claimed that Hungary prospered from its contact with the Levantine trade, based essentially on the import of luxury goods such as spices, silk, dyes, jewelry that were subsequently sold in the privileged market towns to the wealthy nobles, patricians, abbots, and bishops. Pach further argued that the course of Eastern European history underwent a profound transformation with the decline of Levantine trade and the rise of commerce with Western Europe, bringing a shift from the traditional trade in luxury goods to the export of bulk agricultural produce. As Pach summarized, "This role of East Central Europe in international trade (exporting foodstuffs and importing industrial products) limited and hindered industrial-urban growth in the countries involved, where the level was anyway below that of Western Europe in this respect from the beginning of the period."[18]

Why did landlords tap into agricultural sales to the West? Pach was in agreement with Pirenne on this point. Namely, he believed that the favorable situation for agricultural exports, under the influence of the price revolution, stimulated the countries of East-Central Europe to increase agricultural market production. Lords in Eastern Europe, therefore, became eager to participate in exporting to the West because of the price revolution caused by the late medieval demographic drop, increasing the prices of agricultural products to levels that exceeded those of industrial articles. A gap thereafter was created—called the price scissors—between the relative prices of industrial versus agricultural goods. Pach noted three stages in the growing participation of nobles in commerce: "First, they exploited their privileged right to sell wine. Second, they took an increasingly active part (especially the big landowners and the lesser nobility) in the trade in livestock. Third, they developed their trade in wheat and even their own wheat production."[19]

Following these stages, the feudal land tenure system survived and became the dominant feature of the sociopolitical system of East Central Europe. The peasants reacted to their growing oppression by staging a number of formidable revolts, the most serious and famous one led by György Dózsa. However, at each turn, the nobles leading the counteroffensive were able to outmaneuver the peasant resistance with their superior political coordination. Finally, in 1514 the Parliament agreed to laws proposed by Emmerich Verbőczi (sometimes spelled Werbőczi), laying the foundation for the legal imposition of second serfdom. Free peasants became serfs, and free towns were transformed into the *Gutsherrschaft* (estate) of lords.

Challenging the Traditional View

The argument proposed in this work is that urban development and feudalism are not mutually exclusive. Importantly, this was true for Eastern as well as Western Europe during feudalism. Two points will be stressed. On the one hand, towns often lived in a symbiotic relationship with lords, while on the other hand it is clear that the main actors in the towns, namely merchants and artisans, were not the natural allies of serfs. It is noteworthy that evidence even from the Low Countries during the tenth century shows urban growth when Pirenne had predicted decline. Adriaan Verhulst highlighted a number of reasons why Pirenne was wrong. Namely, while Mediterranean trade declined following the Arab conquests, towns in the Low Countries changed to different sources of exchange; such as local and up the river trade. Towns also thrived in the vicinity of monasteries and other ecclesiastic seats. But most importantly, towns grew if they learnt how to trade with the new castle lords of feudalism. Verhulst's detailed study of the topography of Antwerp, Ghent, and Bruges demonstrates that new trading posts emerged within these urban centers in the tenth century, a fact Pirenne did not know. Verhulst writes:

> These new *portus* of the tenth century, in contrast to the Carolingian settlements, were furnished with market-places and owed their development, if not their origin, primarily to local trade with the non-merchant population living within the walls of the new fortifications beside their respective *portus* . . . This sort of fortification was seldom originally built as a defense against the Vikings. Its construction was rather a manifestation of the general spread of fortifications (the "incastellamento") which initiated the feudal period all over Europe. The merchants sought its proximity not for military protection, but for trading possibilities. The castrum therefore was not, as Pirenne put it, a passive element to which towns could become attached, but an active economic factor of attraction.[20]

The symbiotic relationship of towns and feudalism was, of course, a central point in the 1950s debates within English Marxism. As A.B. Hibbert bluntly put it in his 1953 article in *Past and Present*: "There is the simple fact that whatever area and whatever century we may choose to take as being most typically 'feudal' there is still trade and there are still merchants. Feudalism could never dispense with merchants. The very structure, technical level and economic habits of society always made some local and long-distance trade necessary."[21]

The most significant contribution in the debates on the transition from feudalism to capitalism and the origins of capitalism since the 1970s was made by Robert Brenner. Following in the tradition of Maurice Dobb and Rodney Hilton, Brenner is critical of the Pirennian notion that towns were the agents corroding serfdom in the West because: "[the] actual mechanism through which the towns had their reputedly dissolving effects on landlord control over the peasantry in Western Europe have still to be precisely specified." Furthermore, "the viability of the towns as a potential alternative for the mass of unfree peasantry must [also] be called into question simply in terms of their gross demographic weight . . . . It is indeed far from obvious that the medieval towns housed the 'natural' allies of the unfree peasantry. For many reasons the urban patriciate would tend to align themselves with the nobility against the peasantry." In sum, "the historical record of urban support for the aspirations to freedom of the medieval European peasantry is not impressive."[22]

Instead of focusing on towns, Brenner argues that change both east and west of the Elbe issued from class struggle between peasants and lords. Towns are understood, with their artisan guilds and privileged merchant elite, as intricately combined with the system of feudalism, and while towns do make a difference, they are not prime movers of change. Or in other words, it was not the "weakness of towns" but the "weakness of the peasantry" in the East to organize and defend themselves which accounts for the success of the seigniorial reaction and the imposition of second serfdom. As Brenner summarized:

> [E]conomic backwardness in Eastern Europe cannot be regarded as economically determined, arising from "dependence" upon trade in primary products to the West, as is sometimes asserted. Indeed, it would be more correct to state that dependence upon grain export was a result of backwardness; of the failure of the home market—the terribly reduced purchasing power of the mass of the population—which was the result of the dismal productivity and vastly unequal distribution of income in agriculture rooted, in the last analysis in the class structure of serfdom.[23]

In other words, towns are not islands separate from the sea of feudalism. The merchants in the towns were dependent on the demand by lords for luxury products, and instead of working to establish free market economies, were interested in hoarding staple rights. Furthermore, artisans had conflicting interests with cheap rural labor and more often than not tried to limit immigration into towns by strengthening guilds. Towns, therefore, did not try to undermine feudalism, but were in fact privileged members of the feudal club. Or, as Rodney Hilton wrote in 1952, "modern capitalism derived its initial impetus from the English textile industry and does not descend directly from the principal medieval centers. Its foundations were laid in the rural domestic industry which had fled from the traditional urban centers."[24] And as Maurice Dobb noted, "It was precisely in the backward north and west of England that serfdom in the direct labour services disappeared earliest, and in the more advanced south-east, with its town markets and trade routes, that labour services were more stubborn in their survival."[25]

Several questions remain unanswered in light of the conclusions reached by the debates in English Marxism concerning the role of towns in the transition from feudalism to capitalism: If the occidental city was not the single and most important agent corroding feudalism in the West, is it logical to claim a natural correlation between the rise of second serfdom and urban decay in the East? If towns and feudal lords were symbiotic partners in the West, instead of antagonistic forces in a life-death struggle as Pirenne had maintained, why would landlords in Eastern Europe want to subjugate towns and reduce them to poverty in their attempts to restrengthen feudalism? Instead of assuming urban decline under second serfdom, is it not possible that urban development and feudalism coexisted in Eastern Europe in the sixteenth and seventeenth centuries?

By revising the notion of urban decline in sixteenth-seventeenth century Hungary, the work also questions the assumption that Central and East Central Europe's inability to produce stable liberal democratic regimes in the nineteenth and twentieth centuries can be reduced to the victory of the nobility over towns during the seigniorial reaction. The work is especially critical toward historians such as Carsten, Blum, and Rosenberg, who idealized the supposed bourgeois West and exaggerated the hegemony of the nobility east of the Elbe. The argument proposed is that the struggle between towns and lords in early modern Europe was not about capitalism versus feudalism, progress versus stagnation, or democracy versus authoritarianism. Instead, towns and lords coexisted within a system of shared values and norms. Therefore, Carsten's theory that the rise of authoritarian regimes in the modern period in Central Europe can be reduced to the late medieval subjugation of towns by the nobility and the subsequent failure of the bourgeoisie must be revised.

This book traces the history of towns in the Hungarian Kingdom from their foundations in the early medieval period to the establishment of the Austro-Hungarian Monarchy in 1867. In the first part (comprising chapters 2 and 3), the study focuses on the evolution of towns from the thirteenth century through the establishment of second serfdom in 1514, to the end of the seventeenth century and the Thököly and Rákóczi insurrections. In this part it will be argued that contrary to common wisdom, towns grew after the victory of the manorial reaction. There is no contradiction between urban growth and feudalism; towns are not isolated islands of secular rationality surrounded by an ocean of agrarian superstition and irrational mysticism. Lords can and do dominate towns, but this in itself is not a problem.

Lords will allow towns to develop as long as they do not attempt to undermine feudalism, and many towns were able to maintain their autocephalous existence. It is important to remember that towns in the early modern period were not driven by the capitalist spirit of striving to establish self-sustained growth, nor were they trying to increase their population ad infinitum. Merchants in the towns wanted to make a profit, and artisans were interested in new technologies to improve production, but towns were not spaces where proto-capitalist forms were waiting to hatch. Towns were an intricate part of the closed and paternalistic, privileged and exclusive system of feudalism. The internal self-justification and logic of development for towns under feudalism was, therefore, far different than under capitalism.

At the same time, while towns and lords under the feudal political economy lived in a symbiotic relationship, their relationship was by no means always peaceful. Towns and lords were privileged corporate members of the feudal political economy, and each side sought to hoard royal monopolies, often at the expense of the other. There are numerous instances when this conflict led to bloodshed. Under feudalism towns would battle lords, lords other lords, and towns would wage wars against other towns, but these feuds were never intended to undermine feudalism. They were struggles over monopolies and privileges. Furthermore, in Hungary and Eastern Europe in general, there was a noteworthy ethnic component to the urban-country divide. Feudalism, it must be stressed, was introduced late and from above in Hungary, and in contrast to the West, developed its own idiosyncrasies. Hungarian feudalism was far more fragmented along ethnic lines than its western counterpart and, besides the classic division of those who work, those who pray, and those who fight, an eastern caste-like division of society was superimposed. The Germans, Romanians, Magyars, Slovaks, Ruthenians, and Roma, as well as the Jews, Turks, Armenians, Greeks, Poles, Croats, and Serbs, to name some of the larger groups, each had a niche in society. Under Hungarian feudalism, therefore, the classic occidental feudal division of society mirrored ethnic-linguistic and religious differences. And what is most relevant for this study is that many towns were German-dominated. In the Uplands and Transylvania there were towns with a Magyar majority, like Košice (Kaschau/Kassa), Cluj-Napoca (Klausenburg/Kolozsvár), and Alba Iulia (Weissenberg/Gyulafehérvár), but out of the thirty plus royal free towns in the seventeenth century, only seven had a Magyar-speaking majority.[26] This special ethnic-exclusive character of towns reinforced the fact that towns were not the spaces where serfs could escape from bondage to freedom. Towns instead were often spaces of "free air" for the already privileged German burghers.

In chapters 4 and 5 the book shifts the focus from a discussion of towns within the system of second serfdom to analyzing the relationship between towns and the newly emerging Habsburg absolutist state from the late seventeenth century to the rule of Maria Theresa (1740–1780) and Joseph II (1780–1790). These chapters draw attention to the fact that while the bourgeoisie was able to live in a symbiotic relationship with lords and princes during late feudalism, the rise of the absolutist state in the eighteenth century radically altered the balance of the social relations of power in the kingdom. Adding to the tension between town and state were the contradictory ways in which Habsburg consolidation was carried out over the kingdom after the Ottoman expulsion. In 1699 the Treaty of Karlowitz was signed, representing the end of Ottoman rule, as well as Hungary's full incorporation into the Habsburg Empire. At one level, in opposition to the sixteenth and seventeenth centuries when Hungary was divided and confronted by foreign invasion, civil wars, religious turmoil and stagnation, the eighteenth century represented a period of peace, stability, and economic expansion. The number of royal free towns increased from 44 to 61 between 1720 and 1787, and the total urban population during the same period rose from an estimated 171,126 to 484,659. At another level, however, the eighteenth century was detrimental for urban growth. Under Habsburg rule, urbanization in the Carpathian Basin was limited to those towns that tapped into the booming agricultural export market. A division of labor was emerging in the Empire, and while Bohemia's industry was favored, unfair taxes and discriminatory tariffs devastated manufacturing and mining towns of the Uplands and Transylvania. Equally demanding was that Habsburg consolidation was built on renewing practices of the Counter Reformation. Far less violent than in previous centuries, Lutherans, and especially wealthy Lutherans, were being pushed out of the kingdom. Prohibited from holding municipal government positions, Protestant schools became impoverished, and ministers harassed. Unable to compete on the economic front because of unjust tariff laws, as well as persecuted because of their religious beliefs, a significant number fled Hungary for Prussia, Holland, and some to America.

Persecution and unfair economic competition, therefore, stunted urban development in towns that did not become agricultural exporters. However, it was precisely from the elite burgher families suffering most under Habsburg consolidation that champions of Enlightenment reform emerged. Frustrated on the economic front and religiously discriminated on the cultural, within virtually all of the major royal free towns of the Uplands and Transylvania arose a small radical layer of Westernizers. The decades between 1760 and 1790 represented, therefore, the birth of Hungary's modern bourgeoisie. It was at this moment that the Cultural Revolution taking place in France and at elite German Universities filtered into the isolated towns of East Central Europe, forever altering the identity of the German burghers living in them; nothing short of the bourgeoisiefication of traditional German burgher culture happened. Inspired and enterprising burghers established Masonic Lodges, labored to modernize the curricula of the Lyceums, and spread the teachings of Rousseau, Voltaire, Wolff, Locke, and many others to the Magyar nobility and aristocracy. The peak of this period of bourgeois self-affirmation was the short rule of Joseph II (1780–1790) and Leopold II (1790–1792), a brief 12 years. It was brought to a sudden halt following the untimely death of Leopold II in 1792, as the rise of Metternich, the defeat of Napoleon, and the establishment of the Holy Alliance ushered in the long rule of the Counter Revolution, institutional features of which remained an intricate part of the Habsburg system until 1848.

In chapter 6, the focus of the book becomes the history of the Hungarian bourgeoisie in the nineteenth century. As previously noted, Francis Carsten maintained that the Central and Eastern European bourgeoisie, after being subordinated to the nobility following the manorial reaction, raised its head briefly in the nineteenth century, "when once more they were defeated by the forces which had vanquished them four hundred years earlier."[27] In writing these lines, Cartsen was in agreement with a large body of literature arguing that the problems of Central and Eastern European society in the twentieth century were reducible to the "feudalization" of the bourgeoisie. According to this view, the West was home to liberal democratic capitalism, because towns remained autonomous and strong, and the bourgeoisie since the French Revolution seized state-power. The East, concurrently, produced totalitarian regimes, state-capitalism, National Socialism, and Communism, because the bourgeoisie was defeated and subordinated to the nobility. Carsten understood the defeat of the Hungarian and German Revolutions of 1848, the Austro-Hungarian Compromise of 1867, and the unification of Germany by

Prussia in 1871 as reaffirming his theory that stunted urbanization in the late medieval period produced stunted bourgeois development and an aristocratic hegemony in the modern period.

In sharp contrast to the feudalization thesis, chapter 6 follows the new view of Central European bourgeois development advanced by Geoff Eley, David Blackbourn, and Jürgen Kocka. Aspects of the feudalization thesis are kept, but there is strong disagreement with the idealized dichotomy of a bourgeois West versus a noble East. In place of the old dichotomy, this work argues that the bourgeoisie was a radical and progressive force for a relatively short period in European history. Under feudalism, towns and nobles were not caught in a life-death struggle as is often maintained. It is true that during the eighteenth century, there was a short period when the bourgeoisie did become radical and championed democratic reform and liberty, but that came to an end as soon as industrialization began. Chapter 6 shows that following the industrialization of Hungary, and modern nation-state building, the bourgeoisie experienced a golden age of prosperity. It did not play a revolutionary role after 1848, but neither did its Western European counterpart. Throughout Europe after 1848, the rise of industrial capital had replaced agrarian interests as the dominant force. But this did not entail the end of the former ruling class. The bourgeoisie and former lords again formed a common bond—as under feudalism—and their mutual concern became keeping their elite class position intact while containing the newly emergent working class, as well as disgruntled peasantry. This was a Europe-wide phenomenon, and had nothing to do with feudalization. As Ivan T. Berend described the Central European bourgeoisie after 1848: "The burgher middle class, which had been in the vanguard of democratic nationalism in earlier decades, now shifted to the conservative camp. Frightened by the awakened masses, the burghers ceased struggling against the ruling noble elite. They wanted rule, and turned against the dissatisfied, often organized and violent workers and peasants."[28]

By revisiting and revising the notion of a failed bourgeoisie, new light is thrown on the history of towns in East Central Europe. In criticizing Carsten's view that the subjugation of towns by the nobility in the medieval period led to the failure of the bourgeoisie in East Central Europe to establish liberal capitalist democratic regimes, this work does not want to oppose the study of *long durée* processes as critical in understanding the historical dialectic. Instead, in criticizing the "urban subjugation thesis," the goal is to show that there is a tendency in the historical scholarship on the transition from feudalism to capitalism to idealize the modernizing and progressive role of towns, and underestimate how towns and the bourgeoisie coexisted with nobles under feudalism. As is evident in the study of economic history, towns and the bourgeoisie are far more likely to ally with landlords and nobles than with oppressed peasants. Only in the most exceptional circumstances does the bourgeoisie stand up and defend the values of democracy, equality, and meritocracy, and this holds true for both Western as well as Eastern Europe.

2

Urban Development in the Hungarian Kingdom between the Thirteenth and Sixteenth Centuries

In the Hungarian Kingdom, similar to the rest of Eastern Europe, the growth of towns is dated to the period between the thirteenth and fourteenth centuries. In 1100 Kremica (Kremnitz/Körmöcbánya), in 1141 Skalica (Skalitz/Szakolcza), and in 1200 Szeged (Szegedin) were granted royal privileges, but real urban growth was more characteristic of the first half of the thirteenth century. In 1225 Banská Bystrica (Neusohl/Besztercebánya), in 1238 Trnava (Tyrnau/Nagyszombat), in 1242 Levoča (Leutschau/Lőcse), and in 1244 Buda, Banská Štiavnica (Schemnitz/Selmecbánya), and Krupina (Karpfen/Korpona) became royal free towns. In 1291 both Bratislava (Pressburg/Pozsony) and Pest were elevated to royal free standing, but between 1250 and 1320 fewer towns won royal charters. Starting in 1324, another explosion occurred in the granting of royal privileges to towns, when Bardejov (Bartfeld/Bártfa), Prešov (Preschau/Eperjes), Sopron (Ödenburg), Zvolen (Altsohl/Zólyom), Nová Baňa (Königsberg/Újbánya), and Baia Mare (Neustadt/Nagybánya) were raised to royal free standing. By the end of the fifteenth century there were approximately 30 royal free towns, 20 royal mining towns, and over 600 larger settlements that had been granted franchise. The largest town was Buda with an estimated population between 12,000 and 15,000, followed by Košice (Kaschau/Kassa) and Pest with 7,000 to 8,000 (Szeged's population reached this level at the start of the sixteenth century), followed by Bratislava, Sopron, Cluj (Klausenberg/Kolozsvár), Trnava, Bardejov, and many of the royal free towns of Transylvania, with approximately 3,500–5,000 urban dwellers. At the lower end of the spectrum were the small royal free towns with a population of only 2,500–3,500, like Levoča, Prešov (Preschau, Eperjes), Kežmarok (Käsmarkt/Késmárk), and numerous mining towns.[1]

By the end of the fifteenth century urban development had made progress in the Hungarian Kingdom, and some towns reached the size of Ravensburg, Heidelberg, Freiburg, Mainz, and Dresden. The largest towns were almost as large as Frankfurt am Main, Wrocław (Breslau), Zürich, and Ypern, with estimated urban populations of 10,000. But no Hungarian town at the end of the fifteenth century reached the size of Prague with an estimated population of 30,000, nor Nürnberg which in 1438 was 22,800 strong, Strassburg with 20,000, and Lübeck with 18,000 urban dwellers. Hungarian urbanization was on the ascent between the thirteenth and fifteenth centuries, but nevertheless towns remained small in comparison to their larger northwestern and southwestern counterparts, especially those of Flanders and the Mediterranean, where towns had grown to over 40,000 and some as large as 50,000.[2]

Several overlapping factors contributed to rapid urbanization between the thirteenth and fifteenth centuries. Royal free towns developed because of a combination of factors, including an increase in Levantine trade and the direct intervention of the kings, who were prompted into courting German immigrants from the Holy Roman Empire by their interest in developing the metallurgical and manufacturing potential of the kingdom. Other towns, which experienced growth despite their failure to receive royal free privileges, grew because the Roman Catholic Church solidified its position and expanded, building more churches and monasteries (Esztergom and Eger are noteworthy examples here). Last but not least, the hurried castle building drive following the Mongol invasion also contributed to urbanization, and many villages were granted franchise by their castle lords.[3]

An interesting geographical distribution characterized the emergence of various types of towns in the Hungarian Kingdom. The occidental city in the classic sense of the term developed almost exclusively at the foot of the Carpathian Mountain range—in the Hungarian Uplands (today's Slovakia) and the eastern territory (Transylvania)—while the more populated Carpathian basin witnessed a completely different type of urban evolution. Two complementary explanations can account for this discrepancy. First, the mountain regions were rich in ores—notably, silver and gold—and salt, giving way to one of the most important propellers of early urban development: mining. The second and equally significant factor was that the rocky and forested nature of the mountain topography hindered the manorial system from expanding during the early medieval period. Consequently, in the first half of the thirteenth century the northern and southeastern territories remained untouched by the feudal political economy, maintaining scattered Slavic, Magyar, and Romanian settlements, but few signs of state building, lordly castles, or towns. While the crown claimed these lands as its own, royal authority was more conceived than real. Following the shock of the Mongol invasions in the first half of the thirteenth century, however, the Hungarian King Béla IV felt strong pressure to increase the income of the crown's last remaining untouched lands. Béla IV aggressively courted and settled German miners, artisans, and traders and granted generous estates to faithful followers. Of the thirty royal free towns and the over twenty royal mining towns that came into existence by the end of the fifteenth century, the majority were built near the Carpathian mountain range, imported from the Holy Roman Empire, and inhabited by German and Italian burghers. Towns with charters that followed the traditions of the occidental urban heritage were therefore exclusively established on royal land. Naturally, the crown's domain also included large tracks of land in the Carpathian basin, where Buda and Pest are classic examples of urban growth. However, the rapid expansion of the manorial system in the basin during the eleventh and twelfth centuries also meant that land tended to be held and divided among feudal lords. Few settlements found on lords' demesne were able to rise to the status of royal free towns on the plains, and they were granted those charters only in the late seventeenth and mid-eighteenth centuries, such as Debrecen, Subotika (Maria Theresiopolis/Szabadka), Novi Sad (Neusatz/Újvidék), and Sombor (Schomburg/Zombor).

Concurrent to state-sponsored urbanization, a unique type of urban development was also underway on the estates of large landlords in the Carpathian basin. Between the thirteenth and fifteenth centuries, over 300 villages won franchise from their castle lords and the largest among them emerged as *mezővárosok* (agricultural towns). Unlike the transplanted towns on the royal land, *mezővárosok* came into existence by market forces (i.e., they were not imported from the West but bought their freedom from their lords), and the urban dwellers were ethnically Magyar as opposed to the predominantly German and to a lesser degree Italian character of the royal free towns. Agrarian towns were susceptible to lordly subjugation because of their origins as serf-villages, and even after they were granted franchise they almost invariably had an overlord. Nevertheless, Hungarian historians and social scientists consider *mezővárosok* the organic and authentic Magyar towns, because they won their franchise through grass roots struggle against their feudal lords, they produced for an export market and, most importantly, they "usurped the right of illegitimate authority;" meaning that unlike the ethnically exclusive "imported" royal free towns of the mountain region, the enfranchised large villages were places of free air where peasants, commoners, and vagabonds could settle in their escape from overdemanding and oppressive lords. Moreover, some Hungarian historians see the predominantly German-speaking royal free towns as artificial attempts at urbanization, which, throughout their history, upheld the feudal order and never produced a progressive bourgeoisie. *Mezővárosok*, by contrast, are commonly considered the source of a uniquely Magyar antifeudal entrepreneurial Calvinist middle-class.[4]

From the second half of the fifteenth century, the growth of urban autonomy and prosperity in the Hungarian Kingdom experienced a number of reverses. The problem at an important level is related to the inability of the crown to balance its budget. A similar question confronted the Hungarian crown during the late medieval period. However, at the turn of the fourteenth century, emerging out of a civil war set off by a bloody interregnum struggle, the newly elected Charles of Anjou (king of Hungary 1307–1342) succeeded in stabilizing state finances and freeing the crown from demanding oligarchs. Charles of Anjou, among other important initiatives, helped increase the inflow of taxes to the treasury by supporting urban development. He expanded gold and salt mining in the Transylvanian towns and gold mining towns in Transylvania like Baia Sprie (Mittelstadt/Felsőbánya), Baia Mare (Neustadt/Nagybánya), as well as Kremnica (Kremnitz/Körmöcbánya), and Smolník (Schmölnitz/ Szomolnok) in the Uplands. Charles also granted new and strengthened old privileges to other towns. Under his rule the Upland towns of Bardejov (Bartfeld/Bártfa), Prešov (Preschau/Eperjes), Košice (Kaschau/Kassa), Žilina (Zsilina/Zsolna), Sabinov (Zeben/Kis-Szeben), Ružomberok (Rosenberg/Rózsahegy), and Martin (Túrószentmárton), and the Transylvanian towns of Cluj-Napoca (Klausenburg/Kolozsvár), Brașov (Kronstadt/Brassó), Bistrița (Bistritz/Beszterce), Sighetu Marmației (Siget/Máramarossziget), and far eastern towns in what today is Western Ukraine such as Viskove (Visk), Huszt, and Tyacsiv (Técső) developed rapidly. Some older royal free towns like Levoča (Leutschau/Lőcse), Komárom (Komorn/Komárno),

21

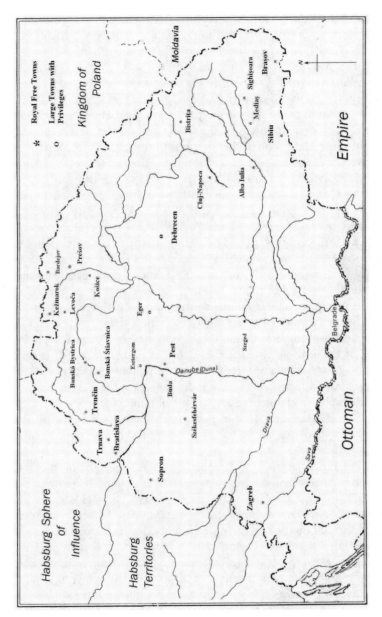

Map 2.1 Map of towns in the Hungarian Kingdom in the late fifteenth century.

Banská Bystrica (Neusohl/Besztercebánya), Banská Štiavnica (Schemnitz/Selmecbánya), Bratislava (Pressburg/Pozsony), Sopron (Ödenburg), Kőszeg (Günst), and Buda (Ofen) also experienced growth.

Charles Anjou realized early that for the state to be independent and strong, it needed the financial backing of towns. More developed towns increased the volume of trade and the prince's affluence. Urban growth under Charles Anjou was, therefore, closely related to the issuance of charters to towns: in the form of mining or market monopolies. In this respect, one of the important initiatives he introduced to improve state finances was to develop the inflow of taxes by expanding and regulating international and domestic trade. Historically, commerce in Europe during the medieval period was governed by the system of *jus stapuli* (staple rights), granting privileged towns a monopoly over trade. Each town strove to secure the greatest possible number of staple rights, thereby creating their private monopolies of trade. Some of the most developed staple rights in the early thirteenth century were enjoyed by Venice, Cologne, and Vienna, privileges that coerced all foreign merchants traveling near the cities to stop and put their goods up for sale from one to four weeks. If the merchants did not stop and attempted to travel by the cities, their goods could be confiscated and the merchants fined.[5] Sometimes *jus stapuli* included all goods being transported for sale, and at other times only certain specified goods. As Henri Pirenne wrote, "in Flanders, Bruges became the distribution center for merchandise entering the Zwyn, and the general staple for woolen goods. Ghent obtained for itself the staple for grain. In Brabant, Mechlin became the staple for salt and fish, while in Holland the staple for all goods going by the river went to Dordrecht."[6]

In the Hungarian Kingdom, under Charles Anjou, the most elaborate and inflated privileges were granted to only a select few towns, like Levoča, Košice (Kaschau/Kassa), Buda, Bratislava, Sibiu (Hermannstadt/Nagyszeben), to name some of the important ones. Traders were often required to put up for sale their merchandise for up to four weeks and to buy all their food and drink within the town walls. This latter clause of the privilege, especially as it forbade merchants from bringing their own food into the town, meant a great profit for the town-dwellers.[7] There were many different types of Staple Rights granted, of course, and every royal free town, and many of the smaller privileged urban settlements, enjoyed some sort of charter and *jus stapuli*. Towns after all provided safety and a market, and merchants had to pay for these things. Despite coercion and monopolies, therefore, the institution of staple rights produced a stable and calculable international network of trade in late thirteenth- and early fourteenth-century Europe, and significantly advanced commerce in Hungary.

The reforms of Charles Anjou brought short-term stability to state finances in the first half of the fourteenth century. However, the new round of revenue problems caused by the increasing cost of military expenditure and leisurely consumption at court under Sigismund (1387–1437) revealed the limitations and contradictions of the existing system. From the time of Sigismund and continuing under any ruler who attempted to centralize state power, up to and including Matthias Corvinus, the court combated the new round of revenue problems by mortgaging away a sizable part of the royal land and selling mining and market monopolies with increasing frequency. The proliferation of new charters, titles, and privileges in circulation naturally gave the impression of urban growth, and the actual number of towns possessing "royal free standing" and *jus stapuli* grew almost continuously from the rule of Sigismund to Matthias; in 1412 Trenčin (Trenschin/Trencsén), in 1468 Banská Belá (Dilln/Bélabánya), and in 1483 Senj (Zengg) were granted royal free privileges. However, the inflation of royal charters in the long run meant that power was increasingly falling into the hands of a new aristocracy in the countryside and the new elite called the Ringbürgers in the towns. This in turn would further enlarge the crown's budgetary deficit, leading to the issuance of more privileges and charters.

In the most immediate sense, the new royal revenue crisis was felt most directly by smaller towns and villages. Under the rule of Sigismund, who was caught up in costly wars and rising luxury spending at court, the crown began to mortgage royal enfranchised villages to nobles on a scale previously unknown.[8] Free and privileged royal villages like Starý Tekov (Bars/Óbars) and Spišský Štvrtok (Donnersmarkt/ Csütörtökhely) in 1388, Tepličany (Tapolcsány) in 1389, Csepreg (Tschapring) and Sárvár in 1390, Sárospatak, and Szina in 1392, Kőszeg (Güns) in 1393, Körmend in 1396, and Şaeş (Schaas/Segesd) in 1394 found themselves, from one year to the next, under Magyar noble control.[9] Furthermore, in possibly the most sweeping transfer of all, in 1412 Sigismund mortgaged thirteen towns in Spiš county plus another three royal treasury towns to the Polish king, towns which in turn were then mortgaged to Polish aristocrats until reverting back to Hungary in 1773.[10] Problems of revenue flow also compelled Matthias Corvinus to follow a similar practice when the need arose, and despite the fact that he is credited with having been a staunch supporter of urban growth, he was also responsible for granting vast lands to the Zápolya family in northern Hungary, including the royal free town of Kežmarok (Käsmarkt/Késmárk) in 1462 as a private fief.[11] Throughout the kingdom, therefore, from the late fourteenth century and intensifying in the fifteenth, towns found their former protector, the king, weakening, and less able and unwilling to come to their defense. Many were left to fend for themselves, often succumbing to noble rule.

State budgetary troubles, as previously noted, also contributed to the crown granting too many charters and monopolies to royal free towns. Already prior to Sigismund's reign, there were problems in the system of granting staple rights, the most obvious being the unfair advantage enjoyed by the towns that had them over those that did not. Under the rule of Sigismund, however, because the financial difficulties at court mounted, the earlier limitations of the *jus stapuli* system became exposed, and a full-fledged bidding war—with its accompanying backdoor dealings, bribes, and conspiracies—started for the monopolies of trade that would make or break a town's future. Towns like Levoča, Bardejov, Bratislava, Sibiu, Košice, and Buda, which were granted the most extensive privileges, prospered, while other towns that lost in the bidding war declined in significance.[12] In a number of cases the animosity became so extensive because of the inequality produced by this regulation on trade that towns went to war against one another, the most famous being the war between Kežmarok and Levoča that intensified around 1435 and continued for one hundred and fifty years.[13]

It is noteworthy, however, that even those towns that were victorious in the bidding wars for trade privileges developed social-structural problems. In his influential work on the town of Sopron between the fifteenth and sixteenth centuries, Szűcs discovered that internal social developments played just as important a role in stunting urbanization, as did external factors (like noble subjugation). Specifically, Szűcs discovered that prior to the seigniorial reaction a growing disparity of wealth and political power was taking place within the urban commune. From the fifteenth century, some merchant families rose in spectacular fashion, buying titles of nobility and becoming owners of large wine lands near the town. Other families, mostly poor artisans, were losing ground economically and politically, and experienced difficulties acquiring membership in the town fraternity.

To illustrate this point, it is useful to look at the evolution of Sibiu, the largest town of Transylvania. When in 1367 the first staple rights were granted to the town, the document stated that all "guild members" could take their produce to the market without having to pay tolls at

Figure 2.1 The town of Sibiu in the seventeenth century. Sibiu was one the most important and biggest towns of Transylvania, as well as the capital of the Saxon Germans. Reproduced courtesy of the Historical Gallery of the Hungarian National Museum (T. 6022).

Vienna, Prague, Venice, and towns in Dalmacia. In the fourteenth century, therefore, there was little distinction between the "artisan" and "commercial" families, and the two occupations often overlapped; artisans could be merchants and merchants could be artisans.[14] However, during the rule of Sigismund, the royal charters on trade began to limit commerce to a select few merchant families. It was at this time that social inequalities increased, as the privileged merchant families rose in spectacular fashion to become the oligarchy in the town and the surrounding towns as well. By the late fifteenth century, the social-structural evolution in Sibiu set off by royal charters favoring special merchant families in opposition to artisans involved in commerce was complete. In the 1472–1477 registry of Sibiu, for instance, the majority of those who lived in the 893 houses were listed according to their guild affiliation, such as furriers, tailors, and smiths. The commercial families, however, were no longer involved in manufacturing, and had distanced themselves from the artisans by moving into the center of town.[15]

The new merchant elite that rose to positions of power in the royal free towns of fifteenth century Hungary presented formidable obstacles for urban growth in the long run. It is true that at first this new merchant elite contributed to the advancement of trade, and the international networks they established were extremely impressive. As Gernot Nussbächer, the leading historian of early modern Braşov, noted on the fifteenth century: "[f]rom as far as London, Ypern, Löwen, Brügge, Köln, came textiles and luxury goods, from Nürnberg knives, from Poland and the Uplands of Hungary metal goods, and from Italian cities like Verona and Bergamo hats and textiles. From the orient carpets, spices and southern fruit."[16] However, as Nussbächer observed, profits increasingly were concentrated in a handful of families of Braşov, such as (spelled as in the original documents) Lukas Rehner, Lucas Czeresch, Johan Groman, and Georgius Hirscher and to a lesser extent Simon Grett, Johan Kylhaw, Andreas von Rosenau, and Peter Schwarz.[17] The urban decline starting in the late fifteenth century was intricately tied to the emergence of these families. After a generation or two of hoarding profits, the new elite came to be known as Ringbürgers, because of their habit of segregating themselves from the rest of the urban commune by moving into the center of town. Following the deterioration of the Levantine trade route and increasing leisurely consumption of the new urban elite, social frictions created by the growth of inequalities stunted urbanization. The consolidation of Ringbürger rule was usually marked by the introduction of stricter laws limiting the settlement of new immigrants into the town, curtailing the number of artisans given full burgher privileges. Towns declined during the rise of second serfdom, therefore, not simply because of external forces (such as noble subjugation), but also internal factors; namely, the rise to power in the town of an elite with vested interest in land and not commerce or manufacturing.

The *mezővárosok* fared the worst during the late fifteenth-century urban contraction. Following a protracted decline in market opportunities, these towns began their slide into debt to their former lords and by the end of the century only a handful were able to avoid becoming part of the lords' demesne again. The success of lords in reversing the trend by which their villages had begun to win their freedom in the late fourteenth century and early fifteenth century apparently lies in their cunning and skill at forming a united front, primarily through county diets but also through Parliament. The peasants reacted to their growing oppression by staging a number of formidable revolts, the most serious and famous one led by György Dózsa. However, at each turn, the nobles leading the counteroffensive were able to outmaneuver the peasant resistance with their superior political coordination. Finally, in 1514 the Parliament agreed to laws proposed by Emmerich Verbőczi (sometimes spelled Werbőczi), laying the foundation for the legal imposition of second serfdom.

Did Towns Develop Under Second Serfdom?

The question remains whether 1514 was followed by a period of urban decline, stagnation, or growth? After formerly free peasants were transformed into serfs, their freedom of movement hindered, and lordly jurisdiction increased throughout the kingdom, did this imply that lords also aimed to stunt urban development? How did lords behave toward towns? Was there urban development under second serfdom?

The answer to the above questions relates directly to the fact that the manorial reaction first and foremost undermined the strength and legitimacy of the king in significant ways. Royal free towns, after all, were the most important source of cash flow for the crown. When towns were either subjugated to lordly rule or a Ringbürger oligarchy, the king received less in taxes. Consequently, as a political-economic system, the early stage of second serfdom entailed the collapse of the state and the emergence of highly fragmented, de-centralized local sources of power. The obvious structural limitation of such a system was its vulnerability to international military competition. And when

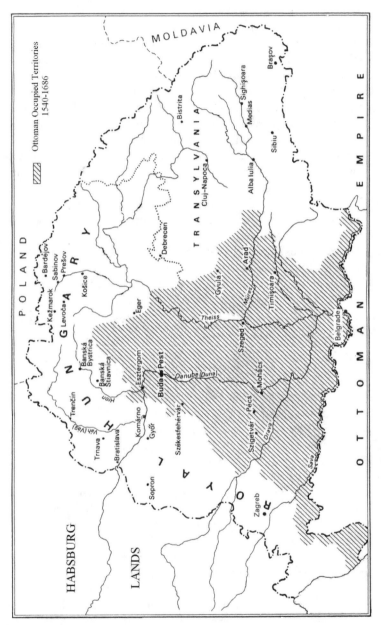

Map 2.2   Map of partitioned Hungary between 1540 and 1686.

the first serious threat of an organized and disciplined state presented itself, in the form of the army of Suleiman the Magnificent, the weak Hungarian king was unable to field significant resistance and was miserably defeated at the Battle of Mohács (1526). As the immediate consequence of the rise of second serfdom, therefore, by 1540 the Greater Hungarian Kingdom had ceased to exist as known formerly and was partitioned into three parts; the plains coming under the direct suzerainty of the Sultan, the eastern territory known as Transylvania becoming a vassal Principality of the sultan, and the western and northern Uplands consolidating into the Independent Hungarian Kingdom. From the 1540s onward the crown of the Hungarian Kingdom was inherited along the Habsburg line, though most of the judicial administrative authority lay with the two chambers of Parliament in Bratislava and the numerous county noble diets.

The complete collapse of central authority followed by the partition initially strengthened the already strong centrifugal tendencies within the social structure. However, the military defeat at Mohács also contributed to the political-economic system of second serfdom undergoing considerable sophistication, which favored towns. Namely, the geo-political military situation forced lords into making concessions to urban growth. As the former Greater Hungarian Kingdom became a military frontier region for 150 years, over which the Muslim and Christian powers fought fiercely for supremacy, new men were invited into the towns to carry the sword in times of war, to help in the introduction of new military technology and, last but not least, to assist in the overall modernization of urban centers ravaged by the hoarding that had followed the manorial reaction. Such a mutation of the political-economic regime of second serfdom was, of course, also a natural progression of the feudal system itself. In the West it was precisely identical factors that prompted princes and lords to bolster urban development in the ninth and tenth centuries. Occidental feudalism is an exclusively rural-based regime only in its embryonic stages. As a result of struggles between landlords and international military competition, it quickly evolves into a more complex order, including a degree of urban autonomy.

The example of the relationship between the Zápolya family and the town of Kežmarok is illustrative of the complexities involved in the evolution of towns at the onset of the manorial reaction. Kežmarok had been granted a number of royal privileges during the thirteenth century (the earliest in 1269), including the right to hold a market and to elect a judge. The town's name probably originated at this point, reflected in its spelling *Kaisermarkt* (meaning "emperor's market") in the earliest documents. In 1380 Kežmarok was granted royal free standing and regularly sent representatives to the king's court. Shortly thereafter, the Hussite revolutionaries invaded. The scant records that survived indicate that Czech and Polish mercenaries entered the town during the first half of the fifteenth century and formed an alliance with the urban artisans and the poor against a coalition of Ringbürgers, local Magyar nobles, and the Hungarian king. After a long, harsh, and indecisive clash of swords and ideology that spanned three decades, in 1440 victory was achieved by the Hussite leader Giskra, the homes of the merchant-elite were looted and burnt, and a popular Republic was established with a mercenary-captain at its head. Neither the mighty János Hunyadi (voivode of Transylvania 1441–1446 and regent of Hungary 1446–1453) nor his famous son Matthias Corvinus (king of Hungary 1465–1490), were able to bring the town and territory under royal control until Matthias sent Imre Zápolya to defeat Giskra. For his success against Giskra and the Hussite followers, Zápolya was granted vast estates in northern Hungary, including the office of *Schloβrichter* of Kežmarok (Castle Judge).[18]

From 1465 to 1485 the Zápolya family consolidated its rule over northern Hungary, attaining a vast estate spanning over four counties and a dozen towns. In 1485 Matthias Corvinus granted the land to the Zápolya family in perpetuity. Following this move, Imre Zápolya changed the title of his office in Kežmarok from that of castle-judge (*Schloβrichter*) to castle-lord (*Schloβherr*) and referred to the town as his private "*villa*" and the burghers as his "*subjects.*" In classic Eastern European fashion, this newly risen magnate took a free market town and transformed it into his private *Gutsherrschaft*, forcing the town to pay taxes to him personally and not to the king.[19] Ironically, Matthias Corvinus, in his effort to centralize power, was instrumental in the phenomenal rise of the Zápolya family who, in turn, became the leaders of the manorial reaction that was responsible for weakening royal authority while strengthening noble autonomy.

The verdict on whether the Zápolya family was able to subject Kežmarok completely to their private family authority is filled with contradictions. It is true that the rule of the Zápolyas damaged the town's royal free standing and from a judicial-administrative standpoint it experienced noticeable regress. However, it is noteworthy that the town notary throughout the Zápolya period referred to Kežmarok as a Republic (*Respublica Kaisermarkt*), and signs of urban dynamism were also evident. Between 1515 and 1516 a new and stronger wall was con-structed with a new taller tower, a town mill was built, and—the most important symbol of urban autonomy—a town hall was erected. This urban dynamism continued into the 1520s, and in 1521 the town pos-sessed a public bath, a curia for the plebs, a new schoolhouse, and in 1523 a clock was installed in the church tower. Interestingly, in 1526 the town was able to send two ambassadors to the National Assembly to cast their vote on the next king of Hungary (the former king having died at the battle of Mohács), a privilege the Zápolya family suspended when they initially subjugated the town. Finally in 1531 János Zápolya trans-ferred the office of castle lord of Kežmarok to a Polish magnate and mercenary by the name of Hieronimus Łaski. Łaski, Zápolya's ambas-sador to Constantinople in 1527, was an educated humanist and adven-turer who had spent some time in the company of Alvisio Gritti, the rich merchant and son of the Doge of Venice.[20] A onetime condottiere in Italy who traveled considerably in Europe, upon coming into possession of the town castle, this good prince changed the title of the office back to castle-judge (*Schloßrichter*) from castle-lord (*Schloßherr*).[21]

A possible explanation for the Zápolya family's behavior toward Kežmarok (Käsmarkt/Késmárk) can be traced to the events immedi-ately following the collapse of the Hungarian Kingdom after the Battle of Mohács (1526). At Mohács, the Hungarian king died and János Zápolya emerged as the leading candidate to become his successor. It comes as no surprise then that Kežmarok—as the family's town—would be allowed to send representatives to an ad hoc meeting of the National Assembly convened quickly following the death of the king, where Zápolya was crowned Rex of Hungary. Yet Kežmarok experi-enced urban dynamism already between 1515 and 1523, and it can be argued that János Zápolya was able to become a leading candidate in 1526 because he realized early on that his support for urban growth could help him in becoming wealthy and powerful. He had learnt the secret of how to become a powerful and good prince.

János Zápolya changed his political position several times in his lifetime. In 1514 he was one of the military leaders who defeated the peasant rebellion of György Dózsa and played a leading role in the ratification of the Verbőczi laws, which limited peasants' right to move freely. He was one of the leading figures laying the foundations for the establishment of second serfdom. After Mohács, however, he emerged as a claimant for the Hungarian crown against Ferdinand Habsburg. The House of Habsburg had the genealogical right to the crown, but Hungarian kings were elected by a National Assembly at the time, and the office of the king was not constitutionally inheritable. When in 1526 Zápolya convened an ad hoc National Assembly shortly after the debacle at Mohács, he was elected king. Ferdinand, to counteract this bold move, summoned another National Assembly in Bratislava and had himself elected king. Two kings of one kingdom quickly led to civil war. Then rumors began circulating concerning Ferdinand's plans to organize an army of disgruntled peasants against Zápolya. Zápolya, now acting as head of state, quickly reversed his earlier position and reintroduced the freedom of movement to the peasantry and even requested towns to open their gates to migrants from rural areas. Further, after "King" Zápolya settled in the capital of Buda, in order to win over the bourgeoisie of that town, he ennobled all the burghers in a memorandum drawn up in 1531. Such a mass ennoblement, with the granting of freedom of movement to the peasantry, and the request to the towns to accept the settlement of serfs, meant the judicial end of second serfdom. Paradoxically, then, the same man who led the manorial reaction when he was an oligarch also brought an end to it when he became king. Zápolya's reversal, however, only applied to a small part of the Hungarian Kingdom, basically those territories that came under Ottoman occupation and administration from 1540 until 1686. Ferdinand had secured the northern Uplands and in the Principality of Transylvania the nobility maintained its control over rural labor.[22] Yet Zápolya is a good illustration of how the partition of the Hungarian Kingdom altered the attitudes of nobles and magnates toward towns, and how the fortunes of towns changed because of the impact of international military competition.

The strength of urban autonomy in the sixteenth century is arguably most visible in the long drawn out struggle over the right of nobles to settle within the walls of royal free towns. These attempts intensified shortly after the military debacle at Mohács, and the fall of Szeged (1541), Pécs (1543), and Visegrád (1544). Each successive defeat forced nobles to migrate in ever-increasing numbers north and west into the Independent Hungarian Kingdom or east into the Principality of Transylvania. Severed from their land and homes, these nobles were clamoring for both the security and the economic opportunities available in the royal free towns of the Uplands and Transylvania.

An important corollary to this point is the unique historical evolution of the Hungarian nobility. Unlike throughout most of Europe, with the exception of Poland and to a lesser extent Spain, in the Hungarian Kingdom the nobility accounted for approximately 4.4 percent of the total population at the turn of the fifteenth century. This contrasted greatly with the classic Western European pattern, where the title-holding nobility never accounted for more than 1 percent of the populace in the early modern period. Possibly the most important difference in evolutions can be found in the large number of poor nobles in Hungary versus their relatively rich western counterparts. Of the roughly 150,000 nobles living in the Hungarian Kingdom in 1494–1495, out of a total estimated population of 3.5 million, two thirds (100,000) had no serfs, were in possession of only small land holdings, and lived in the villages with the peasants. The manor-holding nobility who benefited from robot service numbered 50,000 at the end of the fifteenth century, and they actively distanced themselves from their poor, but noble-titled brethren.[23] The one and important advantage the title of nobility held was tax exemption, and for the majority of serfless, landless, village-dwelling impoverished nobles who could scarcely be distinguished from the peasantry, it was an advantage they clung to dearly. And it was precisely because the Ottoman administration did not respect and accept the tax-exempt privilege of the occidental feudal title that the nobility living on the newly occupied lands flooded north and east, where the title could still be used to advantage.

The conflict between royal free towns and nobles in the sixteenth century was therefore multifaceted. The actual mass of the nobles who wanted to settle within the towns is an important factor to consider and while at first one or two arrived at the gate, soon thereafter came a flood of impoverished noble-peasants, who possessed little of the skill and know-how required for city living. With the exception of towns like Bratislava—which became the new capital of the Independent Hungarian Kingdom—Trnava (Tyrnau/Nagyszombat), Košice, and Alba Iulia (Weissenberg/Gyulafehérvár) to name some important ones, many municipal governments reacted to this mass immigration by closing their gates.

Realizing that they could not settle successfully in the royal free towns if they waged the struggle on a case-by-case basis, the shunned nobles looked increasingly toward the National Assembly, hoping that what could not be achieved at the local level might be done at the national one, and through national legislation the towns would be forced to open their gates. However, as Gyula Szekfű noted, in the second chamber of Parliament problems awaited the nobility because, according to custom, "delegates from royal free towns had an equal vote to delegates sent from county diets, and there were periods, under the rule of Maximilian and Rudolph, when the number of representatives

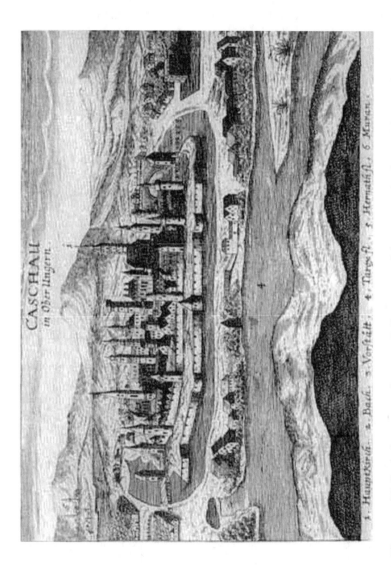

Figure 2.2 The town of Košice in the seventeenth century. Košice was one of the important border towns between the Ottoman occupied territories, Transylvania, and the Independent Kingdom of Hungary under Habsburg administration. Reproduced courtesy of the Historical Gallery of the Hungarian National Museum (T. 505).

sent by the towns equaled those sent by the nobles."[24] Consequently, the nobles could not be assured of winning the battle in Parliament unless they were able to decrease the number of urban representatives. Their best strategy was to petition the king to intervene and force the towns to open their gates. They acted accordingly when in 1552, they asked "your Highness to give the command to the royal free towns and the mining towns, that those nobles and others who are escaping from the war, who can no longer live in the safety of their home, to be allowed to settle, and in 1562 they again petitioned for the right to buy homes in the towns."[25] But these and many other attempts were defeated with the exception of a handful of places, and it was only after 1647 that nobles were able to settle within the walls of royal free towns in limited numbers.

Perhaps the boldest move by frustrated nobles to open the gates of the towns was made in 1608 when, in the second chamber of Parliament, they declared that from that time forth the number of towns that could send representatives was to be reduced from over thirty to twelve: the seven most important mining towns, and the royal free towns of Košice, Levoča, Prešov, Bardejov, and Sibiu. Soon after, however, the towns of Bratislava, Sopron and Kežmarok were quickly added, bringing the total to 15. At the same meeting (1608) the nobility further declared that only those towns were to send representatives that were serf-owners, that is, landlords in their own right. Since it was the task of the Assembly to pass legislation regarding serfs, it was argued that only those with a vested interest in serfdom should be able to participate. In short, the nobles were making their best effort to limit urban representation and the towns that could not be excluded outright were pressured to become feudal lords and required to become serf owners.[26]

The Magyar nobility did not succeed. Their efforts to form a united political front at the national level failed because Emperor Rudolph used towns to counterbalance Magyar noble autonomy. Illustratively, in 1609 a short year after the nobles had thought they had achieved hegemony in Parliament, Emperor Rudolph invited the towns of Varaždin (Warasdin/Varasd), Modra (Modern/Modor), Krupina (Karpfen/Korpona), Zvolen (Altsohl/Zólyom), Koprivnica (Kopreinitz/Kapronca) to send ambassadors, and by 1655 Trnava, Trenčin, Senj, and Eisenstadt were represented, so that by the mid-seventeenth century there were around 30 royal free towns, equaling the number of nobles sent by the county diets.[27] At the national level, therefore, urban representation had never been stronger than during the early seventeenth century, and compromise rather than subjugation characterized the relationship between nobles and towns.

The conflict between the nobility and towns during the sixteenth and seventeenth centuries can also be understood as a struggle of German burghers versus Magyar nobles. In the Zipser towns of the Uplands and the Saxon towns of Transylvania, at least, this too was an important element of the feud. Urban representatives at Parliament would claim that they were not willing to replace their German-burgher laws with Magyar-noble laws, and nobles did not hesitate to criticize the exclusive German culture of the towns. Many towns had a mixed ethnic composition, but only about 10 percent of the urban population enjoyed burgher privileges and these were often Germans. At the same time, while the elite burghers were German, the cottagers, servants, and day laborers who moved into the town from the countryside, were often Magyars, Slovaks, Ruthenians, and Romanians. Esztergom was unique here, because well into the fifteenth century, there was a sizable Italian urban population, due in large part to the fact that the city was one of the centers of the Roman Catholic Church in Hungary. In mixed towns like Bratislava, Buda, Cluj, and Braşov in the fifteenth century the Magyars are often listed as living in a separate quarter of town from the Germans. The Magyar and German conflict within the towns did increase in the late fifteenth century, when concurrently there were more Magyars moving in. It was at this time that Magyars reached a majority in Košice and Cluj. In 1438 the Germans of Buda arrested, tortured, and killed János Ötvös, a leader of the Magyar camp in the town. They hung a rock around his neck and threw his body into the Danube. In reaction to this, the Magyars of Buda forced the Germans of the town to accept the custom whereby the mayor of the town would be alternatively Magyar and German, and that Magyars would represent half of the senators in the municipal government. The ethnic balance of power in some towns shifted back and forth. Cluj in the fifteenth century had a German majority, in the sixteenth Magyar, and then quickly back to German, and from the late sixteenth century the Magyars enjoyed a continuous majority.[28]

However, even in those towns that had a large Magyar urban population, such as Cluj-Napoca, the nobility encountered resistance, and so the issue of barring the entry of nobles was more complex than simply ethnic exclusion. It is instructive to look at, for instance, a decree from Cluj-Napoca in 1603, which was used to exclude nobles from entering and living in the town. The decree starts by praising the wisdom of the early Hungarian kings for separating the nobles and serfs from the burghers. It goes on to say that because within the town walls, all burghers are equal before the law, allowing nobles to live in the town would upset that balance. And while members of other ethnic groups may settle in the town, they may do so only if they come from a burgher background. A noble person may not marry into the town, and if he takes a burgher woman as wife, she would forfeit her civic rights and property.[29] The point being that the legal wrangling between towns and nobles at the end of the sixteenth century was not a struggle of progressive burghers versus backward feudal lords. Towns willingly reverted to defending their autonomy by referring to the feudal division of labor established by the first kings. They were not agents corroding feudalism, and it was just as difficult for a serf as a noble to find sanctuary within their protective walls.

The evolution of the *mezővárosok* (agrarian towns) was distinct from that of royal free towns and royal mining towns. In the agrarian towns that came under the jurisdiction of the Independent Hungarian Kingdom or the Princedom of Transylvania a trend begun in the late fifteenth century continued, wherein nobles moved in, subjugating the towns. The partition of the Hungarian Kingdom and the mass exodus of nobles from the occupied plains even intensified this shift because the nobles who were shunned by the royal free towns had nowhere else to settle but in those agrarian towns that did not come under Ottoman occupation. In general, many agrarian towns that had won their franchise in the fourteenth century were now flooded by a deluge of dispossessed nobles, who quickly monopolized the offices of the municipal administration and the merchant professions. It was from these subjugated agrarian towns that the figure of the Eastern European wholesale grain exporting noble of the sixteenth century emerged.

Exceptions to this pattern were those agrarian towns of the Independent Hungarian Kingdom (the Uplands) and the Princedom of Transylvania that specialized in wine and cattle production. Because cattle and wine production does not require the use of servile labor as grain, agrarian towns with a strong wine and cattle manufacturing base did not follow the same pattern many of the agrarian towns had. Peasants were less frequently reduced to the level of serfs and evidence exists of even the growth of free wage labor in the wine-growing agrarian towns during the seventeenth century. Among these latter agrarian towns, many are found on the present territory of Hungary, such as Pásztó, Mezőkövesd, Mezőkeresztes, Aszaló, Sajószentpéter,

Szikszó, Gönc, Szerencs, Magyarszó, Tokaj, Tállya, Tarcal, Tolcsva, Erdőbénye, Sátoraljaújhely, Bodrogkeresztúr, Olaszka, and some in present-day Slovakia, such as Mad and Santovka.[30] In general, however, aside from wine-growing towns and some that concentrated on cattle production, most agrarian towns that fell under the jurisdiction of the Independent Hungarian Kingdom or the Princedom of Transylvania felt the full brunt of second serfdom and experienced "urban decay" in the sixteenth and seventeenth centuries.

A unique and far different type of urbanization characterized the agrarian towns that came under Ottoman political administration. The most noticeable effect of the imposition of Ottoman rule on the Carpathian basin was the dramatic decline in the number of inhabited settlements. As evidenced by István Rácz, a leading Hungarian urban historian, while in 1522 there were 264 settlements in Bács-Bodrog County, by 1720 only 55 of them remained populated. Similarly in the administrative district of Jászkunság, while in 1557 there were 49 settlements, by 1720 only 23 were inhabited. In the three counties of Békés, Csanád, and Csongrád combined, while at the turn of the sixteenth century there were 188 settlements, by 1720 there were only 23. The most extreme case was in Csanád County where, before the arrival of the Ottomans, 76 settlements were inhabited, a number that fell to a dismal 3 by the end of Ottoman rule, representing a 96.1 percent decline.[31] These figures have led many Hungarian historians to believe that the Ottoman period represented 150 full years of dearth and decimation. Complementing the decline thesis is the mass exodus of nobles from the occupied lands (due to their loss of tax exempt privileges) and their extensive accounts of mass persecution, suffering, and torture at the hands of the "barbarians." Evidence is abundant in support of the claim that the Ottoman period signified the imposition of Eastern despotism on a more developed Western Christian feudal order. As László Makkai—the distinguished early modern historian of the region—noted that even though the Hungarian feudal system was significantly less developed in comparison to the rest of Europe and that the development toward capitalism in the sixteenth and seventeenth century had made only miniscule headway, nevertheless these humble beginnings were still far more advanced than the complete stagnation and immobility which the Turkish empire represented.[32]

Contrary to Makkai's opinion, however, there is every reason to believe that the introduction of Ottoman civilization and administration actually represented an advance over the preceding era. It should be remembered that laws sanctioning the imposition of second serfdom had been enacted only a decade before the Ottoman arrival, and the respect for human liberty was at an all time low in the kingdom. It is also important to note that in contrast to what has been characterized as Ottoman "barbarism" stands the example of the Magyar feudal class, which punished the conspirators of the 1514 Dózsa peasant rebellion by forcing Dózsa's followers to eat their leader's burnt flesh. Antal Verancsics, an eyewitness to the execution of Dózsa, described it thus: "They took György Dózsa's clothes off up to the waist and tied him to a red-hot iron chair. Then they forced his soldiers to dance the heyduck around his throne. After the completion of every round they had to take a bite out of his flesh."[33] There appears to be scarce evidence, in other words, to prove that Hungarian conditions were more advanced in terms of tolerance, hygiene, the sciences, urbanization, trade, manufacturing, state administration, and military technology.

It is true that the immediate impact of Ottoman rule was the decline of smaller settlements and the exit of the nobility, and even the abolishment of royal free privileges to distinguished towns. Yet this was paralleled by the growth of large settlements, the increase in individual liberty (including religious toleration), and the rise of municipal government autonomy. The decline of small villages was therefore not the product of Turkish slash and burn tactics, but signified the aggrandizement of many small villages into larger settlements. Fear of raiding bands of Turkish warriors propelled peasants living in small hamlets to move to larger villages. The result was that the Plains became the most urbanized region of the Hungarian Kingdom, albeit in reality this represented extremely large villages rather than what would, in the classic sense, be considered cities. István Rácz has shown that the effects of this process were felt into the late eighteenth century and in 1784, while in the entire Hungarian Kingdom 58 percent of the population lived in settlements with fewer than 1,000 inhabitants, in three of the largest counties of the Plains 50 percent lived in settlements with populations of over 5,000 people.[34] Consequently, although many villages of fewer than 100 inhabitants declined in the sixteenth and seventeenth centuries, large settlements such as Nagykőrös, Cegléd, Makó, Hódmezővásárhely, Békés, Kiskunhalas, and Mezőtúr doubled in their size. The largest of the agrarian towns, Debrecen, grew from 5,000 to 15,000 and Kecskemét witnessed an increase from 4,000 to 9,000.[35]

The most impressive aspect of Ottoman rule was that noble privileges no longer had legal binding authority. That is, the arrival of the Ottomans meant that lordly jurisdiction over serfs was broken, and the peasantry was left to organize their own self-governments. This represented a strong reversal of the events leading up to the arrival of the Ottomans, whereby the imposition of second serfdom manifested itself by increasing the burden on peasants and decreasing the autonomy of agrarian towns. Notwithstanding the fact that after the arrival of the Ottomans, bands of Magyar nobles did periodically descend on Ottoman-dominated territories from the north and east to demand taxes—and some peasants as Ferenc Szakály has shown, were forced to pay "double taxes" (to the Magyar nobility as well as to the Ottomans)—without an entourage of mercenaries, they had little success.[36] Interestingly, the troops of the sultan never settled in the agrarian towns and if the taxes were paid in full on time, there would be no interference in the internal affairs of the municipal administrations.

The collapse of lordly control did not mean that the agrarian towns of the lowlands became completely devoid of nobles. As noted previously, the Hungarian nobility had followed a different road than their Western European counterparts and their numbers were significantly inflated. Furthermore, in the fifteenth century many of them lived inside the villages and their fate was little better than that of the peasants. A number of these impoverished nobles did not move north or east, but instead took up residence in the agrarian towns. Indeed, altogether only two counties, Békés and Csanád, became completely free of nobles in the sixteenth century. But descending from a noble background appears to have been a disadvantage to someone applying for town citizenship. In Kecskemét, for instance, between 1564 and 1647 there were only eight families of noble descent and in Nagykőrös, only 10.[37] Agrarian towns were definitely anti-noble, and they gave permission for nobles to settle only if they renounced their privileges and took an oath of loyalty to the municipal governments.

The largest agrarian town with a noble presence was Debrecen, where between 1564 and 1640, 118 nobles were granted burgher rights. Many of these families played a prominent role as merchants and occupied seats in the town senate. The most famous judge of the sixteenth century, Ferenc Duskás was also a noble. The nobles' status in the town, however, did not derive from their feudal titles, nor did it entail judicial immunity from the civic courts, or tax-exemption. It was primarily their merchants' skill and capital that accounted for their rise and lofty positions. Moreover, the advantages of "burgher rights" significantly outweighed the benefits of a noble title. Without burgher rights, a family could not receive part of the community land, nor could it use the common lands, and hence could not be in possession of their own means of subsistence. Such a disadvantage would invariably hurt one's chances of success and was the fate that befell the unfortunate class of day laborers and servants.

Towns that lay within the stretch of territory that is commonly referred to as the "military border zone" underwent a further unique urban evolution in the sixteenth century, as exemplified by Tata, Győr, Pápa, Veszprém, Keszthely, and Zalaegerszeg. A high proportion of these towns' urban-dwellers were professional soldiers. In sixteenth century Győr, for instance, 265 of the 731 houses were occupied by soldiers and next to the 3,000 burghers lived a soldier population of 2,000.[38] Because these soldiers were not always fighting, there is significant evidence that they played a critical role in the commercial and manufacturing development of these towns, and are possibly the best examples of how continuous military conflict in the sixteenth and seventeenth century could coexist and even spur urban growth.[39] Furthermore, because of the length of military conflict (the region remained a military border zone for 150 years) in these border castle-towns, resembling Spartan-like urban fortresses with the core of their identity centered on the soldier-burgher ideal, a distinct military caste-like element emerged. The Kuruc army, used by Imre Thököly and Ferenc Rákóczi II in their struggles for Hungarian Independence against Habsburg rule in the late seventeenth century, was recruited from this soldier-burgher population.

In sum, the imposition of second serfdom was legally ratified in the year 1514. This inaugurated the introduction of the first stage of second serfdom, signifying a decline of state authority and a corresponding fragmentation of political power. As it first emerged, the political-economic order of early second serfdom was a highly unstable social system and contributed significantly to the partition of the Hungarian Kingdom in 1540. While the arrival of the Ottomans initially strengthened the centrifugal forces within society, shortly thereafter, lords were forced into a more conciliatory position toward towns and urban autonomy. Consequently, from the mid-sixteenth century onward towns were making a comeback. The second stage of second serfdom was a more complex order and resembled late occidental feudalism in its social organization, where towns, lords, and princes shared power. The agrarian towns in the lowlands followed a different evolution, although interestingly they too made a comeback. Ottoman rule on the plains eliminated the institutional features of second serfdom and feudalism. Free from lordly control, peasants on the plains aggrandized their small villages into large urban-like settle-ments, developing on the way a sophisticated form of self-government with which the Ottomans did not interfere. Consequently, towns, both where second serfdom continued to thrive and where it was broken, made significant strides in the partitioned Hungarian Kingdom of the mid-sixteenth century, and were embarking on a robust ascent that would stumble only in the late seventeenth century.

3

The New Burghers

The mid-sixteenth century brought profound changes to Hungary's royal free towns. Much of this was a product of the Italian and German Renaissance, but there were also important internal factors involved. The agents of change were predominantly young men who studied abroad at universities in Vienna, Wittenberg, Krakow, and Prague, and returned with the new ideas of the age. Also represented were natives of Western Europe and Italy, who decided to migrate eastward escaping religious persecution or simply inquisitive individuals exploring the wild eastern frontier. The two elements, of course, complemented one another and crossed roads at Central European universities, sometimes even traveling eastward together. They represented a new generation, a new worldview, a new burghertum that introduced the main tenets of the Reformation, rewrote the customary laws of the towns, revitalized the urban economies, and established new trading networks and merchant houses.

The new burghers who arrived in the sixteenth century were different from the preceding Germanic immigrants. The earlier wave of German colonists in the twelfth and thirteenth centuries was a mass flow of people. Whole villages and large extended families were courted, assembled, and transported together across Europe, and while these early twelfth and thirteenth century pioneers led the way in building the foundations of towns, they were a community dominated by agrarian and plebeian interests. This form of settlement of whole communities continued into the fourteenth century when, with the exception of a few wealthy merchants from the Hansa cities and southern German trading towns, most newcomers arrived in large extended families.

Changes in immigration patterns occurred as a consequence of the manorial reaction, the Ottoman invasion, and the partition of the kingdom, when the territories of the Greater Hungarian Kingdom lost their mass appeal. The Ottoman occupation, the continuous wars between the Habsburgs and Ottomans, Habsburgs and Magyar nobles, Magyar nobles and Ottomans, led many to think twice before moving east. In contrast to previous times, therefore, the new German immigrants of the sixteenth century tended to arrive alone, individuals of adventurous spirit and entrepreneurial talent, bravely trekking east. They were craftsmen who were also mercenaries, evangelists who were social revolutionaries, merchants from new and rising merchant houses looking to tap into the Levantine trade. Demographically they were almost imperceptible in comparison to their thirteenth and fourteenth century counterparts. Nevertheless, they made a profound impact on the social organization of life in the border towns of European civilization.

The surprising ease whereby newcomers could settle and prosper is indicative of the internal turmoil engulfing towns. Ringbürger rule had increased social inequalities and produced a rift between the artisan and merchant families. What made the period so critical was that from the outbreak of peasant revolt in 1514 to the miner revolts in 1525–1526, the defeat at Mohács in 1526, and the civil war for the Hungarian Crown between Ferdinand and Zápolya (1526–1540), towns became desperate for reforms to reverse their fortune. Furthermore, revolt and civil war were accompanied by the outbreak of disease, depleting towns and fueling the need for new immigrants. Last but not least, similar to their Western European counterparts, new burghers in the East were able to enter formerly closed urban communities because they bridged the growing gap between the Ringbürgers and Plebeians; or in other words, they entered towns by filling the function of *Mittelbürgers*.[1]

Peter Haller (1500–1570) stands out as an important example of how outsiders were able to enter and transform urban life in the town of Sibiu in Transylvania. The Hallers were an influential Nürnberger merchant family with ambitions to establish an international network connecting Central Europe with the Levantine trade route. By the turn of the sixteenth century, there were three Hallers carrying out business in the Hungarian Kingdom: Ruprecht in Buda, Bertalan in Pest, and Conrad in Košice. One of the wealthiest Hallers in Hungary was Johann Haller, who was granted the right to mint money in Bratislava in the 1530s. Peter Haller was born the son of Ruprecht Haller in Pest in 1500. In 1526 he supposedly participated in the Battle of Mohács, and after the defeat moved to Sibiu to become, with Christopher List, the manager of the Fugger gold and salt mining interests in Transylvania. In the 1530s he furthered his business ambitions by expanding his trading network into Ottoman-held Moldavia and Wallachia. To establish strong local ties, around 1530 he married the daughter of the Braşov merchant and judge Johan Schirmer. In Sibiu he had a remarkably successful career in the municipal government and, despite his outsider status, was elected to the town senate at the age of 29, and became the judge of Sibiu in 1543. During his first term as judge between 1543 and 1546, he organized the rich Saxon archives and created an index of all the documents. In 1547 he was sent by the town to Vienna to discuss with Ferdinand the future of the Hungarian Kingdom following the death of János Zápolya. Peter Haller must have made a good impression on Ferdinand because in 1552 he was promoted to the political office of Royal Judge (*Königsrichter*) of the Saxons, a political office sometimes referred to as "Count of the Saxons."[2]

During Peter Haller's tenure, Sibiu adopted Lutheranism, and his notary, Thomas Bomelius, rewrote the town's Customary Laws. The legal reforms Bomelius introduced in Sibiu were carried out by Johann Honterus (1498–1549) in Braşov. Honterus had studied in Vienna, and was active as a printer and humanist in Krakow and Basel in the 1520s. In 1533 he traveled back to his home town of Braşov and in 1535 founded a printing press, considered the first of its kind in Transylvania. Toward the goal of developing the legal system, Honterus co-founded a School of Law in Braşov. One of its first pupils, Matthias Fronius (1522–1588), composed the *Eigenlandrecht der Siebenbürger Sachsen* in 1583. This legal code, based in part on the work started by Bomelius, was adopted shortly thereafter and served as the law governing the Saxon towns of Transylvania until 1853.[3]

Changes introduced to the legal administration of towns, such as those made by Haller, Bomelius, Fonius, and Honterus, represented a critical turning point in the history of urban life east of the Elbe. Towns were entering a new period in their history. Urban dwellers who settled in the Hungarian Kingdom between the twelfth and thirteenth centuries, it must be noted, were organized into what were called Bruderschafts, or brotherhoods. The Bruderschaft was a patri-archal social organization in which the male head of household, or more appropriately clan, represented the interests of the extended family at the communal meetings. During this embryonic stage of urban development, the concept of private property had not yet fully developed, and the municipality would not hesitate to dip into its members' pockets by the means of direct taxes and forced loans. The individual in the legal administrative sense was subordinate to the interests of the fraternity, and a burgher could not take his belongings with him if he left the town without paying for an expensive permit to depart. These societies reinforce the analogy put forth by Pirenne that nothing among all the social organisms created by man recalls more strongly the societies of the ants and bees than do the medieval communes. In both cases, Pirenne noted: "there is the subordination of the individual to the whole, the same co-operation for the sake of livelihood, for the maintenance and defense of the community, the same hostility towards strangers."[4]

The extended power of communal authority was also a legacy of the unique early history of towns in the Hungarian Kingdom. Royal free towns and mining towns were, as previously noted, transplanted from the various parts of the Holy Roman Empire, ranging from Lombardy in the south to the Netherlands in the north. Complete boroughs were courted by Hungarian kings and settled as united communities. Naturally, this unique experience of moving across Europe left a marked imprint on the identity and solidarity of each transplanted settlement, and for a long time the immigrants maintained a strong sense of their prior regional life. The strength of this identity can be measured by the fact that even in the early modern period some towns maintained the distinct dialect they had brought over when they arrived, paving the way for modern linguistics to reconstruct the communities' points of origin. The rugged nature of the new world must have also served to strengthen and elevate community interests over individual needs. Upon arriving, the settlers divided themselves into large complex households, composed of multiple nuclear families living under one roof with their unmarried siblings as well as the elderly and the servants. A patriarchal order emerged on these foundations, and the head of the household would also represent the household's interest in the municipality. In short, a diversity of factors account for the existence of strong communal solidarity and regulation in the medieval royal free and mining towns.

The earliest written urban constitutions in the Hungarian Kingdom date from the 1350s. Only a handful of such documents exist, and these come from the most advanced towns of the kingdom, such as Sopron and Buda. In general, however, towns did not possess written customary laws until the late fifteenth century. Urban life, therefore, underwent a profound advance in the legal administrative sense between 1450 and 1550, with the peak of change occurring concurrent to the spread of the Reformation. It was at this time that the judges and notaries were no longer simply recruited from influential wealthy patrician families, but instead both offices became assigned to the "learned" in the town. Their role changed from the mundane copying of documents left by their predecessors, to a need for interpreting and possessing a scholarly understanding of law and administration. Complementing this transformation was the growing number of students from the towns who traveled to the West and studied at the leading universities. After a year or two abroad, they brought back with them a modern understanding of urban administration, like Haller and Honterus, and would work to rewrite the urban constitutions, spread the word of the Reformation, and establish schools and literacy.

From the sixteenth century onward, the office of notary was filled by individuals with experience and training in law and administration, and inspired judges worked to reword and in some instances recodify the system of law. The new laws had their primary impact on the question of inheritance and strengthened the idea of private property both conceptually and legally. However, it is important to remember that communal land remained a dominant part of urban life well into the nineteenth century, and on a number of occasions in the seventeenth century, the municipal government intervened and confiscated the inheritance of wealthy burghers. As a catalyst for the industrial revolution, different laws would have to be implemented that once and for all destroyed the dominance of the commons. The impact of the customary law reforms can be reduced to two important developments. First, the patent regulations on the rights of individuals to private property allowed for a greater mobility of burghers between towns, strengthening interurban ties both domestically and internationally. They sanctified a more open policy toward entry and exit into and from the towns because new burghers interested in settling could rest assured that the capital they brought into or made in the town would not be appropriated and thereafter distributed by the municipal governments. Second, the reforms and advancement in urban administration, allowed for what Max Weber would call a greater predictability and rationalization of economic action.

The example of Albert Łaski and Emmericus Sonntag is illustrative of the complexities involved in the relationship between new burghers, notaries, nobles, and towns, at the onset of the manorial reaction. Emmericus Sonntag appeared in the town of Kežmarok in the 1560s in the company of the castle lord of the town, Albert Łaski (1536–1605). The Łaski family was one of the most important Polish aristocratic families of sixteenth-century Central Europe. Albert Łaski was the son of Hieronymus (1496–1541) and the grand-nephew of Jan Łaski (1466–1531). Jan Łaski was the Chancellor of Poland, who produced and had printed *The Statute of Jan Łaski* in 1505, which codified all the legal and social regulations of the Polish Commonwealth.[5] Albert was also the nephew of another Jan Łaski, otherwise known as Johannes a Lasco (1499–1560), a leading religious reformer who in the 1550s tried to establish the Reformed Church of Poland. Albert Łaski's father became famous for his diplomatic and military adventures. Hieronymus Łaski came in possession of the Castle of Kežmarok for his diplomatic services to János Zápolya during his struggle against Ferdinand of Habsburg for the Hungarian Crown. In 1527 Łaski had represented Zápolya's interest before Suleiman the Magnificent, and for these services was granted the title of Count of the Zips, including the Castle of Zipser County as well as the town castle of Kežmarok. In 1532 Łaski also traveled to France to request support from the French king. During these decades the town of Levoča was on the side of Ferdinand, and Kežmarok on the side of Zápolya, and in a number of military engagements Hieronymus Łaski distinguished himself as a military leader. He is credited with forging the first cannons from church bells and using them in battle in the county.[6]

The fortunes of Hieronymus Łaski changed when he conspired in the 1530s with Louis Gritti (the son of the Doge of Venice) and Suleiman the Magnificent, against János Zápolya. The plan supposedly called for Gritti to become the king of Hungary, and Łaski to be awarded Transylvania. But nothing came of this, because Zápolya had discovered the plot, arrested Łaski and imprisoned him in 1534. In 1535 Łaski was freed with the help of influential friends, and it was at this time that he openly changed his allegiance and became an ally of Ferdinand. In 1539 Ferdinand sent Łaski to Constantinople to work out a plan against Zápolya, where he was threatened by Suleiman the Magnificent with having his ears and nose cut off for his new alliance with Ferdinand. But he escaped harm, although he was imprisoned shortly thereafter in Belgrade until 1540, for the murder of Suleiman's supporter, Ricon in Italy by the men of Ferdinand. Hieronymus Łaski died in 1541 when Albert Łaski was only six years old.

When Emmericus Sonntag arrived with Albert Łaski in Kežmarok in 1560, the town was emerging from a relatively long period of military turmoil and civil unrest. From the end of the Battle of Mohács in 1526 to the death of János Zápolya in 1540, Kežmarok had been involved in a bitter struggle against its greatest rival, the town of Levoča some 25 miles south. The conflict between the towns ended in a stalemate, but from 1520 to 1540 they fought a drawn out war, draining the treasuries, disturbing each other's commerce, and periodically contributing to devastating fires.[7] The leading ideology of Kežmarok in the 1560s was communal republicanism based on a strong sense of civic pride and patriotism. The origins of this ideology date to the Hussite Revolution, when the town came under the control of the Hussite general Giskra and the rule of the Ringbürgers was broken. In 1542 the Plebeians clearly had the upper hand. Of the 13 senators, six were artisans while the professions of the remaining seven remain unknown. There were only four merchants among the 259 burghers in the House of Plebs, while 81 percent of those whose professions can be identified were craftsmen. The most important sign of plebeian control was that no single district in the town dominated political life. While districts two, three, and four sent over 20 delegates to the House of Plebs, and districts six and eight only 10 and 11, respectively, political power was not concentrated in one or a few districts. Of the four merchants listed as representatives in the House of Plebs, each lived in a different quarter of the town.[8] There were, of course, many more merchants in the town than the four listed in the 1542 records. War between Kežmarok and Levoča was essentially about each town trying to establish commercial hegemony in the region. The absence of merchants listed as representatives in political administrative offices is, therefore, an indication that unlike Levoča, where the merchant-patricians seized control of the town's political machinery through their monopoly of the senate, in Kežmarok artisans and the handicraft guilds represented the dominant political force.

Despite the uniquely plebeian character of Kežmarok's political administration, upon his arrival, Emmericus Sonntag experienced a rapid rise in the town because of his advanced education. First starting as Łaski's private accountant, Sonntag was soon appointed town notary. These were critical years for Kežmarok, as Protestantism spread and Łaski is said to have promoted the teachings of Erasmus and Melachton in the town. Sonntag's fortune, of course, depended greatly on that of his patron, Albert Łaski. In the 1560s Łaski was a rich man, and things were looking good for Sonntag. Łaski had just inherited the great wealth of his father, and enjoyed some military success in Moldavia, coming in possession of a castle and around 10,000 Florins. In 1566 he supposedly was able to assemble 3,000 Polish officers to fight on the side of Emperor Maximilian II at the castle-town of Győr. He also played an influential role in the struggle for the Polish crown following the end of the Jegiellonian dynasty in Poland with the death of Sigismund II Augustus in 1572.

Emmericus Sonntag's life changed dramatically when his patron Albert Łaski's fortunes turned for the worse. In Łaski's attempt to influence the Polish royal elections in 1573 he borrowed 42,000 Gulden from János Rueber, an important Magyar noble of the Uplands. To borrow this money, Łaski mortgaged the castle of Kežmarok to Rueber. But Łaski's candidate Maximilian lost, and he began to fall into serious debt. Adding to his misfortune was that the new king of Poland, Stephan Báthory (1533–1586) was angered by Łaski's opposition to his candidacy, and sent troops to attack Łaski's castle in the Polish town of Lacko. Events turned even worse when Rueber fell into debt himself and passed Łaski's debt onto Sebastian Thököly. Thököly gave Łaski three years to pay the debt, or forfeit his right to the castle of Kežmarok. When Łaski was unable to pay, Thököly took control of the castle and the town.[9]

Sonntag, who was elected judge in 1582, did not remain quiet during this period. Upon hearing that Thököly would take control of the town castle, he devised a plan to keep his patron as the castle captain. He convened a meeting of the leading burghers in his home and conspired against Thököly, telling those privately assembled that in exchange for their help, Łaski pledged a 10-year tax exemption to the town. Spurned on by this promise, many accepted the proposition and proclaimed their allegiance to Łaski. By this time, however, Łaski was in serious financial trouble. To raise money, Łaski traveled to England, where he came into contact with the English alchemist John Dee and his colleague Edward Kelley. John Dee had started his career as a respected scientist and chemist, but later in life became involved in black magic and witchcraft. John Dee and Edward Kelley would regularly gather together in Dee's house, where Dee spoke to apparitions, in the form of little girls, or angels sent by God. When Łaski arrived at Dee's house in May, 1683, Dee, Kelley, and Łaski performed a number of séances, in which Dee was informed that the apocalypse was nearing, and the Antichrist would rise. On June 14, 1583, Dee asked an apparition to tell him about the future of Łaski. The spirits replied that: "I say unto thee, His name is in the Book of Life; The Sun shall not pass his course before he be King. His counsel shall breed Alteration of this State; yea of the whole World."[10]

Following the advice of the spirits, Dee and Kelley concluded that their future was tied to Łaski, and in September 1583 they embarked on a journey to Poland, where Dee was going to make gold and help Łaski pay off his debt to Thököly as well as help him become the king of Poland and Moldavia, and possibly Hungary. None of these dreams materialized, of course, and by 1584 Thököly was firmly in control of the town of Kežmarok. Thököly arrived with his own private army, and routed the meager opposition of the burghers of the town.[11] Naturally, Thököly was angered by the burghers' treason and when he arrived to take control of the office of Captain of Kežmarok, he took possession of the keys to the town armory, appropriated the common pasturelands, forced the town to sell a certain amount of his wine, and decided that he would personally make the choice of who could be elected judge of the town. Thwarted, Emmericus Sonntag—the leading conspirator—fled for his life. On August 24, 1584 Sonntag was in Prague where, as secretary to Albert Łaski, he delivered letters between the Spanish Ambassador and John Dee. A close relationship formed at this time between Dee and Sonntag, and Sonntag was asked to arrange a meeting between Dee and Emperor Rudolph. Łaski and Sonntag were convinced that Dee would be able to use his skills to make enough gold for Łaski to become king one day. On September 12, 1584 Emmericus Sonntag succeeded and Dee did meet with Rudolph. But the relationship between Dee, Łaski, and Sonntag soured by late 1584. On February 28, 1585 an apparition appeared before Dee and warned him of the betrayal by Sonntag, and prophesied that "he shall have his reward: and shall perish with his own hand."[12]

In the end, most of these characters died without having achieved anything spectacular. Dee and Łaski died in poverty, Kelley died in the dungeon of Emperor Rudolph, and Emmericus Sonntag disappeared from the pages of history.[13] But they are, nevertheless, classic examples of how the internal everyday life of towns in East Central Europe in the mid-sixteenth century was filled with intrigue and energy, as well as inquisitive and searching minds. Instead of thinking about towns in Eastern Europe as progressing toward a state of slumber and decline from the sixteenth century onward, therefore, greater attention should be focused on the dramatic changes that were taking place on the cultural as well as spiritual front, and more specifically, the triangular relationship between towns, new burghers, and nobles, that was driving much of the transformation.

New Burghers as Evangelists and Social Revolutionaries

Changes in the administration of towns occurred simultaneously to the spread of the Reformation, and few aspects of sixteenth-century urban life in the Hungarian Kingdom illustrate better the dynamism of towns than the spread of Protestantism. East Central Europe, after all, was one of the focal points of religious dissent since Jan Huss was burnt at the stake in the early fifteenth century. The Hungarian Uplands (today's Slovakia and southern Poland) were especially vibrant in religious dissent, as for most of the second half of the fifteenth century it was controlled by the Polish Hussite military leader Giskra. In the first half of the sixteenth century, countless Protestant dissident groups were scattered across East Central Europe. There were Anti-Trinitarians and Unitarians, Polish Brethren, Socinians, Racovians, Lutherans, Anabaptists, Calvinists, to name some notable and less well-known ones. These dissident groups often intersected, and the Polish Brethren considered themselves Unitarians, but they sometimes became strongly antagonistic toward one another as reflected, for instance, in the struggle between the Racovians and the Unitarians in Poland, or the Anti-Trinitarians and Calvinists in Transylvania. Often, religious dissent was tied to class antagonism. This was most certainly the case with Jan Huss and the Hussite revolution of the early 1420s, as Czech artisans joined the struggle because of their hostility toward the rising German patricians of the towns in Bohemia and Moravia. It was also true of the Racovians, who established a communistic social order in some Polish villages. In other words, besides the classic Reformation led by Calvin and Luther, in East Central Europe the Radical Reformation, as George Hunston Williams put it, was especially strong.[14] Weak kings, tied to the tendency of power to be concentrated at the local level following the manorial reaction, allowed greater freedom for religious dissenters to establish sects according to their utopian visions.

The life of Andreas Fischer in the town of Levoča is an important example of the religiously charged atmosphere of the time. In the years leading up to the arrival of Andreas Fischer from Moravia, the political life of Levoča was already in a state of violent flux. The roots of unrest relate to the growing rift that was developing in the town between the Senate and the House of Plebs, a debate that boiled over in the election of the unpopular Conrad Spervogel as judge by the Senate in 1517. Although historically the Senate had reserved the right to elect the judge from its ranks, shortly after coming to office, Spervogel was forced to resign owing to *"infidelitatis fraternitatis."* The plebeian success in ousting an unpopular judge evidences the important fact that the patricians never mastered hegemony. From the ranks of the wealthy senators, leaders with a populist inclination would periodically rise to prominence and base their legitimacy on pushing plebeian interests in and against their own class position. In the person of Paulus Oestreich, such a charismatic judge came to power after the overthrow of Spervogel. Paulus Oestreich, supposedly the wealthiest man in town, enjoyed the popularity of the town folks, and under his rule two corrupt senators were removed from office, including a member of the influential sixteenth century Henckel family.[15]

Oestreich's popular rule was short-lived, however, and in 1522 Spervogel was again judge of the town. Similar to his first term, upon taking the oath to office, Spervogel was soon entangled in controversy. In the larger picture, the early 1520s was a period when the Hungarian king was increasingly finding it difficult to collect revenue for his ongoing wars against the Ottomans. The resulting revenue crisis played no small role in the king's inability to field a large enough army to battle Suleiman at Mohács. Urban elites, having lost faith in the legitimacy of the king, or having realized that the king had no more power, started pocketing a larger portion of the taxes. Corruption and bribery ran rampant as the Ringbürgers strived to establish oligarchic control over the royal free towns. This was exactly what transpired in the case of Spervogel. In 1522 the royal tax collector arrived to receive 350 Florins from Levoča for the war against Suleiman. After he left, it came to light, however, that the taxes were not paid in full and suspicion immediately fell on Spervogel. Rumors circulated that the night before, Spervogel had disappeared with the tax collector into the town hall wine cellar, and got him drunk on the best wine. The full details of the controversy were never disclosed, but the scandal further rocked the already fragile social peace of Levoča as blame was flung across all corners of the town. This set the stage for Gregorious Mild's election as judge.

Spervogel despised Mild and in his diary described his rule as *adversum* (hostile) and *superbus* (tyrannical, despotic), and Mild personally as *sordidus* (filthy) and *arrogans* (arrogant). Like Oestreich before him, Mild also based his legitimacy on popular rule. However, unlike his predecessor, he was also more willing to take chances and showed signs of being caught up in the chiliastic attitude of the times. Mild's great crime, according to Spervogel, was inviting Andreas

Fischer into the town in 1529, a figure whose life was surrounded by a tremendous amount of mystery and controversy. It appears that Fischer was a successful demagogue, as both he and his wife took to the streets and preached to the people with a dynamism that had long been unheard or unseen. He also began to baptize adults. As Spervogel put it, "[Fischer teaches] that one should not baptize anyone younger than thirty years of age, and those who have already been baptized [as infants] should be baptized again."[16] Fischer's fortune changed, when accusations were cast upon him for denying the divinity of Christ, and forming a secret society of religious followers. The seventeenth-century judge of Levoča, Gaspar Hain, noted in his *Chronicles* that Fischer had formed a secret sect of Anabaptists, preached the end of the world and the end to differences in wealth. Perturbed by Fischer's apocalyptic visions and radical communal utopia, the majority of the senators deserted Mild and sent for the Royal Judge of the County to come to their aid and arrest Fischer.

Fischer was arrested with his wife in 1529, and taken to the castle at Tschitschva. At this time the Royal Judge of the County also wrote a letter to Levoča that those senators who invited Fischer into the town should be "burnt at the stake."[17] The senators escaped harm, but Fischer and his wife were sentenced to death; Fischer by hanging and his wife by drowning. In September, 1529 the unnamed wife of Fischer met her death by drowning, and as a sympathetic historian of Hungarian Anabaptists and Sabbatarians put it, she died "a martyr to the cause of religious liberty and free conscience." Fischer, however, miraculously escaped hanging, and while Spervogel wrote that his body hung in the square for several hours, after he was cut down, he was able to flee. This represented, according to Daniel Liechty, a radical turn in Fischer's theology. When Fischer returned to Levoča to preach, "this time he was not only seen as a great preacher but also a living martyr. Spervogel's *Diarium* reports that many people saw Fischer's escape from death as a sign of God's favor and verification of his message."[18] Fischer's largest following appears to have been in the town of Sabinov [Zeben/Kisszeben]. After Fischer had escaped execution, he moved to Sabinov and challenged the local pastor Anton Philadelphus to a theological debate, which Fischer won and Philadelphus moved out of the town. "At this point, the end of February 1530, the Sabinov council did an extraordinary thing. They sent an official envoy to Levoča requesting that Levoča Anabaptists (some of whom were still in jail) be allowed to move their families to Sabinov. Thus Sabinov became a sort of haven for Fischer's beleaguered followers."[19] Fischer continued to preach until 1540, when he was caught and killed in a neighboring county by the Royal County Judge Bebek, for the crimes of bigamy and blasphemy.[20]

It is not clear why Mild invited Fischer into the town. At first glance, it appears contradictory that a wealthy senator would welcome a spiritual leader who, in turn, would form a secret society and preach the end of the world and the blessings of a society without distinctions in wealth. It is possible that Mild was taken by the apocalyptic visions of Fischer and became an enthusiastic follower. It is also possible that Mild intended to take advantage of Fischer's presence in outmaneuvering the leading oligarchs in the Senate by forming a popular front and establishing his private rule over the town. What is clear is that internal crisis, the struggle between elites and plebeians, opened the door for new burghers like Sonntag and Haller and Fischer to enter and make an impact on urban life. Fischer failed, but two decades later the town did become Protestant. Countless school rectors, town priests, notaries, and judges made their entrance into the urban communities in this way and, as outsiders, emerged as the leading forces of change.

Religious turmoil in sixteenth-century Hungarian towns was, therefore, a confluence of both external and internal forces. New burghers with radical views from all over Europe traveled eastward because they could find spaces where the Catholic hierarchy had less control and the inner life of the urban communes was in serious spiritual crisis. The impact of the Ottoman invasion, tied to the growing wave of religious dissent, led to the strengthening of Chiliastic feelings that the world was coming to an end, the Apocalypse was near, and the Messiah was soon to appear. Evangelists from Italy and Germany found a ready audience in towns of the partitioned Hungarian Kingdom willing to listen to a new interpretation of spiritual life. The spread of the Reformation, therefore, expanded through a dialectical relationship. Andreas Fischer was thrown down a cliff, his wife drowned, and many religious dissidents martyred in one form or another. Yet despite the hardship and bloodshed, towns developed. Second serfdom, which led to the weakening of kings and the strengthening of local sources of power, empowered evangelists in Eastern Europe. In turn, the Reformation led to the building of schools, an increase in literacy, the accumulation of books, and the founding of printing presses. A new rational and critical view pervaded the intellectual world of the towns, even if that view at times merged with a mystical, irrational, chiliastic understanding of events. Most importantly, a new burghertum emerged in the towns, altering the medieval division of power within the urban communes, leading to a profound metamorphosis and a critical transition toward modernity.

Mining Towns in the Sixteenth Century and Change

The dynamics of change was especially noteworthy in the mining towns of the Hungarian Kingdom. Mining had been, of course, one of the great early propellers of urbanization, as towns sprouted up around gold, copper, silver, and salt deposits. During the early period, between the thirteenth and fourteenth centuries, the social division of power within the mining communities resembled that of other royal free towns. Communities were broken down into large multifamily households, the leader of which represented the household's interests at municipal government meetings. Production was carried out by small enterprises, often corresponding to households, employing from one to four wage laborers.[21] Between 1350 and 1450, Hungarian mining towns emerged as globally important centers for gold and silver production. Annually, 1,500 to 2,000 kilograms of gold were produced, representing from 30 to 42 percent of world production. The production of silver was also impressive, accounting for 10,000 kilograms and representing from 25 to 30 percent of world production. These mining towns would remain important until the transatlantic silver developed after 1560 (noteworthy here are the Potosí mines in Peru), forever undermining the value of Hungarian silver and leading to a sharp decline in profits.[22]

Similar to the royal free towns already discussed, the larger mining towns in the second half of the fifteenth century also experienced growing social stratification. Two processes are especially noteworthy. Between 1400 and 1450, the valuable surface ores were depleted. Second, the revenue crisis at court led the kings to raise taxes as well as grant charters and monopolies to wealthy entrepreneurs. The consequences of these dual processes were that from the second half of the fifteenth century small enterprises were going bankrupt, while wealthy burghers emerged who consolidated control and production. In other words, similar to other privileged towns, by 1460 the mining towns also experienced the rise of a new patrician ruling elite. The case of Banská Štiavnica is illustrative of these developments. While in the early fourteenth century mining enterprises employed almost no wage

Figure 3.1 The town of Banská Štiavnica in the seventeenth century. Banská Štiavnica was one of the most important mining towns of the Hungarian Uplands. Reproduced courtesy of the Historical Gallery of the Hungarian National Museum (T. 4178).

labor, with the depletion of surface ores, and increasing capital investment, the size of enterprises grew, and some former owners became
part of the growing mining working class. In 1509 small enterprises
continued to prevail, but larger ones also emerged. Out of the 14 silver
mine enterprises in 1509, some employed one or two wage laborers,
but the three largest enterprises employed 33, 26, and 21 workers. By
1519 the number of enterprises increased to 30, and the total number
of wage laborers to 404, with the three largest enterprises employing
62, 37, and 33 workers. Sometimes the work of consolidation was carried out by local merchants who bought up the smaller mines, such as
István Jung and János Kolomon in Banská Bystrica.[23] Other times consolidation took place through absentee owners, rich and influential
Augsburg and Nüremberg merchant houses that were given or bought
mining charters and privileges from Hungarian kings.

The largest and most impressive mining enterprise in Hungary
between 1495 and 1541 was established by the Thurzó and Fugger
family union in the town of Banská Bystrica. This also represented the
zenith of early modern mining in Hungary. The founder of the enterprise was Johann Thurzó (1437–1508), who lived in Krakow at the
turn of the 1490s, and married Magdalene Beck. Thurzó became
important to Hungarian mining when in the 1490s he was contracted
by the seven largest mining towns in Hungary to help solve the problem of flooding in deeper mines. Between 1492 and 1495, he used his
expertise in mining and combined it with the capital of the Augsburg
merchant house of the Fuggers, to establish the *Ungarische Handel* or
Neusohler Kupferhandlung, the name of the Fugger-Thurzó enterprise. Thurzó was in charge of operating the copper and silver mines
until his death in 1509, when his son Elek took over. Johann's other
son Georg (1467–1521) also strengthened the Fugger-Thurzó family
alliance by marrying Anna Fugger. "In the period 1494–1546, the
mines of Banská Bystrica produced in total 74, 281 tons of copper and
119 tons of silver."[24] The Fugger-Thurzó enterprise transformed the
town into the most important copper producing center of Europe,
using the most advanced technologies available in separating silver
from copper.

Inequality in wealth and growing social stratification within the
mining towns produced similar problems of corruption as in the other
royal free towns. Tensions were especially high in the 1520s. The crown,
desperate to raise money for its foreign wars, clashed with the patricians
in the towns who had formed an alliance with the oligarchs in the country,

with the goal of keeping taxes for themselves and consolidating control over their respective feuds. In Banská Bystrica things came to a head in 1525 when the Fugger-Thurzó enterprise began to mint money with less than the required silver level. The miners protested and went on strike, eventually revolting, and the crown complained that by flooding the market with less valuable minted coins, the enterprise was threatening the outbreak of inflation. In the investigation into the affairs of the town, it also came to light that the Fuggers and Thurzós had stopped paying their municipal taxes. The crown came down hard on the families, banishing the Fuggers from the town, fining them 500,000 Florins, imprisoning Thurzó and fining him 50,000 Florins. Yet these measures had only limited success. After the defeat at Mohács in 1526, the Fuggers and Thurzós were back in power. They were lending money to Ferdinand I in his struggle with Zápolya over the Hungarian crown, and in turn were given a 15-year tax exemption to work the mines. It was during these years when they made some of their largest profits. Between 1526 and 1529 it is estimated that they exported enough copper and silver for a net profit of one million Florins.[25]

The rule of foreign, mostly Augsburg, merchant-industrialists declined in the mining towns from the 1560s. The Fugger family left in 1547. Soon thereafter a number of other Augsburg firms attempted to take their place but failed. There were the Langnauers, Haugs, Links, Weiss, Pallers, and Stainigers. But from the 1560s Hungarian mining entered a depression, and as Braudel noted, "the mines were making losses or at best only modest profits which their backers one day no longer thought worth the candle."[26]

Mining, however, did not decline for long. While foreign merchants lost interest, a home mining bourgeoisie took their place, and experienced rapid economic advancement in the late sixteenth century. It was during this same period that new words were introduced into the Hungarian language, words that are not part of the vocabulary of urban decay. Words and phrases such as *iparkodik és indusztrálkodik* (to be industrious), *gépely* (machine), *órai mesterséggel forgó* (clock work), *magában forgó szerkezet* (automat), and *csinálmányok* (manufactured products), made their appearance primarily in the Upland and Transylvanian mining towns.[27]

Several aspects of the growth of mining in the late sixteenth and early seventeenth centuries are noteworthy. First, the modernization of metallurgy and the tremendous wealth accrued in the hands of a few families took place within the context of a war economy, the

Figure 3.2 Banská Bystrica in the seventeenth century. During the sixteenth century, Banská Bystrica was a major mining town of Europe, where the Fugger family made a fortune. Reproduced courtesy of the Historical Gallery of the Hungarian National Museum (T. 4144).

Thirty Years War first and foremost. But it should also be remembered that the 150-year partitioning of the Hungarian Kingdom, and the continuous wars between Habsburgs and Ottomans, Protestants and Catholics, nobles and towns, as well as the numerous noble and urban feuds, produced an unquenchable thirst for iron, sulfur, and copper. It was the mining towns that profited arguably the greatest from the chaos that engulfed the region. Second, the cooperation between noble leaseholder and venture capitalist in the mining towns was not an alliance of equals. Those burgher families that began to produce for the war economy in time became exceptionally wealthy, while the nobility for the most part was undergoing some economic contraction because of the cost of the wars. However, the mining entrepreneurs needed the political support of the aristocracy, and worked together with the upper class often at the expense of municipal government autonomy. The aristocracy first and foremost helped ambitious miners take control of the town commons, which was a prelude to the concentration of wealth and the building of enterprises on a larger scale. Last but not least, the iron mining and smelting operations were for domestic consumption and not exported abroad. This was a home-bourgeoisie, producing for the home-market.

In conclusion, what has been presented in this chapter underscores the importance of viewing Hungarian urban evolution in the sixteenth century as a period of dynamic change and even growth. Among the most fundamental cultural changes that took place, urban constitutions were modernized, the family and social organization of the communal brotherhood was reformed, schools were established, literacy increased, and towns converted to Lutheranism. Throughout towns in the Independent Hungarian Kingdom and Transylvania, everyday life was filled with energy and vitality from the mid-sixteenth through the seventeenth century. Of course, it is counterintuitive to think that towns grew and prospered. The wars and the partitioning of the Hungarian Kingdom, the religious strife between Protestants and Catholics, and the numerous instances when cholera broke out should have stunted urbanization. But nevertheless, despite the hardship, bloodshed, and even the decline of international trade, towns experienced the Reformation, with its intellectual as well as architectural splendors. Indeed, the transformation of the region into the border area or frontier zone separating the Muslim from Christian civilization following the Ottoman occupation, led to the increase of the immigration of enterprising and entrepreneurial burghers from Central Europe, who now viewed with growing curiosity and interest the towns of the Uplands and Transylvania. Immigration of large extended families declined, but that of new burghers grew. Or in other words, it would be more correct to say that towns in the sixteenth and seventeenth century were actually experiencing their golden age and ascending, rather than maintain the traditional view that they were hollow and descending.

4

The Difficult Victory of Habsburg Absolutism

The Hungarian nineteenth century novelist Kálmán Mikszáth (1847–1910) noted that the seventeenth century was one in which the burghers of the royal free towns were forced to walk on eggshells. Before the town gates might stand the mercenary troops of the Holy Roman Emperor, the Ottoman sultan, or rebellious Magyar nobles. Each day brought its own surprises, dangers, possibilities, and adventures, and it was unclear where it would all end.[1] To survive, towns developed a sophisticated game of diplomacy. On different occasions they appeared as loyal subjects of the Sultan, the Holy Roman Emperor, or Magyar noble rebels. By maneuvering through this maize of alliances, towns could maintain a degree of autonomy, and the most successful were even able to manipulate the different invading armies to consolidate their "local" power. Bribes, conspiracies, and treachery were part of everyday life. The Sultan defended the town of Sibiu when Gábor Báthory in 1610–1611 tried to subjugate it, and Hieronimus Łasky defended Kežmarok in the 1530s when the troops of Ferdinand Habsburg tried to conquer it. Towns also asked for the help of his Holy Roman Emperor and, provided they could deposit a large enough donation, he would come to their defense. Using this strategy, in 1647 Svätý Jur Sankt (Georgen/Szentgyörgy), in 1648 Eisenstadt (Kismarton), in 1649 Kőszeg (Günst), in 1647 Pezinok (Bösing/Bazin), in 1650 Kežmarok, in 1681 Rust (Ruszt), and in 1686 Pukanec (Pukkanz/Bakabánya) were granted royal free privileges.

Of course, tales of misfortune and destruction also abound. As long as Hungary remained partitioned along the Ottoman-Habsburg border, intense violence was never far away. This is well illustrated in the example of Lipova (Lippa) in Transylvania. In the mid-sixteenth century a large army sent by the sultan appeared at the town's gates. To avoid unnecessary destruction, the "Burgomaster" (town judge/mayor) informed the pro-Habsburg castle lord that in the town "there was not one citizen that would hazard the losse of their children, wives, sisters, and revenues, all of them being assured, that if they should stand upon their guard, the Belerbey [the military captain of the Ottoman troops] would without mercy put them all to the sword."[2] Or in other words, the burghers would not man the wall in the event of war.

As related in the sixteenth-century work by Martin Femée (1540?–1590?), *The historie of the trovbles of Hvngarie*, upon hearing this news from the Burgomaster, the castle captain of the town decided to retreat and allow the town to fall into Ottoman hands without a fight:

> Pete [the captain of the town castle] seeing the cowardly resolution of this Burger, and assuring himself, that the Turks being in the towne, hee could not possible defend the Castle, esteemed it better and more profitable for the seruice [service] of Ferdinand [Habsburg], in preseruing [preserving] those souldiours [soldiers] which he had with him, to retire with safetie, then to expect and aduenture [adventure] the losse of all. Upon this deliberation he forshooke the Castle, and the greatest part of the towne, and so departed out of it with all his souldiours.[3]

As soon as the castle lord left, the Burgomaster went to the leader of the Ottoman army and received a reward:

> [T]he Burgomaster went presently to seek the Belerbey, vnto whom he yeelded the towne keyes, with many submissiue [submissive] demonstrations of obedience; in recompense whereof, the Belerbey receiued [received] it kinde thankes, shewing him many pleasant sports, and also bestowing many presents of him, and presently after went accompanied to Lippa with the said Burgomaster, where hee lodged with all his armie, and soiourned [sojourned] there tenned daies, greatly reioycing himselfe.[4]

Fortune was not on Lipova's side, however, because shortly after allowing the Ottomans to enter, a large army sent by the Habsburg Emperor arrived and laid siege to the town for several weeks to oust the Ottomans, leaving the town burnt to the ground. These were difficult times. Some towns declined, others stagnated, and yet others stayed at the level they were before.

Concurrently, however, it must be stressed that the manorial reaction did not logically lead to the noble subjugation of towns. It led instead to the collapse of royal power and introduced a period of contested sovereignty. There was most certainly a process of creative destruction that came as a natural consequence of this atmosphere of near anarchy. After being sacked and burnt, towns had to rebuild and during the rebuilding, the walls were made thicker, taller, stronger, and to avoid the fires caused by the cannons, houses were increasingly built from brick. The examples of Sibiu (Hermannstadt/Nagyszeben) and Braşov (Kronstadt/Brassó) in Transylvania are particularly interesting. Similar to towns across the Hungarian Kingdom, prior to the fifteenth century most buildings were constructed of wood. It was not until 1408 that Sibiu's first brick building, besides the town church, was completed. However, between 1408 and 1599 an architectural revolution occurred, and by 1599 only one wooden house was left on the market square. This architectural revolution was most intense during the sixteenth century; in Braşov the tower to the town hall was constructed in 1528, in 1539 the first printing house was built, in 1545 the Fish Market in the town square was erected, and between 1539 and 1545 the most impressive building to the current day, the Merchant's House, was constructed. In Sebastian Műnster's (1489–1552) eyewitness account, Sibiu was likened in size to Vienna, and in 1683 the *Magyar Simplicissimus* described the towns of Transylvania in the following way: "Transylvania is a wonderful land. It is plentiful in people, gold, silver and other metals, salt, fish, wild game, wheat and honey. The towns are beautiful and in large part Lutheran and German. The capital is Sibiu, which is the largest and in size and beauty comparable only to Wien and Breslau (today in Poland, Wrocław)."[5] In short, the sixteenth and seventeenth centuries represented a dynamic period in the history of towns. Demographically no megacities appeared like London, Paris, or Amsterdam, nor did they reach the size of Augsburg, Nuremberg, or Florence, but economically, socially, and culturally, many were evolving and experienced progress.

In the second half of the seventeenth century, however, a critical change occurred in the position of towns. Much of this change was a response to the long and influential rule of Leopold I (1640–1705), whose reign between 1658 and 1705 was one of the longest in the history of the Habsburg family. Leopold I alienated towns by his efforts to construct an Absolutist state in Hungary. He represented the trend in seventeenth century European history, in which large monarchies were expanding and subjugating independent city-states to their authority. Absolutist states began to interfere in the internal affairs of formerly independent cities throughout Europe, destroying in the process, as Henri Pirenne put it, "the protectionism and exclusivity of the bourgeoisie."[6] Craft guilds continued to function, but their influence was waning. This trend also signified the decline of old towns and the rise of new, younger manufacturing towns. However, it is critical to stress that this conquest of independent or semi-independent towns did not happen without resistance. In Hungary, for instance, towns were openly hostile to Leopold's centralization drive, and this brewing tension was one of the underlying reasons for the outbreak of civil war that raged on and off from 1678 to 1711.

Towns were, of course, not alone in their estrangement from the crown. The Magyar nobility was similarly alarmed and distressed about the policies of the royal court. Among the grievances against Leopold I were his alliance with the Jesuits, the disrespect he showed toward the Hungarian Diet and Hungarian Laws, his attempts to construct a large standing army, increases in taxation, the attempt at greater regulation of trade, and the appointment of officials—mostly foreigners—to important administrative positions in Hungary, both on a kingdom-wide basis and the municipal level. It was in opposition to Habsburg centralization that a circle of leading Magyar nobles formed in the 1660s with the aim of restraining Leopold I. The notable leaders of this group were Ferenc Wesselényi, Earl Ferenc Nádasdy, Earl Ferenc Frangepán, the Prince of Transylvania Ferenc Rákóczi I, and the Viceroy (Bán in Hungarian) of Croatia, Péter Zrínyi. The original plan designed by Wesselényi called for the leading nobles of Hungary to request an audience with Leopold I to discuss their grievances, and if and only after this failed, would they mount an insurrection. In 1667, however, the leader of the malcontents, Ferenc Wesselényi died, and under its new leader, Ferenc Nádasdy, the movement became more radical. Convinced of Leopold I's insincerity toward the Magyar cause, Nádasdy designed a plan whereby the Magyar nobles, with the assistance of the Ottoman sultan, would overthrow Habsburg rule in Hungary. The year of insurrection was set for 1670.[7]

Nothing came of the Wesselényi Conspiracy—as it later became known—because informers had alerted Leopold I of the impending revolt. The ringleaders were quickly arrested, executed (except for Ferenc Rákóczi), and their family estates confiscated. But what angered the Magyar nobility most about Leopold I's handling of the

Wesselényi Conspiracy was that he not only executed the leaders of the plot, but also confiscated their family estates shortly thereafter. It was this policy that most provoked the nobility because, according to the Hungarian constitution of 1222 (the so-called *Aranybulla* or Golden Bull), the king was an elected official and the nobility had the legal right to revolt and resist his authority. By confiscating the property of the malcontents, Leopold I broke the ancient liberties of the Magyars and reaffirmed the suspicion that he aimed to attain absolute rule. In short, the handling of the Wesselényi Conspiracy as well as the continuing state-building drive of Leopold I had disastrous consequences, and Hungary fell into a bloody civil war from 1678 to 1711. These decades were to have a decisive influence on Hungarian history. They marked the period of the last major revolt by the Magyar nobility against Habsburg rule until 1848 and, most importantly, happened concurrent to that tectonic shift in East Central Europe whereby the Ottomans were expelled from the Carpathian Basin after 150 years, and the Habsburgs emerged as the leading power until the end of World War One.

Towns were especially frustrated by Leopold's religious intolerance, which intensified after 1670 as he afforded the Jesuits increasing authority over Hungary. The Jesuits, of course, had long been concerned with the state of Catholicism in Hungary, where in 1670 supposedly only 1 out of 10 people was Catholic, and over 2,500 Protestant Churches served the population. However, the Jesuits were limited in their actions because an all-out assault on the Protestants held the potential of unleashing a renewed round of religious wars across the Holy Roman Empire. Proceeding in a cautious manner was essential. The uncovering of the Wesselényi Conspiracy, therefore, presented the Jesuits with a golden opportunity. They convinced Leopold I that behind the plot lay a grand Protestant design, and all Protestants, especially the leaders of the flock, should be held accountable. Further, to circumvent criticism from Protestant princes and towns across the Holy Roman Empire, the Jesuits told Leopold I that the renewed persecutions were to be understood as part of the inquisition into the Wesselényi Conspiracy.[8]

The persecution began on September 25 in 1672 when Cardinal Leopold Kollonitsch (1631–1717) summoned the Protestants of Liptó, Turóc, and Zólyom counties to discuss the question of religion in Bratislava. Kollonitsch was so impressed by the number of Protestant ministers and schoolteachers in attendance that shortly thereafter he expanded the summons between February and March of 1673 to all

Protestant ministers and schoolteachers of the Hungarian Kingdom. "Of those that were summoned, such as lived under the Turks the Vizier Bassa [Pasha] of Buda forbade their appearance, and they obeyed his commands: but those that were only Tributaries to the Turks, and lived under the Government and Laws of the King of Hungary, as well as those that were solely under his Power and Authority resolved to obey the Citation; and therefore accordingly appeared in great numbers."[9] To the surprise of the ministers and schoolteachers, Kollonitsch's summons was not intended as a meeting to discuss the Catholic-Protestant question. Instead, it was a mass trial of all the Protestants as traitors, accomplices in a conspiracy involving Magyar nobles and the Ottoman sultan in the overthrow of Leopold I. As soon as the Protestants appeared, three options were presented to them:

> 1. That they should lay down their ecclesiastical Employments and ingage [engage] never to resume them again. Or, 2. Depart the Kingdom, never to return again, or preach or teach therein, upon pain of death and lost of Estates. Or 3. Embrace the Popish Religion, denying and foreswearing the Protestants.[10]

No clear evidence exists as to the exact number of Protestants brought to trial. According to the modern historian László Benczédi, 766 Protestant ministers and schoolteachers were involved, while the Catholic interwar period historian Gyula Szekfű estimated the figure at 240.[11] Despite these differences, little disagreement surrounds the events following the trials. Those who did not convert or leave the kingdom were taken by soldiers to Italy on March 18, 1675 and sold as galley slaves for 50 crowns a head. A few weeks later another 20 were added to the list and altogether some 61 Protestant priests and teachers were enslaved until "admiral Ruyter [Reuter] bought their liberty in February 1676," by which time only 26 were alive.[12]

Besides the growing religious intolerance at Court, Leopold I also contributed to the outbreak of civil unrest by his decision to expel Magyar soldiers from the military border towns of Győr, Tata, and Székesfehérvár—to name the most important—and replace them with German ones. His actions were driven by an important discovery during the inquiry into the Wesselényi Conspiracy: Magyar nobles were planning to use the Magyar soldiers in the military border castle-towns to launch their offensive against Vienna. In a hasty move, without ascertaining the guilt or innocence of those accused, in 1670 from

Figure 4.1 The town of Győr in the seventeenth century (also known as Raab in German). Győr was a military border town between the Habsburg Empire and Ottoman Empire. Reproduced courtesy of the Historical Gallery of the Hungarian National Museum (T. 6022).

7,000 to 10,000 Magyar soldiers were expelled. Thereafter, the countryside on the Plains, in the Uplands, but mostly in Transylvania was littered by roaming bands of Magyar soldiers, dangerous because of their military training, and perfect for rebellion because of their willingness to enlist in political adventurism. It was this group that formed the core of the Magyar Kuruc Army, the guerrilla force that would remain a thorn in the side of the Habsburg Imperial army for much of the period between 1678 and 1711.[13]

Discontent turned into open revolt in 1678, when Leopold I formally suspended the Hungarian Diet and attempted to rule solely through Vienna. The leader of the opposition, Prince Mihály Apafi of Transylvania, published a short pamphlet with the title *The Declaration of the Hungarian War* in English in 1682, explaining the reasons and causes of the revolt. Apafi began this pamphlet by claiming that Leopold I had broken the ancient laws of Hungary, was trying to take away the ancient liberty of the Hungarians, and had illegally confiscated the property of the rebels, leaving all their heirs orphaned and in destitution. Many fled into exile, and because the Magyars had found themselves on the precipice of death, they turned to the Ottoman sultan for protection and asked for his assistance to defeat the "tyranny" and "despotism" of Leopold I. Apafi wrote:

> The Exiled Lords, provoked by these and other Inexplicable Injuries, brought to the Precipise of final overthrow of Life and Fortune; destitute of all help from Christians, and perceiving no hope of mitigating His Majesty, dis resolve in this extream necessity to betake themselves to the benignity of the Illustrious Ottomans, Soveraignity, and implore his Protection against most unjust violence, for the relief of the Kingdom, and the safety of many innocents.[14]

Apafi published the reasons for the revolt because he hoped to garner English support and because he was well aware that in order to succeed it was crucial to explain why the Christian Magyars have formed an alliance with a Muslim power against the Holy Roman Emperor. Apafi noted in the pamphlet:

> I know many do misconstruct this Act of Extream Necessity, and preposterously slander the Hungarian Nation, as degenerate, and making defections from Christians; but such are either ignorant of Hungarian Liberty, according to fundemental constitution, or too active promoters of the Aufriack [Austrian] interest.[15]

Apafi notes that it was not without precedence in European history that Christians turned to the sultans of the East to assist them against a Christian ruler, and the Magyars should not be judged unjustly:

> Neither are the Hungarians the first who have implored Ottoman assistance in their defence: Henry and Fredirick, Brethren to the King of Castil, in the time of Pope Clement the 4th, when associate with the Sons of Conradus, did call the Saracens by Sea and Land, not to defend their Country, but to expell the French from Italy. Maximillian of Austria, that he might repell Force carried on against him, but especially that he might destroy the Venecian Common-Wealth, was active to procure the Turks assistance; Francis the first of France, when he perceived the ambition and dangerous Power of Charles the fifth, did not question the accepting help from the Turks; neither was it unglorious in our time, for the famous State of Polonia to call the Tatars to their defense against Christians.[16]

The agreement between the Magyar malcontents and the Ottoman sultan stressed that after the defeat of the Habsburgs, Hungary would become a vassal state of the Ottomans. Unlike under the Habsburgs, however, there would be freedom of religious worship, the Diet would elect the king of Hungary, no foreigners would be allowed to hold political offices, there would be no interference in the administration of laws, and the sultan would not try and subjugate any of the towns or castles.[17]

Initially, the Ottoman-Magyar alliance enjoyed tremendous success. Under the able leadership of Imre Thököly (1657–1705) and Grand Vizier Kara Mustafa (1634–1683), between 1678 and 1682 the Habsburg Imperial forces were repeatedly defeated. Thököly reached the peak of his success in 1682, when he ruled Transylvania and the Uplands, and controlled the gold and silver as well as the cattle, wine, and grain towns. It was in the same year that Leopold I made arguably the most important political decision of his life. Understanding that his support in Hungary had all but evaporated, in 1682 he made a compromise with the Hungarian nobility. He re-granted the Hungarian constitution, the Diet was once again endowed with the right to elect the king, and he promised to stop the persecution of Protestants. When in 1682 Thököly convened a National Diet in Košice to discuss the final assault on Habsburg rule in Hungary, he was surprised to find the Hungarian nobility abandoning him in large numbers. They claimed that all their demands had been met, and continuing the war was no longer necessary. Furthermore, many nobles were concerned with the direction the revolt had taken, strongly questioning the placement of Hungary under the sovereignty of the sultan. Rumors also circulated about Thököly promising freedom to all serfs that joined his cause to boost the number of his troops. Nobles feared that after the Habsburgs were defeated, this serf-peasant army would be difficult to control, and reminded themselves of the danger of the Dózsa peasant revolt.[18]

Disappointment at the National Diet of Košice did not stop Thököly. He could still count on the support of Protestant merchant capital in the towns, and his army was stronger and larger than ever. In 1683 Thököly led one of the largest armies at the time to the gates of Vienna with Kara Mustafa which, according to some accounts, was composed of 50,000 janissaries, 30,000 sphahis, and 200,000 accompanying troops. Arriving on July 14, 1683, the troops were camped outside the gates of Vienna until September 12, 1683. On that day, however, the King of Poland, Jan Sobieski (1629–1696), led a counter attack and defeated the Ottomans, driving them back into Hungary. Kara Mustafa was beheaded for his incompetence by the Ottoman Sultan, and defeat at Vienna also spelled the end of Thököly's prospects for becoming king of Hungary. The troops of both the malcontents and the Ottomans were, from that time forth, on the retreat, and in 1683 Bratislava, in 1685 Košice, Prešov, and Gran, and in 1686 Buda and Pest were taken by the Habsburg forces. Finally, in 1699 the Treaty of Karlowitz (also spelled Carlowits) was signed, forever ending the Ottoman occupation of Hungary, and establishing the Habsburgs as the supreme masters of the kingdom.[19]

The defeat of the Ottomans did not mark the end of unrest. As soon as the malcontents appeared to weaken, Leopold I aggressively reintroduced his centralizing drive. In 1687 he convened a National Diet in Bratislava, where he declared the office of king no longer elective but inheritable, personally appointed the Palatine of Hungary (the second most important political office after the king and historically elected by the Diet), increased taxation, and gave legitimacy to the confiscation of Protestant schools and churches. What further alienated the towns about the National Diet of 1687 was that from thenceforth royal free towns could collectively cast only a single vote (previously each royal free town had their own vote). Discontent with Leopold I, therefore, continued to be strong, and the limited number of rebellions between 1687 and 1700 was due, first and foremost, to the overwhelming superiority of the Imperial troops, rather than to the malcontents' lack of will.[20]

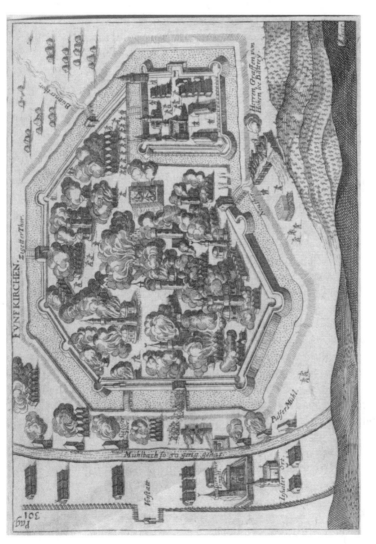

Figure 4.2 This seventeenth century print captures the destruction of the many Minarets of Pécs by Christian forces as they expelled the Ottomans from the territories of the Hungarian Kingdom. Reproduced courtesy of the Historical Gallery of the Hungarian National Museum. (T. 2955).

Following the fall of Thököly, who retired and died in Nikomedia in the Ottoman Empire in 1705, his foster son Ferenc Rákóczi II, Prince of Transylvania, became the leader of the rebels. Like Mihály Apafi before him, Rákóczi and the rebels demanded that the office of king be restored as an elected office, churches and schools confiscated from Protestants returned, and greedy councilors at court removed. They also called for the establishment of a Hungarian Office of Treasury instead of the "foreign illegal chamber" that administered Hungarian taxes, demanded the reappointment of Hungarian magistrates who had been removed in favor of foreigners, the primacy of Hungarian Law, tax reduction, improvement of commerce, and consultation of the Diet about domestic policies. Until these conditions are met: "the Hungarians have a Right to cast off the obedience to his [Leopold I] tyrannical Government."[21]

The revolt led by Rákóczi enjoyed some striking victories. Between 1703 and 1709, as the Habsburgs became distracted by the War of the Spanish Succession (1701–1714), the Hungarian rebels gained a strong foothold over most of the kingdom. However, in the long run, this last decade of the civil unrest also produced some of the highest death tolls. Between 1703 and 1711, the opposing armies marching back and forth across Transylvania and the Uplands spread disease and devastation. Certain towns declined by as much as two-thirds of their former populations. Few records document the actual number of deaths because in many places the town priest also perished, and no one was left to keep record. Mass graves were dug, and whole families disappeared. In the Uplands and Transylvania many towns would not recover demographically until the 1740s and 1750s.

It is unclear what course Hungary would have followed if the malcontents had succeeded. Nobles led the revolt, but there was a promise to end the robot for those serfs who joined the movement, and the struggle was also about religious freedom, the reestablishment of the constitution, defeating tyranny and, what most impressed the merchants, relaxation of taxes and improvement of commerce. From an urban perspective, the greatest benefit would have been to the mining towns of the Uplands and Transylvania, such as Baia Mare, Baia Sprie, Brezno (Bries/Breznóbánya), Kremnica, L'ubietová, Nová Baňa (Königsberg/Újbánya), Pukanec (Pukkanz/Bakabánya). If the rebels had succeeded, these towns would have formed the industrial center of Hungarian manufacturing, fulfilling initially the demands of the Hungarian war economy, but also that of the agricultural sector (plows, pitchforks, wheel-frames, etc.). It is noteworthy that under

Habsburg consolidation, it was precisely these mining towns that suffered the most severe decline because the Habsburgs relied on Bohemian manufacturing, and it was only in the second half of the nineteenth century that a few of them made a comeback.

Despite the obvious advantages of a potential victory by Thököly or Ferenc Rákóczi, it is noteworthy that neither of the rebel leaders, for all their emphasis on the importance of religious toleration, restricting the authority of the monarch, and improving trade and commerce, were commensurate with the leaders of the Glorious Revolution in England. Hungarian historians have a tendency to romanticize the "what ifs" of a victory by Rákóczi. They argue that maybe Hungary would have followed the course of Western European countries, and become the England of Eastern Europe.[22] Yet the usefulness of such speculations is highly debatable, for even if Rákóczi had been victorious, it is difficult to see how Hungary could have remained independent for any significant time. The late seventeenth and first half of the eighteenth century was a period of territorial consolidation, aggrandizement, and Empire building in East Central Europe, where the three Absolutist states to emerge—the Habsburgs, Hohenzollerns, and Romanovs—divided the territory among themselves. The partitioning of Poland first in 1772, second in 1793, and third in 1795, by Austria, Russia, and Prussia, is an excellent example of this point. Poland, like Hungary, had an overbloated class of nobles that ruled through a National Diet, which in turn elected the king. Yet the uniqueness of Poland, namely its elective monarchy and large nobility, was also its greatest weakness, and Poland—like Hungary if it had followed that road—could simply not oppose the international military competition of the newly rising absolutist states. Absolutist states were expanding in Eastern Europe in the seventeenth and eighteenth centuries at the expense of smaller kingdoms or elective monarchies precisely because they represented a superior concentration of military resources.

The intention here is not to idealize the state-building project of Leopold I, or even his successor Charles VI (Charles III in Hungary). At the end of his reign, Leopold I had made only modest gains in constructing an absolutist state in his Empire. The weakness of Habsburg absolutism would of course become exposed during its wars with Prussia. The Habsburgs, as Perry Anderson in his *Lineages of the Absolutist State* (London, 1974), had pointed out, were never able to construct a truly absolutist state and instead, Habsburg absolutism remained a hybrid of eastern and western forms. Much of this was because of the independent and rebellious nature of the Magyar nobility, and the compromise that characterized the end of the Rákóczi Revolt. Recognizing his inability to win the war, Rákóczi sued for peace with Charles VI (Charles III in Hungarian), and in what became known as the Peace of Szatmár (1711), the Magyar malcontents put down their guns and swords, not raising them again in a similar manner until 1848. The Peace of Szatmár was a success for the Habsburgs because the Magyar nobility agreed to make the office of king inheritable, rather than elective. Further, the king was to appoint the Palatine, and while the Hungarian Diet continued to meet periodically, it lost its law-making power. From 1711, critical decisions concerning Hungary were made in Vienna and the cameral politics of court. However, the Magyar nobility was not defeated like their Czech counterparts at the Battle of White Mountain. They kept their lands and serfs and, most importantly, were allowed to maintain their noble county diets—the real source of local Magyar noble political power. It is precisely in this compromise where the distinguishing features of western versus eastern absolutism can be detected. Namely, while in the West, Absolutism "was the redeployment of the political apparatus of the feudal class which had accepted the commutation of dues, as a *compensation for the disappearance of serfdom*, in the context of an increasingly urban economy which it did not completely control and to which it had to adapt. The Absolutist State in the East, by contrast, was the repressive machine of a feudal class that had erased the traditional communal freedoms of the poor. It was a *device for the consolidation of serfdom*, in a landscape scoured of autonomous urban life and resistance [. . .] The Absolutist State in the East never lost the signs of this original experience."[23]

Royal Free Towns at the Turn of the Eighteenth Century

The preceding section surveyed the critical political-military changes that transpired in the Hungarian Kingdom during the final decades of the seventeenth century. Important events included the revolts of Thököly and Rákóczi, the expulsion of the Ottomans (1686–1699), the signing of the Treaty of Karlowitz (1699), and the establishment of Habsburg hegemony over Hungary after the signing of the Treaty of Szatmár (1711). In contrast to this focus on political-military history, the following will be devoted to an analysis of the economic as well as demographic situation of Hungary's royal free towns from the start of

Habsburg consolidation in 1699 to the outbreak of the French Revolution. The data upon which the analysis is based are drawn from the censuses of 1715 and 1720, as well as the larger kingdom-wide survey of 1784/87. The censuses of 1715 and 1720 have many limitations, especially in comparison with the more sophisticated surveys of 1784/87 or 1805. Nevertheless, they remain the most important source of empirical knowledge about the demography and economy of early eighteenth-century Hungary.

After the Ottomans were expelled and the Habsburgs reunified the Uplands with the Carpathian Basin, the Habsburgs did not allow for the unification of Hungary with Transylvania. In part, this policy was based on the belief that a strong Hungary would undermine Habsburg hegemony in Eastern Europe. But it was also based on the conviction that throughout its history Transylvania had existed as a distinct politically administered territory within the Hungarian Kingdom, or in other words, the Transylvanian Diet had a legitimate claim for a certain amount of political administrative autonomy. The political administrative structure of Hungary and Transylvania were, after all, very different. Hungary proper, for instance, was divided into 47 counties in 1720, and had an estimated population of 1.7 million. Over 50 percent of the registered households in 1720 were serf families, while nobles accounted for 6 percent of the population. There was a tremendous amount of variation in the different counties. Some were thoroughly rural and agricultural, while others were urban and progressive. Among the most rural and backward regions were Árva and Torna counties, neither of which had any royal free towns. These counties were not alone. In 1720 Hungary there were 36 royal free towns in comparison to 47 counties. Altogether, in 1720, 27 counties had no royal free towns at all. At the same time, some counties had more than one royal free town. The most urbanized counties were Bratislava and Zvolen, each with five royal free towns, followed by Hont, Sáros, Sopron, and Szatmár counties, each with three royal free towns.[24]

Transylvania had a very different political administrative structure. Instead of the county system that characterized Hungary, it was divided into three distinct administrative units, corresponding to the so-called Three (privileged) Nations of Transylvania: the Magyars, the Székelys, and the Saxons. The Magyar region comprised eight counties, with two royal free towns (Cluj and Alba Iulia). In Székelyland, instead of counties, the region was divided into what were called seats. There were five seats altogether, with one royal free town called Tîrgu

Mureş. The third administrative unit of Transylvania was referred to as Royal Land, and this included the privileged Saxon towns of Transylvania. Royal Land was divided into 11 units, two of which were called districts, and nine others were seats. Royal Land contained five royal free towns, which were also some of the most impressive towns of Greater Hungary, like Sibiu, Braşov, Bistriţa, Madiaş, and Sighişoara. In 1720, Transylvania had an estimated population of 806,000 individuals, with over 50 percent of the households registered as serf-families, and an estimated 28,500 nobles. The eight royal free towns of Transylvania had a combined population of approximately 61,000, comprising 7.5 percent of the total population, a percentage point higher than in Hungary proper.[25]

When discussing Hungary's royal free towns at the turn of the eighteenth century, an important factor to consider is the strong ethnic diversity that shaped their collective existence. Out of the 44 royal free towns of Hungary and Transylvania in 1720, 21 had a German, 12 a Slovak, and 11 a Magyar majority. Interestingly, while more royal free towns (12) had a Slovak than a Magyar majority, those dominated by Magyars accounted for a larger urban population (almost 2 to 1). There were many Slovak towns, but they were much smaller than their Magyar counterparts. Indeed, three of the smallest royal free towns of Hungary had a Slovak majority: Pukanec with an urban population of only 698; Banská Belá (Bélabánya/Dilln) with 614; and L'ubietová with 745.

Royal free towns with a German majority ranged a spectrum from the petit towns such as Ruszt with an urban population of only 956, to the largest royal free town of Braşov, with 16,816 inhabitants. The German presence in large towns was especially marked, however, and three of the four largest towns of Hungary and Transylvania had a German-speaking majority (Buda, Braşov, and Sibiu). Possibly the most distinguishing feature of towns with a German majority, versus their Slovak or Magyar counterparts, was their wide distribution across the kingdom and Transylvania. Slovak royal free towns were limited to the Uplands, and Magyar-dominated towns to Transylvania or the Carpathian Basin. In contrast, German-speaking royal free towns were scattered from the southeastern corner of Transylvania bordering the Ottoman Empire to the northeastern corner and border with Poland, to the western border of the Habsburg Hereditary Lands.

While the German-speaking archipelagos were one of the few culturally unifying entities in the heterogeneous and decentralized Hungarian Kingdom and Transylvania, it must also be stressed that they did not form a single unified German burgher culture. For example, the so-called Zipser Germans that lived in the towns of Kežmarok and Levoča, were very different from the so-called Saxons of Sibiu, Mediaş, and Sighişoara, and the so-called Swabians that lived in the towns of Buda, Pest, Kőszeg, and the other major urban centers of the Carpathian Plains. The majority of the towns with a German-speaking majority were Lutheran, and from the late sixteenth century interurban ties were strengthened, especially among the Zipsers and Saxons. Yet these different urban and regional identities never fused. The difference between the Swabian towns of the Carpathian Basin and the traditional Lutheran towns of the Uplands and Transylvania was especially marked in this respect. The Swabian Germans settled in Buda, Pest, and other towns of the Plains after the Ottomans were expelled. They tended to be Catholic because the Habsburgs wanted to counter the growth of Protestantism under Ottoman rule, and often they were upwardly mobile peasants, small holders, artisans, and craftsmen, looked down upon by the old Zipser and Saxon burgher families.

German burgher influence in Hungary reached its zenith in the sixteenth and seventeenth centuries and by 1720 it was clearly on the wane, as an unmistakable ethnic shift was occurring within the town walls. This transformation is best illustrated by examining the growth of royal free towns with a Slovak majority. In 1720, 12 towns had a Slovak majority, but only five had an overwhelming majority. These were Skalica (Szakolcza/Sklaitz) with 93 percent of the urban-dwellers having Slovak family names, Trenčin with 80 percent, Pukanec and Zvolen with 72 percent, and Brezno with 70 percent. The remaining seven royal free towns had a Slovak majority that had formed only in the late seventeenth century. The town with the smallest Slovak majority was Trnava, where residents with Slovak names accounted for only 37 percent of the urban population, while inhabitants with German and Magyar names represented 31 and 30 percent, respectively. In the other six towns with a Slovak majority, like Banská Bystrica and L'ubietová, those with Slovak names comprised barely above 50 percent of the total population, while in Krupina, Banská Belá, and Sabinov, Slovaks were the largest ethnic group, but did not constitute an absolute majority.

The largest concentration of Slovak-dominated royal free towns was in the two Upland counties of Hont and Zvolen. Combined, Hont and Zvolen counties had eight royal free towns, all important medieval mining towns, following a similar trajectory from the thirteenth to the eighteenth century. Granted royal free privileges in the medieval period, when they emerged as important centers of gold, silver, or copper mining, they reached their Golden Age between 1450 and 1650. At their height, they were ruled by affluent German patricians who built their wealth on the export of valuable ores to Western Europe, and produced the elaborate and impressive renaissance houses furnishing these towns today. Urban decline set in simultaneously to the outbreak of the Decades of Revolt (1678–1710), and urban support for Thököly and Rákóczi was strongest among those frustrated German burghers who were feeling the pinch of declining profits. By 1710, the towns of Hont and Zvolen counties had undergone a significant economic and ethnic transformation. Abandoning their roots as German mining towns, they became part of Hungary's budding cottage industry in the Uplands, home to weavers and tailors, instead of merchant capitalists or industrialists. The affluent German patricians moved out, their place taken by landless Slovak cottagers and weavers. These towns never regained their early modern affluence, and in 1720 the combined population of the eight royal free towns of Hont and Zvolen counties (15,298) was smaller than the population of Braşov.[26]

Royal free towns with a Magyar-speaking majority were radically different from their Slovak counterparts. In the first place, Magyar royal free towns were greater in size, the largest being Cluj-Napoca, with an estimated population of 10,500 in 1720, followed by Debrecen with 8,200, and Tîrgu Mureş (Marosvásárhely/Neumarkt) with 5,000 residents. But most importantly, while many of the Slovak-dominated royal free towns were declining mining towns of the Uplands, towns with an overwhelmingly Magyar population were often expanding agricultural centers in the Carpathian Basin. Under Ottoman rule, towns of the Carpathian Basin, like Debrecen, were freed from their feudal lords and practiced self-government. Some nobles lived in the towns, but noble titles had no legal binding authority under Ottoman rule. All this changed when the Ottomans were expelled from the Carpathian Basin and the Habsburgs consolidated their control over Hungary. With the expulsion of the Ottomans, the descendants of nobles who left in the sixteenth century returned and hoped to reestablish their lost feudal privileges. Most of these nobles did not own estates and wanted to settle in the towns. While agrarian towns were able to fend off the entrance of nobles under Ottoman rule, they found it increasingly difficult to do so under the Habsburgs. Illustratively, while only 132 noble families lived in Debrecen in 1715, by 1787 their numbers increased to 207, and by 1840, to 794 families.

In Kecskemét, the stronghold of peasant-burgher resistance, in 1647 there were only 8 nobles in the town, while by 1730 there were 22, and by 1787 there were 192 noble families. A similar picture unfolded in Nagykőrös, where in 1647 there were only 10 noble families living in the town, in 1728 this grew to 42, and by 1787 there were 317 noble families.[27]

The struggle between nobles and the peasant burghers in the agrarian towns, therefore, intensified with the establishment of Habsburg rule, to the detriment of peasant-burgher autonomy. Many of the nobles who moved into the town were landless and poor, and it is estimated that only 1 to 2 percent had any significant estate holdings. The struggle consequently can be narrowed down to the attempt by nobles to maintain their feudal land tax-exempt privileges and to avoid having to partake in any civic duties. A classic example of this was a letter written to the court at Vienna collectively by the nobles of the agrarian town of Orosháza: "It is true that we are poor nobles of Orosháza, but in our veins flows noble blood. And we request from your most honorable highness, that we may practice the freedoms and immunity that any other noble or ecclesiastic order in the nation has. A noble, wherever he lives, according to the laws granted by the privileges, should be able to practice those freedoms and immunities as any noble, magnate, and priest."[28] István Rácz coined the term "double life," in respect to what the nobles were trying to accomplish. They wanted to move into the large as well as small towns, but they also wanted to bring their rural-feudal legal privileges with them. One of the more extreme attempts of the nobles to live this dual existence took place in Vásárhely in 1803, when they attempted to set up a private court of appeals in the town separate from the municipal government.

The ability of the Magyar nobility to take control of the municipal governments of the agrarian towns was enhanced by the Counter-Reformation policies of Maria Theresa. During Ottoman rule, many of the agrarian towns of the Carpathian Basin had converted to Calvinism, and when the House of Habsburg was consolidating its control over Hungary, it pressured the agrarian towns to rejoin the Catholic faith. Until 1715 Debrecen was able to defend its Calvinist tradition, but in that year one of the prerequisites the court made for the renewal of the town's royal free charter was that Catholics be allowed to settle. Yet it was in 1755 that the greatest damage was done. In that year Maria Theresa was able to force the town to elect two Catholics to the municipal government and in 1774 and 1781,

6 and 7, respectively, of the 13 senators were Catholic. At the same time, Calvinists in the town outnumbered Catholics 27,598 to 680. It was this shift that helped the aristocracy and nobility become the de facto political class of the towns by the end of the eighteenth century. In Debrecen in 1785 out of the 12 senators only 2 were peasant-burghers and 10 nobles. Similarly, by the end of the eighteenth century, in Nagykőrös three-fourths of the municipal administration was in the hands of the nobility, and in Kecskemét in 1836 out of the 67 persons in municipal office, 46 were nobles.[29]

The rise to power of the nobility within the Magyar-dominated towns of the Carpathian Basin was not as grim as it may at first sight appear. On the one hand, it is noteworthy that big towns were able to fend off the nobles' attempt to live a double life. There is, for instance, the classic example of the municipal government of Kecskemét in 1790, when it declared that "all those who live in the town must serve their civic requirements as is naturally ordained in the laws of 1723 paragraph 90."[30] Further, while the nobles had become the political ruling class, and had formed strong lobby groups, only in the villages were they able to practice their feudal laws. All the large agrarian towns—that is, Debrecen, Kecskemét, Nagykőrös, and Mezőtúr—defended their civic standing and the nobility was unsuccessful in its bid to establish political hegemony. It is also important to stress that many nobles who moved into the towns were poor, and some humbled themselves before the municipal governments in their attempts to gain permission to settle. The example of the noble Samuel Prikkel's letter to Kecskemét attests to this trend. Prikkel, in his letter to the municipal government, wrote: "I had worked some lands for Count Károlyi, but the most honorable lord wants this land for himself. I no longer want to live there and my great wish is to settle in this great noble city. I most humbly request the most honorable Magistracy, that this wish of their most humble servant be granted, and allow me to settle. I will be an active servant in the common good and partake of all civic requirements requested."[31] In short, within the Magyar royal free towns, the flood of nobles and even the noble takeover of the municipal governments did not signify the classic noble subjugation of towns, as described by Carsten in the case of Brandenburg towns of the sixteenth century. The nobles made a tremendous impact, but some of this was beneficial for urbanization. Magyar towns, after all, in the nineteenth century, grew on the strength of the export of agricultural produce to the West (mostly the Habsburg hereditary lands), and nobles and peasants living in the town enhanced the connection between town and country.

As is evident from the preceding, Hungary's royal free towns at the turn of the eighteenth century represented a tremendous amount of diversity on an ethnic, economic, and social level: Slovak towns had a large percentage of cottagers, Magyar towns had a large number of nobles and peasants, while German towns were divided along strong provincial identities like the Zipsers and Saxons. In short, each region had its individual specificities. This heterogeneity can be further illustrated by comparing the smallest with the largest royal free towns. As previously noted, in 1720 there were forty-four royal free towns in Hungary and Transylvania, with a total urban population of over 170,000. However, only four towns were home to over 10,000 individuals (Buda, Braşov, Cluj, and Sibiu). These four towns had a combined population of approximately 50,000, greater than the number of persons inhabiting the 24 smallest royal free towns. There were many royal free towns, therefore, but most were very small. Indeed, in 1720 five towns had urban populations of less than 1,000 persons, and 10 additional towns had populations below 2,000. Royal free standing was a privilege, which did not reflect demographic size, and throughout the kingdom (but mostly in the Carpathian Basin) many villages were significantly larger than the royal free towns of western and northern Hungary, with the classic example being Győr, which in 1720 had an estimated population of 7,300, but was granted royal free standing only in 1743.

It is also interesting that while four of the five largest towns in Hungary and Transylvania were in Transylvania, four of the five smallest towns (Banská Belá, Ľubietová, Pukanec, Zvolen, and Ruszt) were in the Uplands. The five smallest towns combined had a population of only about 3,700, and four of the five were declining medieval mining centers. Their decay started in the second half of the seventeenth century, and while they were able to put a halt to a complete demographic collapse by allowing Slovak cottagers to settle, none of them made a successful transition into modernity. They were not alone in their failure. In the early eighteenth century, a division of labor was emerging in the Habsburg Empire, as the Western territories like Bohemia emerged as centers of industry and Hungary, as the breadbasket of the Habsburg Empire. Accordingly, formerly important urban centers were experiencing a long cycle of stagnation, as Hungary's mining and manufacturing had a difficult time competing with western imports. The oldest and at one time most prominent towns, were withering as new cities were sprouting up in the Carpathian Basin. Many of the smallest towns were, therefore, also the oldest, such as Krupina, which was granted royal free privileges in 1244, but in 1720 had a population of only 1,503, Ľubietová, granted royal free standing in 1379, with only 745 inhabitants, or Zvolen, which was granted royal free privileges in 1342, but had an urban population of only 980. Other old towns which remained small were Banská Bystrica (privileges granted in 1225), Baia Mare (privileges granted in 1238), and Nová Baňa (privileges granted in 1345). Up to the sixteenth century, these towns had shown great promise, but after the defeat of Thököly, they never recovered. They failed to become cities and made a difficult transition into modernity.

Urban evolution between 1720 and 1787, consequently, evidences a number of contradictory tendencies. On the one hand, the Habsburg court was clearly interested in promoting urbanization, because it granted 16 new royal charters between 1700 and 1780. As a result, the total estimated population of royal free towns more than doubled from approximately 171,000 (44 towns) in 1720 to 484,000 in 1787 (61 towns), an increase of over 300,000 people. Concurrently, however, the overall proportion of town dwellers dropped from 6.8 to 5.7 percent of the total population. Indeed, the dramatic rise in the absolute number of urban dwellers was due first and foremost to the increase in the number of towns with royal free status. Furthermore, 14 out of the 16 new towns were situated on the territory re-conquered from the Ottomans on the Carpathian Plains, many of which grew on the strength of the export of agricultural produce to the western Habsburg lands. Meanwhile, the historic towns in the mountainous Uplands and Transylvania experienced minimal growth and some even saw considerable decline. In Transylvania, Bistriţa decreased from 5,292 to 4,637 during the period 1713–1787 and Sighişoara from 5,565 to 5,517 between 1723 and 1787, while Braşov and Mediaş experienced less than 5 percent growth.[32]

In political-economic terms, Habsburg consolidation favored those towns of the Hungarian Kingdom that tapped into the agricultural export sector, and were less beneficial, if not outright detrimental, for the historical mining and manufacturing urban centers. Hungary in the eighteenth century had entered the road of dependent development. The stagnation of the mining towns was especially acute. In 1720 the combined population of the eight mining centers of Baia Mare, Baia Sprie, Banská Bystrica, Banská Štiavnica, Pukanec,

Kremnica, Ľubietová, Nová Baňa was around 22,000. This increased to approximately 43,500 by 1787, and to only 60,000 by 1867. In comparison to the rest of the kingdom, such growth was equivalent to decline. For example, the towns of Debrecen, Győr, Pécs, Pest, and Szeged in the Carpathian basin had only 25,400 residents in 1720, but almost 100,000 in 1787, and over 304,000 by 1867. Of course, urban stagnation was not limited to the mining sector. It included virtually all the towns of the Uplands and Transylvania that had experienced a unique urban dynamism in the sixteenth and first half of the seventeenth century. It included the important manufacturing and merchant towns of Bardejov, Prešov, Kežmarok, Levoča, and Trnava of the Uplands, which in 1720 had a combined population of around 12,000 and grew to only 21,700 by 1787. None of these towns made a successful transition into modernity, and in 1868 they collectively accounted for only 32,700 urban dwellers, or less than half the size of Debrecen.

The old towns of Hungary were dying and new cities were rising. It is true that Buda, Pécs, Pest, and Szeged claimed the status of "old towns." They had all enjoyed special privileges in the medieval period, and some of them had even been sites of Roman settlements. Yet the reality was that Buda, Pest, Pécs, Szeged, and Timişoara were the youngest towns of the Hungarian Kingdom. After the Ottomans were expelled, virtually all the urban dwellers were killed or fled for their lives, and new immigrants filled the vacant urban space. These towns attest to the dynamic population movements that characterized the urban history of the Carpathian Basin throughout its history. Home to Italians in the thirteenth century, Germans in the fifteenth, Turks and Sephardim Jews in the sixteenth and seventeenth, in the eighteenth century the Habsburgs settled Swabians, Serbians, Croatians, and Magyars to again rebuild these centers. They grew because of the strength of agricultural export, and while they expanded, the old towns of Transylvania and the Uplands declined. The old towns did not fit into the division of labor the Habsburgs worked to create in their Central European Empire. The level to which many of the historic towns declined is illustrated by Henrik Marczali's reflections on Maria Theresa's last year as empress:

> The inhabitants of the royal free boroughs, the centers of trade and industry, on an average paid no more taxes per head than the wretched peasants of the rural districts. I believe the case is unparalleled; and whether it serves as a proof of the poverty or of the selfishness of the

towns, it at any rate refutes any statement tending to create the impression that towns of Hungary rendered eminent services to the country.[33]

In conclusion, as the eighteenth century came to an end, the historic Hungarian bourgeoisie was undergoing a dramatic crisis. Habsburg consolidation had produced uneven urban development, and while some towns were growing, the majority of towns in the Upland and Transylvania were home to a great deal of bitterness toward Vienna. The Habsburgs not only introduced special taxes that made it difficult for Hungary's home industry to compete, but they also prohibited Protestants from buying land in the countryside, as well as holding political offices. The landlords who traded in grain and cattle prospered, while the producers' and manufacturers' profits slipped away. Faced with discriminatory laws and declining economic standing, many leading Protestant families left Hungary for Prussia, never to return. Hungary's historic bourgeoisie at the time of the French Revolution was, therefore, a small and discontented entity. From the establishment of Habsburg rule to the outbreak of the revolution, the old towns had seen minimal growth, while many underwent demographic stagnation and decline. Martin Schwartner, organizer of Hungary's first modern census, recorded 484,659 urban dwellers in 1787. This represented around 5.6 percent of the total population of 8 million. The majority were German speakers employed in handicraft production. Schwartner also mentioned a noticeable decline in the number of German burghers employed as merchants, while Greeks and Armenians were taking over the kingdom's commercial activities.[34] According to the modern historian Kálmán Benda, however, the number Schwartner noted as urban dwellers was inflated, because day laborers and, in some cases, agricultural villagers were also registered as such. According to Benda, a more realistic estimate of the actual size of the Hungarian bourgeoisie would be between 200,000 and 250,000, representing from 1.5 to 2 percent of the total population. This low percentage was equaled in Poland, but surpassed significantly by France's 12 percent. Furthermore, while the nobility in France accounted for 1 percent of the total population at the time of the revolution, that of Hungary numbered approximately 390,000—making them a larger demographic block than the urban dwellers.[35]

Given their small size, it is not surprising that the Hungarian bourgeoisie has been neglected by Habsburg historiography. The majority were, after all, artisans or apprentices and not enthusiasts of the Enlightenment. Benda estimates that the number of "Josephine intellectuals," that is, those who supported radical reform, was between 15,000 and 20,000, representing only 0.3 percent of the population.[36] As an entity, they could never have overthrown the Old Regime. Nevertheless, it is important to stress that while much smaller than their West European counterparts, as will be highlighted in the following chapter, the Hungarian bourgeoisie was introduced early to the ideas of the Enlightenment, experimented with the ideas of reform and was ready to enlist in a movement to overthrow the system of feudalism. True, when it came to military action, they could never have produced a force substantial enough to defeat an organized army, but as educators, they were able to radicalize Hungarian society by teaching and spreading the "culture" of revolution. Yet the question arises: Given their support for the ideas of the Enlightenment, what would their relationship be to the "nation" and which new "imagined community" would they champion? Would the towns' German-speaking Hungarian subjects become propagators of German or Hungarian nationalism? Or, as German burghers in the Habsburg Empire, would they work to create a Habsburg national identity?

5

Enlightenment from the Towns

A Catholic aristocratic perspective has dominated the literature on the spread of Enlightenment reform in Hungary. Accordingly, Enlightenment ideas in Hungary are understood as having originated at the court in Vienna, where Prince Wenzel Anton Kaunitz was especially influential. It was during Kaunitz's stay in Paris as ambassador that Vienna opened its doors to the salons of the skeptics and atheists. Kaunitz introduced the young Austrian aristocrats to these salons—where, as Gyula Szekfű noted, the body (meaning passions) as well as the mind were liberated—and he publicized Voltaire as well as many others (like Diderot) working for the Encyclopedia in Vienna. Maria Theresa distrusted the irreligious and immoral ways of the new ideas, but after the death of her husband, the empress turned increasingly inward, and interfered less. Szekfű wrote of the period:

> It became, accordingly, fashionable for young Austrian aristocrats to travel to Paris, visiting Voltaire and Rousseau, corresponding with them, and coming back and reading nothing else but French books; from the works of the great thinkers to Baron d'Holbach's materialism, to the most obscene sentimental frivolous French novels. In the Viennese royal and aristocratic salons they no longer believed in God, nor morals, and it was only for the Queen's sake that appearances to the contrary were kept at all.[1]

The Magyar aristocracy was introduced to the new ideas almost immediately. The precondition was knowledge of French, which they learned either at the new educational institutes established by Maria Theresa (the so-called Theresianum), the Military Academy, or the Savoy Cavalry Academy. Everyday life in Vienna also exposed many to the fashionable new cultural currents. The numerous salons, theaters, and operas all played their role. "These young Magyar aristocrats," Szekfű noted, "grew up in a much different world than their fathers and grandfathers, whose worldview was not only dominated by the late Baroque but who also, aside from Latin, knew no foreign languages."[2] The ideas of Voltaire first emerged only in these high circles intricately tied to the royal court, such as the Pálffy, Eszterházy, and Erdődy families, and subsequently trickled down to the "more talented members of the middle class."[3]

Contrasting with the traditional and dominant view that the Enlightenment and Civilization were introduced from above exists the contribution of Éva H. Balázs, Domokos Kosáry, George Barany, and Moritz Csáky.[4] While accepting the civilizing influence of the court, these historians argue that in the Hungarian Kingdom, the Enlightenment had multiple—even if at times intersecting—points of dissemination. Namely, simultaneous to the court's awakening, an equally important movement emerged from the royal free towns advocating liberal reforms. This second source came from a small elite within the Lutheran towns: schoolteachers, merchants, doctors, rural industrialists: the class that had been agitating against Habsburg rule since the re-introduction of the Counter Reformation following the Treaty of Szatmár in 1711. It was the voice of frustrated Protestants who had supported the Magyar noble-led rebellions of Thököly and Rákóczi against the Habsburg state, and who continued to be deeply mistrustful and alienated from rank and file Catholic intelligentsia that came to power after the defeat of the malcontents. Some Catholic burghers joined the chorus especially around Pest, but many of the early radicals originated from either the Protestant royal free towns of the Uplands, Transylvania, or the Calvinist towns of the Carpathian Plains. The paucity of enlightened Catholics, is most evident in the fact that when Joseph II sought to introduce radical reforms, he was forced to reach out to the Protestant urban estate. Most importantly, much like in seventeenth-century England, religious dissent in eighteenth-century Hungary played a key role in the spread of ideas that were parallel and complementary to the ideas propagated by the Enlightenment. Ideas such as the freedom of religious worship, the inalienable rights of man, and the sanctity of private property had gained popularity in Protestant salons struggling against the intolerance and tyranny of the Habsburg state.[5]

The early agitators of reform within the towns represented a tiny fraction of the overall urban population, and a disproportionate number came from the richest families: the children and grandchildren of wealthy urban Lutheran wholesale merchants, miners, jewelers, private bankers (i.e., usurers), wine and grain producers, or in other words that entrepreneurial proto-capitalist and proto-industrialist class that flourished in the environment of contested sovereignty in partitioned Hungary. These families usually rose to prominence in the seventeenth century, when they were often ennobled. It was these ennobled Lutheran burghers who had experienced the most significant setbacks under Habsburg consolidation and it was they who began to seek alternative ways of understanding and reforming state and society. There were, of course, others: the students who enthusiastically embraced the words of their teachers, and a number of bright minds who seemingly figured it out all by themselves. Yet the reality was that in the towns the size of the purse determined the size of the family library, and because the best Lutheran Universities of Wittenberg, Leipzig, and Jena were all at a considerable distance, mostly the wealthier burghers could afford the luxury of a good education.

The ennobled Lutheran burghers were in an unusual class position within Hungary's social structure. As nobles they had one foot in the Magyar rural world, and as Lutherans, the other foot in the German urban world. Yet they belonged fully to neither of these estates. They bridged the gap between town and country, traveling between these vastly different worlds, yet wherever they went, they were seen as outsiders. A case in point is the old nobles' perception of these ennobled burghers, viewing them with mistrust because they had secured their titles in the market square and not on the battlefield. While in France nobles shunned engaging in trade, in Hungary a title of nobility was a necessary prerequisite to be a successful merchant. It was the means to gain tax immunity when trading across county lines. Ennoblement in the seventeenth century from the merchants' perspective was, accordingly, spurred on by a calculating drive for profit, and not a compulsion to mimic and parrot the aristocracy.

The position of ennobled Lutheran burghers within Hungarian society is best understood in the context of the tremendous internal differentiation that characterized the Hungarian nobility and bourgeoisie at the end of the eighteenth century. In 1786–1787, the Hungarian nobility was estimated at 330,000 individuals, with an additional 64,000 living in Transylvania.[6] Included in this group were the Székely nobles of Transylvania, who lived in villages and were not always distinguishable from free peasants. Further, those nobles in Transylvania who had fewer than two serfs were obliged from the turn of the eighteenth century to pay taxes, significantly reducing the worth of their titles. At the top of the hierarchy were the aristocrats, of whom there were few. In 1786–1787 approximately 3 princely, 80 countly, and 95 baronial families lived in Hungary proper, together with an additional 11 countly and 20 baronial families in Transylvania. A large step down from this "castled-elite" stood the propertied nobility who, in the course of the nineteenth century—as a reaction to their growing impoverishment and downward mobility—contributed the rank and file state-builders to Hungarian society. In contrast to these wealthy nobles, many were poor and commonly referred to as "seven plum-tree nobles," a derogatory reference to their humble life, often-times no better than that of peasants. It is difficult to obtain an accurate figure of their proportion in the nobility, but the Hungarian historian Károly Vörös estimated that in certain counties the "*kisnemesek*" (little-nobles) accounted for about 90 percent of all nobles. This petit-noblesse lived in the villages next to the peasants and, most significantly, some of the most indebted nobles lived at the level of serfs. They lost the last vestiges of their privileges in 1800, when it became legally permissible for a non-noble peasant to physically beat an indebted noble-peasant; a peasant beating a nobleman was a world greatly different from Voltaire's France.[7] The ennobled Protestant burghers could neither match the pomp and wealth of the aristocracy, nor were they as poor and uneducated as the "*kisnemesek*."

The urban estate, like the nobility, was also strikingly ridden with division. According to the census of 1787, there were 61 royal free towns in Hungary (including Croatia and Transylvania), with a total estimated population of 485,000. The vast majority of urban dwellers, however, did not have franchise within the towns. The most down-trodden were the women, who could not vote, nor hold political office. The male population of the towns in 1787 was approximately 222,800. But even within the male population only a minority had burgher privileges. Out of around 222,800 males, almost 70,000 were children under the age of seventeen (meaning they were not yet burghers of the town), over 5,200 were peasants, 22,600 peasant-burghers, and over 66,300 were servants or cottagers. In the royal free towns of Hungary in 1787, therefore, only approximately 44,000 persons (9 percent of the urban population) had full burgher privileges and franchise in the towns.[8]

Conflict and tension in the town was not only between the haves and have-nots, but also among the elite 44,000 franchised burghers. In 1787 this urban elite could be divided into three sub-groups. Out of the 44,000 privileged urban-dwellers, approximately 31,200 were burghers, 5,000 were priests, teachers, and government officials, and 7,800 were nobles. Guild masters comprised the core of the 31,200-strong registered burghertum. Of course, there were numerous guilds and different guilds behaved in different ways. Yet many of the guild masters were some of the staunchest defenders of feudalism. They were against opening the town gates to the immigration of peasants, and defended the system of strict price controls and production quotas. Some guild masters in the second half of the eighteenth century began investing capital into the rural industry, thereby also drifting toward the reformers' side, but many remained locked in their petit world, opposing change and fighting to maintain the rigid wall separating town from country. Their resistance to the entrance of peasants often also signified ethnic tensions, and guilds in many of the Upland and Transylvanian royal free towns made it a regular part of their behavior to give membership only to German-speaking Lutherans, excluding in the process Slovaks, Romanians, and Magyars.

Early supporters of the Enlightenment in the towns emerged mostly from the ranks of the 7,800 urbanized nobles. City nobles represented a tiny but unique element within Hungarian society, and were very different from nobles living in the countryside. Nobles that lived in the royal free towns were often Lutherans or Calvinists and, in order to settle and gain acceptance within the burgher world, forfeited their feudal privileges: meaning that they could not defer to noble law to protect their interests, but submitted to the supremacy of the municipal administration. Ennobled Protestant burghers intermarried with both the town burghers and the country-living Protestant nobles. Yet in the second half of the eighteenth century, their economic interests increasingly clashed with guild regulation in the towns, as well as noble control of rural labor. The entrepreneurial ennobled burghers who became involved in rural industry wanted the freedom to decide how much of their capital they can invest in an enterprise, how great their profit margin will be, and how many workers they may employ. This element was a small minority in the towns. Out of the estimated total urban population of 485,000, they represented approximately only 1.6 percent.

The allegiance of the 5,000 priests, teachers, and government officials living in the royal free towns in 1787 was split. Many invariably sided with the guild masters to become the bulwark of tradition. The conservative worldview of the late baroque could not be overthrown overnight. Concurrently, however, Lutheran Lyceums did produce some outstanding reformers, and under Maria Theresa individuals like Samuel Brukenthal from Sibiu rose to prominence. Lutheran and Calvinist ministers and teachers had historically been antagonistic to the Habsburg state, and it was within their ranks that some outstanding progressive thinkers emerged. Within the Catholic Church the Jesuits were losing their influence and were expelled, but they had trained many teachers who occupied leading positions within the educational system. In short, Enlightenment from the towns was based on propagating *Bildung* (education), but there were many teachers—first and foremost Catholic priests—who opposed the idea of freedom of thought.

At the heart of the origins of Enlightenment from the towns was that ennobled Lutheran burghers were experiencing increasing difficulty finding their position within the feudal division of labor that dominated Hungarian society. They bridged the void between town and country, but belonged to neither world. In significant ways, the Weltanschauung of the ennobled Lutheran burghers had much in common with the ennobled Jews in nineteenth century Hungary. Similar to their ennobled Jewish counterparts a century later—who felt internally torn and outside of both the Magyar noble estate and traditional Jewish society and who were similarly struggling to come to terms with their multiple identities—these German burghers had the ability to rise above any one class, estate, or ethnic-linguistic interest. Adopting Karl Mannheim's terminology, the term that possibly best describes them is "socially unattached class."[9] And as a socially unattached class, they were one of the few groups in Hungarian society at the end of the eighteenth century that could become agents of westernization and Enlightenment reform.[10]

The growing alienation of the ennobled burghers from the guilds in the town and nobles in the countryside led to a critical reevaluation of their alliances and allegiances. If reforms were impossible through the guild-dominated municipal government and the noble-dominated county diets, the only other significant ally was the court in Vienna. However, an alliance of Lutheran burghers with the Catholic Habsburgs was not an easy step to take. The Habsburgs, after all, were enthusiastic supporters of the Counter Reformation, and Lutheran towns had suffered egregious bloodshed at the hands of Jesuits and religious fanatics sent by the court. At the same time, those convinced of the necessities for Enlightenment reform had few alternatives, but to try and find support within the progressive aristocratic and royal circles in Vienna and Bratislava.

One of the path-breaking intellectuals trying to create a court-urban alliance was Joseph Benczúr (1728–1784). Born in the Uplands, Benczúr, like many supporters of the Enlightenment in Hungary, studied abroad in the 1750s at Jena and Halle. Upon returning to Hungary, Benczúr was first appointed Professor at the Lyceum of Kežmarok, where he introduced reforms in the curriculum and presided over the general modernization of the school. His reform efforts were soon noticed and earned him an appointment at the famous Lutheran Lyceum in Bratislava. This was a critical move because Bratislava at the time was the capital of Hungary, where the Hungarian Diet was convened. It was in Bratislava that Benczúr made contacts with the salons of the reformers and Joseph II, and where he began building the social networks connecting the urban intelligentsia with the court. His influence increased with the coming to power of Joseph II in 1780, and he was first elected councilman in Bratislava, and in 1784 was appointed by Joseph II personally to be the court librarian. Arguably his most important contribution was helping aspiring Lutheran intellectuals from Hungary's royal free towns win positions in the emerging modern bureaucracy.[11]

Benczúr was author of three notable works: *Ungaria Semper Libera* (1764), *Commentatio juridical critica de haereditario jure* (1771, under the pseudonym Eusebius Verunus), and *Jurium Hungariae in Russiam minorem et Podoliam* . . . (1772). The common theme in each of these works is the positive image of the Habsburgs. In *Ungaria Semper Libera*, Benczúr argued that the Hungarian feudal estates do not have the legal right to restrict and interfere with the prerogative of the Habsburg court. In *Commentatio juridical critica de haereditario jure* he contended that the Habsburg family had a legitimate right to the inheritance of the Hungarian Kingdom, and in *Jurium Hungariae in Russiam minorem et Podoliam* . . . Benczúr traced the legitimate claim of the Habsburg family over that part of Poland which fell under their control after the first Partition of Poland. The most overt praises toward the Habsburg family by Benczúr can be found in an unpublished manuscript he wrote in Kežmarok sometime between 1756 and 1757. In the work Benczúr stresses that since the time of Matthias Corvinus, the Magyar nobility was a force retarding development and hindering progress in Hungary. Fortunately, after the Ottomans were expelled the Habsburg family consolidated its power over Hungary, and was responsible for bringing about a golden age in the kingdom. In other words, Benczúr strove in his published works to establish the legitimacy of Habsburg rule over Hungary and, more specifically, to extol the progressive influence of enlightened absolutism.[12]

Enlightenment reform in Hungary also found allies in individuals such as Johann Schneider (1745–1818). The case of Schneider is very important, because his family had historically been opposed and oppressed by the Habsburgs, but by 1760, nevertheless, became a supporter of Enlightened Absolutism. The Schneider family rose to power in the mid-seventeenth century as wine and grain merchants. In a 1675 testament written by Rosina Kletzer, the wife of Mathias Schneider, her wise last words read: "As the family business is in wine, cursed be the Schneider who drinks from his profits."[13] The family reached its pinnacle of power under Georg Schneider, who was granted nobility in 1681, and in 1686 listed as the richest man in Košice, and elected as the first president of the newly reestablished Merchants Guild of the town.[14] In the same year, he also started to hoard grain in his three homes of Košice, grain that he subsequently sold to Kuruc soldiers during their battle for Hungarian independence against the Habsburg court. Upon the defeat of Thököly, Georg Schneider, with other leading Lutheran merchants of Prešov and Košice, was dragged before a court for conspiring against Leopold I. General Antonio Caraffa, one of the most infamous figures of the Counter Reformation, led the persecution of the conspirators. Caraffa's methods earned him the unflattering distinction of being one of the most innovative and brutal torturers of the Inquisition in Hungary. Interestingly, Georg Schneider was able to escape without injury. This was not from the lack of effort by the jury appointed by the Habsburg court. The judge of Košice, David Féya, alias Rakovszky, was tortured for a confession and implicated Georg Schneider as a conspirator.[15] The most probable reason for Georg Schneider's acquittal was that during the time between the start of the rebellion and his trial, he had married the daughter of Paul Sonntag, Dorottya, and later his son Mathias Schneider married the daughter of Gaspar Sonntag, Susan. This marriage alliance conjoined the leading wine, copper, and iron interests of northern Hungary and was the most financially powerful family network in existence in that part of the kingdom. As the jury was deliberating the fate of Georg Schneider, Dorottya Sonntag's uncle, Joseph Okolicsányi—Al-Ispán (Judge of the Noble Diet) of Arva County—delivered 10,000 Forints to the most honorable judges of the jury, so that 'no ill fate should befall the relatives of the Sonntag family' (i.e., Georg Schneider).[16] Others were not as fortunate. In March of 1687, 20 burghers and nobles were executed in Prešov for conspiring against the Habsburg state, among them Simon Feldmajer, Sigismund Zimmerman (the rich burgher and senator of Prešov), and members of the Keczer, Medveczky, and Palásthy families.[17]

While Georg Schneider escaped major harm, the family from that time forth was on the decline, and much of the resentment was against the Habsburg re-conquest of Hungary. If Thököly or Rákóczi had been victorious, the family could have emerged as the leading wine and grain merchants of eastern Hungary. But with the defeat of the Magyar malcontents, the family lost its power, prestige, and patronage. Nevertheless, despite these past hostilities, Johann Schneider became a supporter of the Habsburgs' drive to establish enlightened absolutism in Hungary by 1760. Schneider's political philosophy is captured in his one and only significant work, *Definitiones propositiones Wolffinae*.[18] Published in a small printing house in the royal enfranchised village of Velká Lomnica (Grosslomnitz/Kakaslomnic) in 1769, the book was a synopsis of Christian Wolff's ideas, one of the most influential philosophers on Joseph II's impending reform initiatives.[19] Schneider was in agreement with several aspects of Wolff's philosophy. He embraced the idea that a strong central government should take an active role in promoting industry and trade, limiting luxury spending and advancing education. He also approved of Christian Wolff's advocacy for the key features of the Scottish Enlightenment. Schneider argued that the question of dogma should not be of concern to the state, and while the ruler has an obligation to maintain the moral standards of the kingdom, the guiding policy should be religious toleration for non-Catholics and support for the freedom of thought. Not only were the reorganization, unification, and centralization of the Hungarian political administrative system crucial for the monarchy's future, but he also advocated the state's involvement in the defense of the inalienable rights to private property. Consequently, followers of Wolff, like Johann Schneider, were eager to see the establishment of a strong state, which at the same time was an adversary to the urban guild control of production and the Magyar noble estate.[20]

One of the most influential and prolific Lutheran Philosophes to emerge at this time was Johann Genersich (1761–1823). A number of similarities exist between Genersich and Schneider. Like the Schneiders, the Genersich family witnessed its most dynamic financial growth during the seventeenth century when, under the guidance of David Genersich, a famous goldsmith, they were awarded nobility. During the Rákóczi Revolt, a series of disasters struck. First, the

Genersichs lost a substantial sum of money they had loaned in support of the Rákóczi (1703–1711) rebellion. Then in 1710 cholera decimated the population of Levoča, resulting in a decline from over 7,000 urban dwellers in 1680 to barely over 3,000 in 1720.[21] The Genersich family was hard hit by the epidemic and all but one branch of the family survived.

Johann Genersich's first significant work on political philosophy was *Von der Liebe des Vaterlandes*, printed anonymously shortly after Leopold II's death in 1792. The work in part was intended as a guide for the new emperor Francis II on how to continue with the Enlightenment reforms of Joseph II and Leopold II, as well as to extol the virtues of Enlightenment in general and the advantages of enlightened absolutism. *Von der Liebe des Vaterlandes*, spanning some 700 pages, appears to have been inspired by Thomas Genersich's 1761 work *Von dem Tod furs Vaterland*. Johann Genersich begins by proclaiming himself a child of the Enlightenment and compares the enlightened with the unenlightened. He argues that enlightened individuals are those who base their membership in a nation on a specific constitutional relationship to a state. Unenlightened people, by contrast, are those who base their national-ethnic identity on some mysterious connection to the land and who make a distinction between the culture of the nation and the administration of the state. Accordingly, peasants and nobles are unenlightened, for they understand their relationship to a nation by their proximity to the soil of the land, and see the modern state (the Habsburg state) as a foreign entity with no connection to the "blood" of the nation. Those enlightened, however, understand that there is no separation between nation and state and indeed, the two categories are identical. *Von der Liebe des Vaterlandes*, therefore, implies that nationalism and patriotism are inseparable phenomena.[22]

The second part of Genersich's work suggests a series of reforms Francis II should undertake in order to remain on the enlightened path. Like Joseph II and Leopold II before him, Genersich proposed that Francis I continue to support educational reforms in the Hungarian Kingdom. Educational reformers, he noted, "the scientists of society," are the best allies the emperor can rely on in his attempt to extinguish the anachronistic legacies of the feudal system and to modernize Hungarian society. Genersich's emphasis on *Bildung* was by no means an endorsement of popular democracy. Rather, he explained that membership in the state needed to be based on one's educational merit, not on some inalienable right given at birth. Reforms must subscribe to the social reality of the masses, but ultimately, decision-making should always be in the hands of the social scientist.[23] Consequently, Genersich, like Schneider, avoided the question of ethnicity and nationhood. He saw "Enlightenment" as the prerequisite for membership in the nation.

A contemporary and complementary figure to Schneider and Genersich was Johann Molnár, a Lutheran minister in Pest in the 1780s. Molnár did not publish extensively, but his political pamphlet called *Politisch-kirchlich Manch Hermaeon* (1790) did win him some fame. Molnár, like Genersich, urged the German-speaking Protestant middle class to impose Enlightenment reform from above because, according to Molnár, reforms were not coming from below. This goal could be accomplished only by defeating the two pernicious enemies of progress: the nobles and members of the clergy. Nobles hindered reform because they reaped the benefits of serfdom and the Catholic clergy robbed the peasants while keeping them mesmerized by false sermons. For Hungary to advance, radical measures like the abolishment of the privileges of the first two estates (the Aristocracy and Clergy) had to be undertaken.[24] Molnár, therefore, advocated the alliance of Lutheran German-burgher with Catholic Emperor to bring about the complete overhaul of the Hungarian feudal land tenure system. Similar to Genersich, this alliance would find institutional unity in the newly constructed modern efficient state-bureaucracy and administration. Ethnicity was not reducible to birth for either Genersich or Molnár. Instead, ethnic identity was understood as something plastic, easily malleable, a question of internal self-affirmation rather than external imposition. While the language question was important for nation-building, for Genersich, Schneider, and Molnár, more critical were the laws and institutions of the state. They shared a civic (laws, constitution, patriotism), rather than ethno-linguistic understanding of nationalism.

For the budding Lutheran Philosophes of Hungary, the victory of Enlightenment reform hinged on education (*Bildung*), advocating the building of more schools, the reading of new books, and enlightening the ignorant. Especially important in this respect is that Genersich started his education as a student in the Kežmarok Lyceum during its most formative years since the advent of the Reformation. Under the direction of József Benczúr (1728–1784), the school reforms of Empress Maria Theresa were introduced, converting the Lyceum into an institution where for the first time the country nobles studied together with the city burghers.[25] Previously these two estates had only limited contact, primarily through the intermediation of the ennobled burghers. The reforms were aimed, therefore, at bridging the gap between town and country. During the first decade of these educational experiments, between 1760 and 1770, the Lyceum was of course poor and Johann Genersich reports that when he attended the school some of the windows were broken and during the winter it got very cold. Because of this, students were required to bring firewood to the school on winter days. Yet despite the lack of means, as a young student at the Lyceum, Genersich was already confronting the leading problem of modern European society: how to bring about a merger between the noble and urban worlds, and one of the future problems of Hungarian society: how to forge a common identity between Magyar noble and German burgher. Following his studies in the Lyceum, Genersich continued his education at the University of Jena, Germany, where he was armed with the intellectual tools that would make him one of the leading pedagogues of the Hungarian Kingdom.[26]

At Jena, Genersich was deeply impressed by the reform ideas of the famous German pedagogue Johann Bernhard Basedow (1720–1790). Basedow argued that a complete overhaul of the education system in the German Princedoms was necessary. Instead of grit memorization of Latin texts and exclusively focusing on the old and new Testament, Basedow evidenced the need to introduce physical education (to develop the body as well as the mind), and to focus on modern subjects, such as agronomics, physics, mathematics, history, and political philosophy. He was a strong advocate of the creation of new institutions that would train a new generation of leaders deeply influenced by the Enlightenment. In 1770 he founded such an experimental school called the Philanthropinum in Dessau, in which schoolchildren from both noble and burgher backgrounds studied together. This school greatly impressed, among others, Immanuel Kant, Johann Wolfgang von Goethe, and Frederic William of Prussia. Basedow's ideas were based on the writings of John Amon Comenius, John Locke, and Jean Jacques Rousseau, and his emphasis on bringing a new sense of realism into the schools played a fundamental role in the development of German public schools in the nineteenth century.[27] Genersich had first-hand knowledge of these institutions as a student in Jena, because very close to Jena in the town of Schnepfenthal, the German pedagogue Gotha Salzman founded an experimental school modeled along Basedowian lines. As proposed by Basedow, the student body was composed of children from both the noble and urban estates and education aimed to be more natural, realistic, and humanistic.

The focus was on practical subjects and greater attention was given to the development of the students' physique.

Upon returning to Kežmarok, Genersich published *Beiträge zur Schulpädagogik* (Contribution to school education) in 1792.[28] This book was essentially a synopsis of the 16-volume work edited by Campe and published in Hamburg between 1785 and 1791 called *Allgemeine revision des gesammten schul- und erziehungswesens* (Hamburg, 1785–1792). The work is a collection of essays from Campe, Locke, Rousseaù, Trapp, Struve, and Unzer. At this stage in his career, Genersich hoped that experimental institutions like those proposed by Basedow could also be established in Hungary. It is important to note that Genersich was not alone in proposing radical reforms. Between 1780 and 1800 a number of exceptional Lutheran pedagogues across the Hungarian Kingdom (many of whom coincidentally also studied at Jena) were experimenting with education reforms, like Marton Liedemann in Levoča, Mathias Sennovitz in Prešov, Thomas Tsisch in the town of Štitnik (Csetnek), and Samuel Ambrózy in Banská Štiavnica.[29]

The experiments advanced by Genersich and other Hungarian pedagogues were closest in structure to Oxford and Cambridge. They were to be boarding schools, where students from both noble and urban backgrounds were to live under the same roof for most of the year. Prior to this, the boarding school as such was unknown in the Hungarian Kingdom. Although inter-status institutions had already been established under Maria Theresa, noble-born and burgher-born children did not live in the same building. According to the new proposal, they were to eat, sleep, and exercise together. On one day, classes were to be conducted in Hungarian, while the next day in German. As in Oxford and Cambridge, the teachers were required to live with the students. Although classes on traditional topics such as the Bible and Latin classics were to be continued, a third of the curriculum was concerned with instructing students on new innovations in industry, horticulture, and comparative European political economy.[30] In a sense, the boarding school was a total educational experience, where each minute of each day served an intended goal of transforming the habits and tastes of the students. Divorced from their home environments, students were to live life in a bubble, continuously inundated with the advantages of middle class culture and civilization.

The experiments in educational reform had three complementary goals. First, Lutheran pedagogues hoped to revive the fortune of the Upland towns by turning them into centers of education. Joseph II first proposed this idea, and Genersich wanted to convince Francis II to continue with the project. Second, the new pedagogues were interested in creating a new common identity between German burghers and Magyar nobles. What they were attempting—using Benedict Anderson's terminology—was to create a new "imagined community" from the fragmented multiethnic/linguistic elements of the Hungarian Kingdom; or using Ernest Gellner's formulation, they sought to vertically connect Hungary's horizontally divided feudal society. They referred to this new ethno-national group as *Ungarndeutsche*.[31] The third and complementary goal of the experimental schools was to train this new class and new ethnicity created by the merger of Magyar noble youths and German burgher children to become leaders of progress, liberty, and Enlightenment in the Hungarian Kingdom. The curricular emphasis on the advantages of the English model, private property, and the need to introduce new technologies, was aimed to ideologically inculcate "provincial minds" to the advantages of Westernization. In the clearest terms, they were to be the training ground for the vanguard troops of the Enlightenment, and they were expected to fill the expanding administrative branches of the State, as well as be involved in modern industrial and financial development.

Arguably the most famous and widely recognized Hungarian bourgeois reformer of the time was Johann Samuel Liedemann (1756–1812). The success of Johann Samuel Liedemann as a businessman was intricately tied to his emigration to Pest in 1786 from Spišská Nová Ves in the Uplands. While in the early seventeenth century the Upland towns could be a source of significant capital accumulation for ambitious entrepreneurs, by the end of the eighteenth century this was no longer the case. A deep and lasting recession set in, which improved only slightly between the decades 1867–1900. Pest was emerging as the overwhelming dominant financial and commercial center of the kingdom. And it was not long after Liedemann moved to Pest that he took advantage of the opportunities available. He settled in 1786 as a small "retailer," but four years later was regarded as one of the most influential merchants in town. By 1790 he was a major actor in the textile trade, having built a warehouse in Pest, and being in contact with firms in Milan, Holland, Augsburg, Vienna, and Cluj. In 1790 he was also elected president of the Pest Wholesalers Association, and personally met with Emperor Leopold II to discuss the grievances of the Pest merchants. In 1809 he made the all-important transition from merchant to industrial capitalist when he built a textile factory in Pest, called the Gácsi Cloth Factory, the first textile factory built on the territory of the Hungarian Kingdom. As the historian Vera Bácskai noted, by that time Liedemann was most probably the wealthiest industrialist of Pest, with an estimated net worth of between 700,000 and 800,000 Forints.[32] In 1812 the family was ennobled.

Johann Samuel Liedemann was the author of two pamphlets, *Vorschlag zur Aufhilfe der Ungarische Handlung* in 1790, and *Merkantilische Bemerkungen und Vorstellung in Bezug auf das königlichen Ungarn* in 1802. These works are complementary in their emphasis on what economic reforms were needed to modernize Hungarian commerce and manufacturing. They both start out complaining about the poor postal service, the bad roads, and the lack of commercial shipping and conclude with a series of reforms that could bring about prosperity. Liedemann notes that the postal service must be expanded, and delivery of mail between Vienna and Pest reduced from two weeks to a week; the roads are in such poor condition that trade in the winter months is all but impossible; roads must be constructed for year-round use; shipping is underdeveloped and must be expanded; autarchic guilds' regulations should be curbed; investment and saving banks built; taxes reduced and unfair taxes on Hungarian manufacturing abolished.

In terms of the *Bildung's* project, Liedemann's most important contribution came as president of the Pest Wholesalers Ethics Committee. In this capacity, Liedemann embodied and expressed the goals and aspirations of the enlightened Protestant burghers of the Hungarian Kingdom. He heavily fined any merchant belonging to the association who acted, dressed, and behaved like a Magyar noble, and under his guidance the Committee prohibited businessmen from visiting cafés after ten at night and smoking tobacco on the street.[33] Furthermore, keenly aware that businessmen were lacking respect in a society just waking from its post-feudal slumber, he worked energetically to enlarge the merchant community. And while he did hold certain anti-Semitic stereotypes—like the idea that Jewish second-hand salesmen form secret societies, steal, and ruin the goods of other merchants—he argued before the Wholesalers Association that those of the Hebrew faith should be allowed to settle and join the merchant community as equals. The one qualification he put forward was that the "Jewish traders [that settle] be transformed, so that with time they can come closer to the bourgeois sphere, and one day be transformed into a proper bourgeoisie."[34]

The Hungarian Jacobins

It is important to reemphasize here that at the time of the French Revolution, few individuals supported the new ideas of the age. The historian Kálmán Benda estimated the number of "Josephite Intellectuals," that is, those who could be counted on to support Enlightenment policies, at between 15,000 and 20,000 individuals. There were few Philosophes in the Hungarian towns like Johann Schneider, Johann Genersich, or Johann Liedemann. Josephite intellectuals accounted for no more than 0.3 percent of the kingdom's total population.[35] It was precisely for this reason that reformers were trying to establish boarding schools with such haste, hoping that a massive push from education would exponentially increase the number of supporters of the Enlightenment. In the 1780s the Hungarian Philosophes within the towns were convinced that only with the help of the Habsburg Court could this radical change be accomplished, while simultaneously the court shared a similar view toward the emergent secular intelligentsia of the towns. Prior to the outbreak of the French Revolution, the Hungarian bourgeoisie did not conceive of any other alternative for rapid modernization except within the confines of enlightened absolutism.

The court-bourgeois alliance—which Benczúr, Molnár, Genersich, and other leading Lutheran pedagogues championed—survived the initial shock of the French Revolution. Few individuals in Hungary realized the significance of the revolution when it exploded onto the European stage in 1789, even if in the long run the ideas unleashed by the revolution would undermine the partnership. In 1789, however, there was confusion about what direction the Revolution would follow, and what had caused it. This misunderstanding was, of course, not unique to Hungary. Alexis de Tocqueville noted in his famous work *The Old Régime and the French Revolution*: "Despite all his political acumen even Frederick the Great had no inkling of what was in the air. He was very near to the Revolution yet he failed to see what was happening under his eyes. More remarkable still, his management of public affairs fell in line with the new ideas; he was a precursor, one might almost say a promoter, of the Revolution." Tocqueville further noted: "The European Kings and their Ministers . . . completely failed to realize the way events were shaping and regarded the French Revolution as one of those passing maladies to which all nations are subject from time to time and whose only practical effect is to open up new political possibilities to enterprising neighbors."[36]

In Hungary the confusion and misunderstanding surrounding the significance of the French Revolution is perhaps nowhere more apparent than in two works written by Leopold Alois Hoffman: *Babel* (1790) and *Ninive* (1790). Hoffmann, an agent provocateur sent to Hungary to assist the court in raising allies against the Magyar nobility who were blocking efforts to implement reforms, advertised the French Revolution as having freed the French king from the grips of the feudal aristocracy. For Hoffman the revolution was the liberation of the monarch, and signified the unity of the bourgeoisie and peasantry with their king. In his work *Babel*, for instance, Hoffmann writes: "While in Hungary nobles try daily to take away the rights of the burghers and are disloyal to the king, in France the burghers joined forces with the king to defend their rights while eliminating the feudal privileges of the nobility."[37] He further writes: "The Hungarian burgher reads newspapers as well as the nobles; he knows as well as his fellows in France that he is not the slave of the aristocracy."[38] In *Ninive*, on the other hand, Hoffmann is writing for the purpose of provoking the peasantry against Magyar noble rule. "The peasantry should turn to the Ruler [Leopold II], so that at the next National Assembly their ambassadors may present their grievances. There is no doubt the King will allow this most humble request of theirs to be granted."[39]

The confusion about the meaning and significance of the French Revolution continued throughout most of the short rule of Leopold II (1790–1792). It is important to remember that while the French Revolution had begun in 1789, Louis XVI was not executed until late January 1793, and the Reign of Terror by the Committee of Public Safety began only in early September 1793. When Leopold became emperor in 1790, the French Revolution had already taken place, but the radical phase had not yet begun. Leopold II, therefore, during the first year of his rule, continued to support reform, propagating the values of the Enlightenment, and was even willing to conspire in revolutionary activity to overthrow Magyar noble rule in Hungary. It is true that he had become more cautious in appointing officials, and conservatives like Bishops Imre Okolicsányi and Antal Mándich, who had been dismissed from the Royal Chancery by Joseph II, were reinstated, independent minded individuals like Sándor Pászthory were dismissed, and censorship clamped down on the dissemination of foreign printed books. Also noteworthy is the growing influence of the Jesuits, who in 1791 had again made great advances, and manipulated the state's cultural as well as educational policies.[40] Concurrently, however, and contradicting this conservative turn, Leopold II also sur-rounded himself with agent provocateurs, who continued to plan the overthrow of the Magyar nobility, and the inclusion of the peasantry into the constitution, as well as increasing the participation of the bourgeoisie at Parliament. Leopold II was convinced that he could avoid a repeat of the French Revolution in the Habsburg Monarchy if he made political concessions, especially to the peasantry and bour-geoisie. As Ernst Wangermann commented: "This conviction had not been shared by his elder brother, nor, as it soon became clear, was it shared by his son and successor. It therefore gives the reign of Leopold II a specific, unique aspect."[41]

One of the most ambitious plans to overthrow the Magyar nobility in Hungary was developed by Leopold Alois Hoffmann in 1791, under the proposed title: "The Establishment in the Royal Free Towns of Hungary (Foremost in Buda and Pest) of Urban Militias." The plan called for the creation of urban militias in Pest and Buda, with the strategic goal of arming the bourgeoisie. Joseph II had originally devel-oped this idea in 1788 during his Turkish War. Worried about com-mitting too many troops to the southern frontier, Joseph II thought it best for Pest and Buda to have their own militias in case the Ottomans broke through the front lines. Hoffman's adaptation of the idea was, however, more ambitious. At first the plan called for establishing a 300-strong urban militia in Pest and Buda, of which only a quarter would be Magyar. Afterward, this plan would be applied secretly to all the royal free towns of the Hungarian Kingdom. In arming the urban estate, Hoffmann hoped that at the moment of the insurrection, the bourgeoisie could be used as an internal ally to the king to overthrow those elements that were going to defend feudalism.

Royal support for Enlightenment reform and radical political action in Hungary and throughout Europe suffered serious setbacks when on January 21, 1793, Louis XVI and his wife Marie Antoinette (the sister of Leopold II) were executed. From that time forth, the conservative *Adels* (or Nobles) Party gained increasing influence throughout the courts of Europe, as the Enlightened Party (Aufklärungspartie) lost theirs.[42] In Vienna, the court's anti-liberal shift was cemented when Leopold II died suddenly on March 1, 1792, and the Reign of Terror in 1793 began in France. The People's Tribunals, Robespierre's radical mob rule, and the mass execution of aristocrats and class enemies con-vinced policy makers in Vienna that the liberalism of Joseph II and Leopold II, if continued, would undermine Habsburg rule in Central Europe. The new Holy Roman Emperor Francis II (Francis I of

Austria), in strong contrast to his predecessors, therefore, "abhorred political change," and closed the doors to those elements in society that had hoped the court would be the agent to help in modernization from above. As Ernst Wagermann summarized the transition:

> The books written and distributed according to Leopold's secret instructions were now confiscated and destroyed by the authorities who had been deliberately circumvented in their publication. The pensions granted to their authors were cancelled. The honours and posts promised by Leopold to his collaborators did not materialize. Their political dreams and personal ambitions were thus simultaneously shattered.[43]

Francis II dropped the reform plans of his father like a "hot brick." The new attitude pervading at court can be illustrated in Francis II's view of reforms:

"No," he once said, refusing some Italian demands for political reform, "every concession is dangerous. Man with his insatiable nature always asks for something more. Give him the hand, and he wants the arm; give him the arm, and he wants the whole body. I do not wish to give them my head."[44]

The sudden change following Leopold II's death signified a tectonic shift within the emerging Hungarian educated class. What course of action should they take? Should they retreat from their earlier reform positions and now join the counter-revolution? Or should they continue advancing radical change, even if that meant an inevitable clash with the conservatives in Vienna? The significance of these questions was especially acute between 1793 and 1794. With the Jacobin seizure of power and the mass executions in France, it had become clear that the French Revolution had opened a new chapter in the history of Europe. But where would the revolution stop? Would the revolution be contained within the borders of France, or would its fire spread and engulf Hungary also? It was during these tumultuous times that the Hungarian Jacobins, a radical group inspired by their French counterparts, emerged, wanting to carry out their own revolution.

Who were the Hungarian Jacobins and what was their significance?

The Hungarian Jacobins had very little to do with the Hungarian bourgeoisie. Kálmán Benda found only two members of the Hungarian Jacobins who were German burghers from Hungary's royal free towns in Transylvania or the Uplands. This is not to imply that they played no role in radical politics. German burghers played an important role in the 1760s as pedagogues spreading the ideas of the Enlightenment, and some were active members as founders and propagators of Masonic Lodges. Yet, when in late 1792 the Hungarian Jacobins formed it is clear that few of them participated in political radicalism. The Hungarian Jacobins did not emerge from the ranks of the historic bourgeoisie, but rather, from those of the disgruntled nobility.

The Magyar nobility at the time of the French Revolution—as indeed throughout its whole history—was deeply divided. At the top stood the court aristocracy, like the Esterházy, Erdődy, and Pállfy families, who were committed to the Enlightenment during the time of Joseph II, but were similarly passionate advocates of the counter-revolution after the establishment of the Reign of Terror, the rule of Maximilien Robespierre (1758–1794), and the rise of Francis II and Metternich. The greatest opposition to Enlightenment reform within the nobility came from the county squires who never favored any sort of change. Provincial lords did not trust reforms that aimed to centralize legal and political authority because their own private jurisdictional authority would be undermined both on their estates and within the County Diet system. They opposed taxing the nobility, liberating the serfs, standardizing the laws, removing private tolls on the thoroughfares and highways, and they most certainly disliked the idea of everyone being equal before the law. The Magyar nobles who became Jacobins, therefore, came from a small fraction of all nobles at large. Noble reformers tended to come from the middle nobility, who had traveled and studied abroad and, impressed by developments in the West, was inspired to change society in the East. These Aufgeklärt nobles in the 1780s were drawn into the reform camp of Joseph II, and were willing, if not outright hoping, to exchange their life on their country estates for a political office in the capital. That is, many of the Hungarian Jacobins had started their political careers as supporters of enlightened absolutism. Their disenchantment with enlightened absolutism came at the precise moment when Joseph II declared German as the official language of the state. This language patent was understood by reform-minded Magyar nobles as an attempt by Vienna to block their entry into the modern bureaucracy, while opening the door for a "German" takeover of the state.

The second important element among the Hungarian Jacobins was the emerging Hungarian literati. The spread of Enlightenment ideas throughout the Habsburg Empire advanced the growing interest in the vernacular languages of the many different ethnic-nationalities. Anton Bernolák and Juraj Palkovič among the Slovaks, György Bessenyei and Ferenc Kazinczy among the Magyars, Matija Antun Relković, Adam Tadija Blagojević, and Tituš Brezovački among the Croatians, Samuil Micu-Clain, Gheorghe Şincai, and Petru Maior among the Romanians, started assembling dictionaries, grammar books, and putting on paper the history and customs of their respective (adopted/imagined) ethnic minority. The Enlightenment and the emergence of the literati in the Habsburg monarchy, therefore, represented the birth of modern ethnic-nationalism in the region. What made the Magyars distinct from the other groups was the accelerated pace at which they jumped from the ethno-linguistic revival phase of the 1770s into the modern militant ethno-nationalist phase. By 1790 the broad outlines of Magyar nationalism are observable, placing it far ahead of most other ethnic minorities in the kingdom, including the Germans.[45] Indeed, German nationalism would not be a serious ideological force in the kingdom until German unification in 1871. The assimilation of so many German burghers into Hungarian society between 1820 and 1860, in large measure, can be traced to the advanced state of Magyar nationalism in comparison to that of its German counterpart.

The leader and self-proclaimed father of the Hungarian Jacobins was Ignác Martinovics (1755–1795). Similar to many of the Hungarian Jacobins, Martinovics came from a noble background and became involved in political intrigue as an enthusiastic supporter of enlightened absolutism. Leopold II recruited Martinovics into the services of the state in 1791.[46] After the death of Leopold II, the fortunes of Martinovics changed dramatically. Francis II stopped supporting the agent provocateurs established by Joseph II and Leopold II, and refused to meet with Martinovics, who was desperately looking for a position in the administration. Greatly disappointed by Francis II, Martinovics in 1793 composed a *Public Letter to Emperor Francis II* (Francis I of Austria) (1793). Initially written in a state of great agitation and anger toward the world, it remained private for a time, before being copied and widely circulated. The Hungarian radical and fellow Jacobin, Hajnóczy, was one of the first to read it and make copies of it, from which moment it became a chain letter, reaching Francis II himself. The first lines of the letter establish its tone throughout:

> The whole of Europe turned its gaze upon you when you ascended the throne to reign over a monarchy of 18 million people, a monarchy

infinitely rich in talents. Those who were acquainted with your talents, with your upbringing, with your heart, had a high opinion of you for they could not imagine that a young Archduke, whom the Emperor Joseph had educated, would ever depart from those philosophical principles which the latter prince had always followed during his administration to the honor and glory of Mankind. But those who have had an opportunity of making your acquaintance more closely immediately said farewell to all prospects of happiness both for your own subjects and for Europe as a whole; which opinion the sad story of your rule to date has justified.[47]

Martinovics concludes his letter to Emperor Francis II (Francis I of Austria) in a similarly aggressive style: "The people do not love you, the whole world says that you are unfit to govern and that you are surrounded by degenerate, evil and stupid advisors. . . . I have told you some harsh and bitter truths as I wish your own good and the happiness of the whole human race."[48]

In late 1792, Martinovics's disenchantment and unemployment led him to use the contacts he had made as an agent provocateur for the state to form the Hungarian Jacobins, with the explicit aim of overthrowing Habsburg rule. However, from the start he was forced into a difficult contradiction. A successful rebellion could only succeed if the Magyar nobility was incorporated into the military wing of the struggle. The Magyar nobility, however, with the exception of a small group of progressives—the notable one being Count Fekete, who wanted to include the peasants in the constitution—was not going to support the abolition of serfdom.[49] A good example of this is György Bessenyei (1747–1811), arguably the most important early propagators of both Enlightenment and Magyar nationalism in Hungary.[50] Bessenyei was famous for supporting the spread of scientific thinking and western literature, as well as the spread and expansion of institutes of learning. Nevertheless, typical of the Hungarian nobility, he was never able to purge himself of his prejudices toward the serfs or, for that matter, the peasantry as a whole. Within the political system of Bessenyei, therefore, it is clear that support for the Enlightenment did not translate into the liberation of the downtrodden. In his work, *Magyar Országnak Törvényes Állása* (The Legal-Administrative Position of Hungary) (1804), he wrote: "Do you know why the mass of peasants cannot vote individually or send collective representatives to the National Diet? Because they do not own land: they are not landlords. Instead they are the leaseholders to the national nobility. The nobles cannot take away the land they live on, but the peasants can never 'not serve' or pay the tithe."[51]

Bessenyei's prejudices become more blatant at a later point of the same text:

"The majority of peasants are to the king and nation from a political administrative point of view nobody and nothing. They are not an estate but an instrument, a tool and condition; plowing, sowing, weaving, boiling, drilling, carving, tailoring, and so on. All these are necessities indispensable to a country; instruments without which the most intelligent valor could neither go forward nor stand its ground. However, [they peasants] should not play a role in governing. If you allow them to rule, under their administration the country would capsize.[52]

The contradiction of using the Magyar nobility to carry out the military phase of the Jacobin revolution was not lost on Martinovics. It was exactly because of this problem that Martinovics formed two secret societies. One, called the Society of Reformers, was composed of rebellious Magyar nobles who did not wish to abolish feudalism, but nevertheless opposed Habsburg rule. The second secret society, the Society of Equality and Liberty, also had a large noble contingency, but its members were committed Jacobin radicals. While the Society of Reformers was to lead the first phase of the revolt, the second revolution was going to be led by the Society of Equality and Liberty with the aim of overthrowing the Magyar nobility. For this reason, the Society of Reformers was unaware of the existence of the second secret society.[53]

Even after Martinovics was arrested, some continued to believe strongly in the possibility of a Jacobin style revolution. The Hungarian Jacobin János Laczkovics, for instance, proclaimed in front of many people: "The arrest of Martinovics happened too late, it cannot help to sustain the monarchy. I would not give one or two months, before we start shooting the princes, counts and barons like rabbits."[54] Yet despite these radical proclamations, it is not at all clear whether Martinovics would have carried through with the second revolution. After all, the Society of Equality and Liberty was clearly smaller in size and did not have the resources of the Society of Reformers. Further, Martinovics realized that if the Magyar nobles were going to provide the military strength of the revolt, the secular intelligentsia had to make compromises. Specifically, success was predicated on reassuring the bulk of the nobles that no drastic change to the system of serfdom was going to be introduced. Martinovics was well aware of the fact that the American Jacobins had made a similar compromise with the

Southern slave owners. When, in 1793, Martinovics and Laczkovics proposed a new Constitution for Hungary, it was mild in comparison to what had transpired in France. According to this proposed Hungarian Jacobin Constitution, after the revolution there was going to be a king, but following the example of the French Constitution of 1791, the monarch would have greatly reduced powers. Real political power would be with the two chambers of Parliament: the first composed of nobles while the second, of representatives from the "Third Estate." Concerned about noble resistance to taxation, the new state would not collect taxes from individuals, but instead sustain itself from the confiscated lands of the Church, aristocracy, and the Habsburg family. Only landowners were going to be allowed to vote and hold office, and no radical change in the serf-lord relations were penned. Further, the Magyar nobility was going to enjoy prerogative over political offices. There were progressive elements to this Constitution. Aristocratic as well as clerical privileges were to be abolished. Every citizen was to be equal before the law. It was also farsighted in terms of the nationalities question. According to the Hungarian Jacobin Constitution of 1793, the Hungarian Kingdom would be divided along "nationality" lines. The northwest would be called "Slavonica," the southwest, with the unification of Croatia and Dalmacia, would be "Illyria," the Bánság and most of Southern Transylvania would be called "Wallachia," and the Central Plains of the Carpathian Basin, "Hungary." The new territories would be administered according to the local language.[55]

In 1794 the leaders of the Hungarian Jacobins were arrested, tried, and in 1795 executed. The precursor of the arrest was growing concern within the Viennese secret police that a revolution was being planned throughout the monarchy. Concern turned to paranoia at court when Joseph Degen, a secret agent for the state, delivered a report on July 21, 1793, about a conversation he had with a known eccentric Francophile Lieutenant Franz Hebenstreit. When Degen's report reached the desk of the Austrian Police Commissioner, Count Pergen immediately convened with Francis II, and recommended the arrest of all known Jacobin agitators in the Habsburg Monarchy.[56]

From hindsight, the scale of the Hungarian Jacobin conspiracy could never have toppled the Habsburg Monarchy. This objective observation was more difficult to make in 1794, as the Reign of Terror continued in France. But Hungarian historians are in agreement today that Martinovics and his fellow conspirators were a fringe movement, whose bark was louder than their bite. The significance of the Hungarian Jacobins, therefore, is not the missed opportunity of revolt. Their significance is far greater. In Hungarian history, the Jacobins represented that critical moment at which the court in Vienna established itself as the ideological defender of the counter-revolution, tradition, and the status quo, while the Magyar nobles' grab for state power became ideologically connected to liberalism. When in 1795 the Jacobin conspirators were hung, the Habsburg side became identified with religious orthodoxy, intolerance, oppression, censorship, tyranny, and the secret police, the Magyar side was associated with the core values of the Enlightenment, such as freedom, liberty, democracy, and progress. The hardening of these lines can be illustrated in the life of Johann Genersich's ill-fated book, *Von der Liebe des Vaterlandes*. The book, written to promote Enlightened Absolutism, was composed between 1790 and 1791, when the radical secular intelligentsia believed in the viability of the court-bourgeoisie alliance. It was the time of Mozart's *Magic Flute*, Leopold II, when the Free Mason Emperor was supposed to lead the citizens of the Habsburg Empire to a land of progress, virtue, and wisdom. The sudden death of Leopold II did not deter Genersich, because he was confident that Francis II would continue on the road of reform. Yet by the time *Von der Liebe des Vaterlandes* reached the coffee tables of the Hungarian secular intelligentsia in 1794 and 1795, the intellectual vanguard was the most disappointed with Francis II, and no longer believed in enlightened Habsburg absolutism. Bad timing by Genersich led to a cold reception of his work, as his book was condemned as a piece of Habsburg propaganda. Hurt and misunderstood, Genersich withdrew from the political-philosophical stage, and his next significant work on political history was published two decades later under the title, *Kurzer Abriss der Geschichte Von Oesterreich, Böhmen und Ungarn* (Tyrnau, 1824).

A deep contradiction characterized Magyar noble nationalism proclaiming itself the defender of freedom, liberty, and democratic western values. On the one hand, for many within the movement, these values were held sacred. On the other, however, the movement also had many hangers on or, more specifically, nobles that talked of freedom but were really after political positions within an independent or semi-independent Hungarian Kingdom. Similar to the German unification of Prussia by the Junkers, Hungarian independence led by the Magyar nobility presented the problem of an outdated autarchic political class in power, while the economy and society were undergoing rapid modernization. The dilemma faced by the German-speaking Hungarian bourgeoisie was therefore similar to its German counterpart. Namely, was the bourgeoisie willing to make a compromise with a backward political class in order to achieve political unity or, as was the case with Hungary, independence? In Hungary, however, this question was compounded by the ethnic-national question. As the interwar period historian, Béla Pukánszky, proposed, the German burghers were torn between three possible roads they could take in the nineteenth century. One, should they join their road with the Magyars, and in the process become indistinguishable from the Magyars? Two, should they follow a separate road which intersected with the Magyars, but which would allow them to maintain some of their prior identity? Or three, should they choose a road completely different from the Magyars, and maintain to the full extent their distinct historical identity?[57] Accordingly, it becomes clear that for the German burghers of the Hungarian Kingdom, the specter of rising Magyar nationalism in the nineteenth century was its most critical challenge to date, possibly even greater than the advent of the Reformation.

6

The Challenges of Ethnic Nationalism

At the beginning of the nineteenth century, the Hungarian Kingdom within the Habsburg Monarchy was one of the most ethnically diverse lands of Europe. It included what today is Croatia, northern Serbia, Slovakia, the Burgenland of today's Austria, and Hungary. Transylvania continued to exist as a separate administrative unit, but in 1867 it was merged with Hungary proper. According to Kálmán Benda, 1804 Hungary, including Transylvania, Croatia, and the southern occupied military border region, had a population of approximately 9.5 million. Of this figure, 1.6 million lived in Transylvania, where in 1804 there were around 580,000 Magyars and Székelys (35.9 percent of the total), 850,000 Romanians (52.7 percent), 140,000 Germans (8.7 percent), and 43,000 persons of other ethnic backgrounds (Armenians, Roma, Greeks, Ukrainians, etc.). In Hungary, excluding Transylvania but including Croatia, Slavonia, and the southern border territories, the position of the Magyars was somewhat stronger because out of the estimated 7.9 million inhabitants, approximately 3.3 million (42 percent) were Magyars, 790,000 Romanians (10 percent), 1.1 million Slovakians, 1.48 million (18.5 percent) Serbians and Croatians, 750,000 Germans (9.2 percent), 280,000 Ruthenians (3.8 percent), and 180,000 others.[1]

The census of 1850 more or less confirms the impression of the 1804 census, namely that Magyar speakers represented the largest minority in Hungary, but that no clear ethnolinguistic group formed the absolute majority. In 1850, Hungary had an estimated population of 11.6 million, of which 4.8 million were Magyar, 2.2 million Romanian, 1.7 million Slovak, 1.3 million German, and 598,000 Croatian and Serbian speakers. The 1850 census also listed 250,000 Jews, even though Jews often spoke a dialect of German, but nevertheless were registered as a distinct ethnic group. In later censuses Jews would no longer be listed as a separate ethnic group, but only as a distinct religious group.[2]

While Western nations such as France and England also had a diversity of ethnic groups living in their states, the level of diversity was clearly immense in Hungary. Adding to the complex ethnolinguistic composition of Hungary was the assortment of religions found in the region. According to Benda, the 1804 census in Hungary, excluding Transylvania, counted approximately 4.5 million Catholics (60 percent of the population), 700,000 Lutherans (9 percent), 1.1 million Calvinists (15 percent), 1 million persons of the Greek Orthodox faith, 126,000 Jews (1.7 percent), and 1 percent of other religions. George Barany's estimate of the breakdown of Hungary's population according to religion in 1819 confirms this distribution, estimating that the country had 4.9 million Catholics, 1.2 million Calvinists, 1.36 million of the Greek Orthodox religion, 820,000 Lutherans, 625,000 Uniates, 130,000 Jews, and approximately 40,000 Unitarians.[3]

At the onset of modern nationalism, the obvious questions emerged: How could so many different ethnolinguistic groups of so many religions be brought together under one national identity? Would the urban estate become the force that holds them together?

It is important to keep in mind that the cultural and ethnic heterogeneity of Hungary was not unusual within the context of occidental feudalism. As Ernest Gellner argued in his book, *Nations and Nationalism*, a common feature of feudal society was that those who worked, those who prayed, and those who fought did not necessarily share the same language or culture.[4] The aristocracy throughout Europe created its own high culture, and often spoke a language different from the rest of the population. The reasons for this are quite clear. Under feudalism the elite had no pressure to pose as defenders of a national culture. Instead, they often subscribed to an "international" "blue blood" high culture. Feudal society, according to Gellner, therefore, is a "culturally horizontally divided" structure, and only during the transition from traditional to modern society did pressures build toward the "vertical-cultural integration of society." In Western Europe this vertical integration proceeded without considerable obstacles. France and England, Holland and Denmark were able to create a united national identity. Elite culture remained elite, but simultaneously a united national identity was forged. In the Habsburg Monarchy, and especially in Hungary, the transition was not so smooth.

A sub-chapter of Gellner's book, *Nations and Nationalism*, entitled: "The course of true nationalism never did run smooth" provides much useful insight at this point. Gellner uses the allegory of an imagined kingdom called Megalomania. This imaginary kingdom—most probably inspired by his Czech national origin—faces problems that were almost identical to those of Hungary. Gellner's Megalomania is composed of three distinct groups: the Ruritanians (who are peasants), the nobility and aristocracy around the Megalomanian court, and urban dwellers. The peasant-Ruritanians speak a language different from the Megalomanian nobility and the urban dwellers, and the Ruritanians and the urban dwellers are of different religious denominations. The picture, therefore, is almost identical to the problems faced by Hungary, where urban dwellers were predominantly German Lutherans, the peasantry Catholic Slovaks or Uniate and Orthodox Romanians, and the Magyar nobility spoke a language different from all of these groups.

In the course of the nineteenth century, Gellner goes on to argue, Megalomania began to industrialize and experienced a population explosion. However, this industrialization took place in regions far from where the Ruritanians lived, and to survive in the new world, many Ruritanians moved to the new industrial cities, where they often assimilated. Gellner writes: "Of course, it was perfectly possible for the Ruritanians, if they wished to do so (and many did), to assimilate into the dominant language of Megalomania. No genetically transmitted trait, no deep religious custom, differentiated an educated Ruritanian from a similar Megalomanian. In fact, many did assimilate, often without bothering to change their names, and the telephone directory of the old capital of Megalomania is quite full of Ruritanian names, though often rather comically spelt in the Megalomanian manner, and adapted to Megalomian phonetic expectations."[5]

Gellner uses the allegory of Megalomania to illustrate that while it was advantageous for the Ruritanians to assimilate—in a sense it would have been the economically rational choice to do so—many did not. In certain areas of Europe, the transition from traditionally horizontally divided to vertically integrated society was not easy. Those Ruritanians who stayed behind in their villages, for instance, remained distant from Megalomanian culture and groups of intellectuals sprouted up speaking of Ruritanian culture as a high culture of its own and a national culture in itself. Belated industrialization, mixed with deep-seated historical-cultural division between those who work, those who pray, and those who fight, made it difficult for Hungary to create a shared "imagined community" in Benedict Anderson's terminology.[6] Interestingly, though, Gellner does not go into detail about what happened to the urban dwellers that were distinct from the Ruritanian peasants and the Megalomanian nobility during the rise of nationalism. In nineteenth-century Hungary, however, this was a critical point of discussion. Should the German-speaking urban dwellers become the voice of the Ruritanians and oppose Megalomanian culture, or should they join with Megalomanian culture and become the ruling elite? Alternatively, should they bridge the gap between Magyar nobles and Slovak or Romanian peasants, and help in developing a new common identity among the conflicting estates?

In a discussion of the position of the urban estate during the process of the vertical integration of Hungarian feudal society, it is useful to start at the microlevel and highlight the different opinions of Johann Genersich, Jacob Glatz, and Johann Asboth in the town of Kežmarok around 1800. While these Philosophes did not become great political revolutionaries or leaders, the three thinkers did outline the three possible roads available to the German-speaking urban estate of Hungary as it merged with modern Hungarian society. On the one hand, Johann Genersich, in his anonymously published work, *Von der Liebe des Vaterlandes* in 1793, advanced an essentially state-patriotic conception of the state, maintaining the belief that enlightened despotism was the best solution to combat backwardness. He believed that membership in a nation should be based on academic merit and national belonging had little to do with birth. At the time Genersich also promoted German as the official language of the state, complimenting the classic Enlightenment position promulgated by Joseph II and his advisor Joseph von Sonnenfels. In 1811 he modified his position, however, and wrote to his friend, Karl Rumy, that while "at the moment the language of the middle class is German, if the appeal of Magyar nationalism continues to grow, Hungarian should be made the official language of the Hungarian state." That summer Genersich also noted that he had begun to study Hungarian, although a year later he wrote to Rumy that he had no time to learn the language.[7]

Many similarities exist between Jacob Glatz's work, *Freymüthige Bemerkungen eines Ungarn über sein Vaterlandes* (1799), and Genersich's *Von der Liebe des Vaterlandes* (1793). Like Genersich, Glatz also published his work anonymously, and began the book by proclaiming himself a supporter of the Enlightenment. From the beginning, the main thrust of the book is clear: Glatz argues that to elevate Hungary into the ranks of the civilized nations of Europe, the enemies of progress, knowledge, and the Enlightenment must be defeated. These enemies he specifically identified as the backward Catholic Clergy, the entrenched aristocracy, and the poverty-stricken county nobility. Other similarities between the two thinkers are also noteworthy. Glatz was also a professor at the Lyceum of Kežmarok and both were members of a special reading group in the town formed to pull their limited resources in order to subscribe to the leading newspapers and journals of Europe. The reading group was composed of enlightened Philosophes who discussed and argued about the significance of the French Revolution, the American Revolution, and developments in Berlin and the Viennese court.

There are, however, noteworthy differences between the philosophies of Genersich and Glatz. Glatz, for instance, was more conscious of his German identity than Genersich. He drew a clear distinction in Hungarian society between those elements that are "nationalungarn" versus those that are not. "Nationalungarn" are those ethnic groups in Hungarian society that lived in the Carpathian Basin prior to the arrival of the Magyars (Slovaks, Romanians, Ruthinians) or who arrived with the Magyar invasion or shortly thereafter (Magyars, Székely, Pecsenegs, Kuns, Palóc). Glatz argues that the "nationalungarn" feel hostility toward the Germans because of the many injustices committed by the Habsburg state (who, in turn, are seen as German). However, the Magyars have also come to accept the German-speaking urban dwellers into the larger national community because the German-speaking urban estate has proven itself loyal to the Hungarian crown throughout history. Unfortunately, Glatz points out, a great deal of misunderstanding continues to engulf the numerous ethnic groups of the kingdom. The Slovaks are mistrustful of the Magyars who, in turn, are mistrustful of the Romanians, and so on. Glatz's solution to the nationality question in the multiethnic and multilinguistic kingdom lies in broad educational reform, whereby each ethnolinguistic group would learn the language of their neighbor. In the process, a greater appreciation of the diversity in the kingdom, as well as respect for each group's intrinsic values would emerge. Glatz, therefore, promoted the idea that Hungary can make a successful transition to the civilized nations of Europe by following the example of the Swiss confederation, where plurality did not interfere with the nation-building process. He was a supporter of the "Hungaricus Conception," which understood Hungarians as a collection of diverse ethnolinguistic groups that were held together by the political unity of the Hungarian Parliament, and not as simply ruled by the "Magyars" (meaning Magyar speakers).

Genersich and Glatz were in agreement on promoting the values and ideas of the Enlightenment, but they disagreed on the image of their ideal state. Genersich remained an advocate of strong central control, while Glatz supported regional and local autonomy. The weakness of Genersich's position is that he fails to address the nationality question, while the strength of Glatz's position lies in his treatment of ethnic diversity as one of the essential problems to solve if Hungary was going to continue on the path of progress.

A third alternative was presented by Johann Asboth, a colleague of Glatz and Genersich at the Lyceum of Kežmarok, and member of the local Philosophes reading group. In a letter to his former student Karl Rumy, Asboth stated: "You should learn to read and write Hungarian perfectly, because only then can you bring honor to your fatherland . . . [Furthermore] . . . In the cultural and scientific field in Hungary, if the Protestant Germans ever learn to read and write Hungarian perfectly, there is no layer that could compete with them and they would become the leading intellectual stratum of Hungarian society."[8] Asboth, therefore, supported the idea of linguistic assimilation into Hungarian society. His letter to Rumy is noteworthy on two interrelated levels. On the one hand, in emphasizing the unique position of the Protestant German-speaking middle class, Asboth understands it as a distinct entity onto itself. On the other hand, Asboth supports its linguistic assimilation into Hungarian society, but supports it because assimilation would insure upward mobility for that "entity."

The common thread in each of these philosophies is the understanding that to attain progress, the linguistic barrier dividing town and country in the Hungarian Kingdom must be bridged. Or, using Gellner's terminology, Megalomanian and Ruritanian cultures have a chance to live in peace if the foreign-speaking urban estate brings them together. However, it is also apparent in the debate among the Lutheran Philosophes that competing ideas of nationalism existed within the towns. Of course, the urban estate was not alone in this, and similar conflicts over the meaning and definition of nationalism raged within the Magyar nobility (or using Gellner's terminology, within Megalomanian culture). The voice of ethnic plurality, for instance, was promoted by documents such as the Jacobin Constitution written by Martinovics and Laczkovics, accepting the languages and cultures of the different nationalities of the kingdom and advancing a federalist solution to Hungary's ethnonational diversity. This voice of tolerance can also be found in István Sándor's periodical, *Sokféle* (Many Types), published in the 1790s and arguing that the strength of

Hungary lay in its diversity. In the periodical, the Croatians are described as brave, the Saxons as hardworking, the Slovaks as great cultivators. Similarly, József Péczel's *Mindenes Gyűjteménye* (1791) (Collection of Many) stressed that the Hungarian state was never controlled by one ethnic-linguistic group, and should not be in the future. There was Gergely Berzeviczy who, "cognizant of Hungary's multireligious composition [. . .] claimed that Hungarians of different creeds ought to be human beings and citizens of one fatherland first. Perhaps reflecting on the Magyarizing tendencies of his compatriots in a multiethnic country, in a letter written in 1808 to a former teacher in Göttingen he stressed that "actually, we here in Hungary are not a nation."[9] There were individuals like Pál Madga who wrote in 1819: "Every citizen of Hungary should be able to choose according to preference, whether to speak and write in Latin, Slovak, or German. If a born Hungarian does not consider it beneath his dignity to learn Slovak or German, the Slovak or German should also not be ashamed to learn Hungarian."[10]

In contrast to those who promoted ethnic plurality stood Magyar noble intellectuals who, inspired by the French Revolution and the power of nationalism, thought that Hungary could become great again if unified by the Magyar language and culture. Magyar nobles like György Bessenyei (1741–1811), Ferenc Kazinczy (1759–1831), and Sámuel Décsy (1742–1816) promoted Magyar nationalism, portraying it as the best way to achieve the goals of progress and Enlightenment in Hungary. As the historian George Barany has pointed out, the birth of Magyar nationalism was intricately tied to the Enlightenment:

> Still the literary-cultural revival in the last quarter of the eighteenth century resulted, under the impact of the twin stimuli of Enlightenment and Romanticism, in an identification of language and national character. The notion that each people must fulfill its peculiar destiny in its own vernacular coupled with the identification of enlightened progress with patriotism and of promotion of the vernacular with dissemination of knowledge were attitudes shared by all backward societies in East-Central Europe.[11]

The classic example of Barany's view is György Bessenyei's proclamation in 1778 that "no nation on the globe has ever acquired wisdom and depth before incorporating the sciences into its own vernacular. Every nation has become knowledgeable by [using] its own and never a foreign language."[12]

The ideology of nationalism does not remain immune to the political context of the existing situation, and the road chosen by the German burghers was deeply influenced by events in Vienna. While under Joseph II and Leopold II, the Habsburg court clearly supported liberal reforms and promoted the advance of the Enlightenment, the inauspicious rule of Francis II (Francis I of Austria) turned many within the German-speaking urban estate away from the court. The execution of the Jacobin leaders, the authoritarian policies of Metternich, and the signing of the Holy Alliance convinced many within the fourth estate that the court no longer supported the principles of Enlightenment. It was at this juncture that the appeal of Magyar nationalism grew within the German-speaking urban estate. This important and critical shift of alliances toward a Magyar-centric politic can be illustrated in two plays performed just two decades apart in the German theater of Pest. In *Das Aufgebot oder die Nation um den Thron* performed in the 1790s, Carl Nitsch stressed that the Habsburg Empire consisted of a mix of nationalities and that the State was independent of the influence of any single ethnic-linguistic group. "At the end of Nitsch's play for instance, representatives from many of the different nationalities of the Habsburg Empire—Magyars, Czechs, Austrians, Moravians, Silesians, Tyrolians, Karinthians, Stirians, Friulians, Istrians, Croatians, Dalmatians, Slovenes, Transylvanians, Bukovinians, East and West Galicians—are seen kneeling before one throne where each declares their loyalty and readiness to sacrifice themselves to the one-state."[13] Less than twenty years later, in Carl Horschetszky's play, the villain is the Austrian censor—a figure that represented Metternich's reactionary politics—and the hero, a young German schoolteacher by the name of Gustáv Fried. "At the end of the play this young German schoolteacher, in a dynamic oration, declares that truth and justice were one with Magyar freedom, and with starry eyes thanks God that he can become a member of a *Greater Magyar Nation*."[14] Thus, instead of looking to the House of Habsburg, this German burgher playwright now turned to the enlightened and cosmopolitan Hungarian aristocracy as the source of modernization. Liberty and progress, ideas associated with the Enlightenment, were increasingly equated with the Magyars and the re-creation of the Greater Hungarian Kingdom.

There were, of course, those who were suspicious throughout the nineteenth century of joining the Magyar road. Indeed, while the liberal German burghers saw no contradiction between being a burgher and a Magyar, many German burghers could not make a similar distinction. The majority living in their hometowns were patriotic to the Hungarian state, celebrated the aristocratic heroes of the Magyars, and showed respect for Magyar noble tastes, but nonetheless considered the imitation of anything Magyar as representing a shift toward ennoblement. The burghers' staunch Lutheran pietism dictated that their children should follow traditional middle-class careers and take over family businesses after completing their studies.[15]

A classic example of the values held by these traditional German burghers can be found in the work of Christian Genersich (1759–1825), the younger brother of Johann Genersich. Christian Genersich was the Lutheran minister in the town of Kežmarok during the first two decades of the nineteenth century. While he was not as intellectually productive as his brother, he wrote one of the first urban monographs in the Hungarian Kingdom, titled *Merkwürdigkeiten der königlichen Freystadt Käsmark* (1806). He dedicated the book to all the good burghers and loyal Hungarian patriots of the town of Kežmarok and in the text highlighted the great contribution these burghers had made to the development of the Hungarian Kingdom. At one important juncture in this work, Genersich raises the question of whether the wall that surrounds the town should be torn down to make way for urban expansion. On the one hand, he writes, the wall had lost all military value with the development of modern military technology. On the other hand, the wall has now taken on a new significance: it symbolizes the historic struggle that the good burghers of Kežmarok had waged to maintain their civic identity, and its continued existence is important to honor the memory of "our ancestors."

In the diaries of everyday people living in the towns, therefore, we see a picture very different from the idealized view of mutual assimilation propagated by the progressive liberals. Indeed, the hoped-for merger between German burgher and Magyar noble *habitus* met with considerable resistance at the micro-level. When, for instance, the young noble Berzeviczy (the grandson of the Jacobin leader) began to court Helena Nendtvich, a distinguished burgher's daughter in Kežmarok, the gulf between town and country proved too great to bridge. While Helena Nendtvich highly praised the young Berzeviczy in her diary, she regretted that he was from a Magyar noble family, and "how can you trust a young Magyar noble?" After a while she stopped opening his letters, sent them back unread and broke off all ties with him. She risked a life without marriage instead of disappointing her parents by marrying a Magyar noble suitor.[16]

This suspicion among German burghers toward the Magyar road can also be illustrated in letters fathers wrote from their hometowns to their sons studying in Pest. As Béla Pukánszky noted:

> One can read touching advice in the letter of a father living in Pressburg written to his son studying away from his hometown; the father praises the success the son is having at school, of having made the acquaintance of many different people, but warns his son not to be seduced by noble society's luxurious habits and frivolous way of life, not to fall in love with a Magyar girl and definitely not propose to her.[17]

Within the urban estate, the strongest opposition to the rise of Magyar nationalism came from the Transylvanian Saxons. The Saxons supported the idea that serious reforms were necessary, but they did not want to become Magyar or, what they feared most, they did not want a Magyar noble takeover of the political offices of the state. The Saxons' fears were centered on a law passed in 1836 by the Hungarian Parliament stipulating that after the unification of Hungary with Transylvania, each part of the Hungarian Kingdom in the new Parliament was to be based on its relative enfranchised population. The Saxons viewed such a state as one dominated by the Magyar gentry, which was first and foremost the largest sector of the enfranchised population. Not only would their German language be unrecognized, but also their middle-class burgher political power would be compromised. Consequently, a form of so-called Transylvanian nationalism emerged among the Saxons, opposing the unification of Hungary. One of the spiritual and political leaders of the Transylvanian Nationhood movement was Joseph Marlin, who wrote in a short piece called "*Politische Aphorismen aus dem Sachsenland*" (1847):

> We Germans should understand our calling and all should learn not only to love Saxonland [an independent province within Transylvania], but also to love Transylvania. It is in the future of an Independent Transylvanian State, where we can see an end to the conflict between the various nationalities and where no one will any longer speak of Hungarianization, Germanization, Romanization.[18]

The tensions exemplified by Marlin's promotion of Transylvania as an independent nation, the letters of fathers warning their sons not to marry into a Magyar noble family, the diary of Helena Nendtvich, and the warning by Christian Genersich not to forget the work of "our [German-burgher] ancestors," illustrate that the transition from feudalism to capitalism in the Hungarian Kingdom was more difficult than in Western Europe. The language of the Magyar nationalists also disturbed Slovak, Croatian, and Romanian nationalist leaders. Sámuel Décsy, for instance, once noted: "those who eat our national bread should learn Magyar," and Ferenc Kazinczy, noted: "the foreigners amongst us either become Magyar, or should starve to death."[19] Traditional minded German burghers like the Saxons, as well as the early leaders of the Slovak, Croatian, and Romanian nationalities movements, would have been in agreement with the historian George Barany's assessment of the problem, when he wrote:

> The gradual but purposeful abandonment of the "a-national" non-Magyar, chiefly but not exclusively Latin, legacy for the sake of the new Magyar "national" literature was a mutilation of the totality of the Hungarian cultural tradition. Although replacement of Latin by the vernacular was one way of making Hungarian cultural life more democratic, the byproduct of the process was an ethnocentric provincialism characteristic of Magyardom's outlook until very recently. The change in emphasis greatly contributed to the transformation of Hungarian essentially pluralistic, patriotism into modern, or exclusive, Magyar nationalism.[20]

Despite the opposition outlined above, Magyar nationalism throughout the 1830s and 1840s attracted the liberal and progressive elements of Hungarian society. Leading burghers in the towns promoted the merger of the urban estate with the nobility, hoping that the union would mutually benefit both estates. On the Magyar side the leading proponents of this school were enlightened Hungarian aristocrats like József Eötvös, István Széchenyi, and Zsigmond Kemény, who argued that the problems of Hungarian society could be solved by copying the English model, which supposedly saw "the aristocracy merge with the upwardly mobile urban class, adopting their industry and diligence, skill and know-how, saving and economizing habits, while maintaining its historic role as the political class."[21] The fervor of revolution was not missed on the urban estate, as they proclaimed their patriotism toward the Hungarian cause. One pamphlet written in German by Alexander Scholtz posted in the town of Spišska Nová Ves at the outbreak of the revolt read:

> From all sides the Fatherland is in danger. Poisonous vermin are attacking our freedom, and its name is reaction.

Comrades! The celebration of Hungary is taking place throughout Europe, a celebration of this nation as a free land, free of foreign rule, foreign interests. Fight for the freedom of your fatherland
Stay loyal burghers
Burghers of a free state.[22]

And the following poems were published in 1863, commemorating 1848 (in German) in the daily *Zipser Anzieger*:

> With all your Saxon blood
> For your new Fatherland
> Stand strong with good heart and hand
> With German assiduousness
> Be one with Hungary
> My true Fatherland[23]

Another poem read:

> In the air of early life
> In the bloody struggle for freedom
> Carry high the holy banner
> Be one with your new allies
> All Classes and Estates
> Old and Young we believe in You[24]

Two aspects of the above revolutionary slogans stand out. First, Hungary is referred to as the fatherland. The dichotomy developed here is one between fatherland (Hungary) versus mother tongue (German). This was an important distinction, for mass support for the revolution among the German burghers could not be garnered without it. Second, national liberation and unity are seen as triumphing over both class/estate and linguistic antagonisms. That is, nationalism is not about a struggle of one ethnolinguistic group against another, but is simply a struggle for liberty from Habsburg tyranny.

Concurrently, it is clear that no agreement existed about the future course of Hungarian nationalism. By 1848, the leaders of the Magyar nationalist movement were clearly under the impression that it signified the victory of the Magyars, and that the other ethnonational groups would fall in line. Ethnic nationalism according to the Magyar intellectual leaders was a transition stage. The mid-nineteenth century political philosopher Elek Fényes argued that ethnic nationalism was going to disappear as the many ethnic-national groups learn to live within one state. Fényes wrote:

> I am certain that the end of the nationalist conflicts will be the same as
> what took place after the war of religions. That is, after long battles the
> people realized that people of different religions could exist with each
> other in one state, under one political system, without it being necessary
> to divide the state according to one's religious views. As with people of
> different religions, so people of different nationalities can live as neigh-
> bors in friendship, without it being necessary to divide and thus kill
> national unity.[25]

Much like Elek Fényes, Mihály Horváth argued in a series of articles
written in 1841 that with the "progress of the Enlightenment, science,
and capitalism there would be a leveling of classes," and consequently
the ethnic-nationalities problem would disappear.[26] At an important
level, the problem was that Magyar leaders confused the demands of
the ethnic-nationalities with that of "class" demands. Kossuth, for
instance, argued that the Croatian peasants of the kingdom should be
given land, and with a vested interest—as property owners—in the
nation, they will feel patriotic toward the Hungarian state. The
Magyar noble liberal position maintained, therefore, that in Hungary
the nation and the state were identical. In Hungary there was only one
nation, that of the Magyars, and within that nation there were
Magyars who spoke German, Serbian, Slovakian, Romanian, or
Ukrainian. Besides the Magyars, only the Croatians were understood
as capable of constructing a nation within the territories of the
Hungarian Kingdom, because the Magyars and the Croatians were
the only groups with a privileged nobility. Kossuth, therefore, aimed
to undermine the Croatian nobles' aspiration by his plan for property
redistribution in Croatia. The Germans, of course, also had their
nobility, but they were scattered and, aside from the Saxons of
Transylvania, this nobility was often disarmed by its co-optation into
the Habsburg system.

Magyar nationalism in the 1840s was an inclusive movement, aim-
ing to incorporate the many different ethnic groups into one united
nation. The radical liberals maintained that the inclusion of the others
had to be achieved by a combination of land reform and a directed
policy of assimilation. Perhaps the clearest manifestation of this position was formulated by the 1848 revolutionary leader Mihály Táncsics
in his work *Hunnia függetlensége* (The Independence of Hungary)
(1847). Táncsics argued for the implementation of land reform and

the end of feudalism to advance the bourgeois revolution, but he also believed that the progress of the bourgeois revolution had to go hand in hand with the progress of the Magyars. The correct way to distribute land, according to Táncsics, was to make sure that no archipelagoes of non-Magyar-speaking communities were created. In districts where there are no Magyars, "only Magyar speakers should be distributed land." Conversely, in those districts where Magyars are the clear majority, non-Magyar speakers should be settled and given land, so that in time they will become Magyars.[27]

The change ushered in by the growth of Magyar nationalism is well illustrated by the fact that while in 1810 the German Theater in Pest could have "*Ungarische Nationaltheater*" inscribed at its entrance without seeing any contradiction between being German-speaking and Hungarian-national, this was no longer possible after 1848, when the force of Magyar nationalism was clearly on the ascent. A new aggressive attitude came to pervade the discourse of assimilation, an attitude exemplified in the comments of Louis Teichgraber—a Hungarian-German burgher—in the *Pesti Divatlap* (The Journal of Pest Fashion) in 1848: "There are no Germans among the Magyar burghers; there are those who appear German . . . But they too are Magyar."[28] When the German Theater in Pest burnt down, and in the 1870s discussions began about rebuilding it, a bitter debate erupted in the Hungarian Press about the secret cultural imperialist goals behind building a German-language theater in Pest. Instead of trying to build a future on the strength of plurality, the prospect of a polyglot Hungarian middle class was no longer a question to be debated. The future new middle class had to be Magyar through and through. Kossuth made this clear when he wrote in the *Pesti Hírlap* (Pest Daily) in 1842:

> [At present] one part of the middle class is made up of nobles, but this must merge with another force. That force could possibly be the burghers of the royal free towns. This bourgeoisie, however, together with its industry and trade is still, to a great extent, German, and is only now starting to be part of the Hungarian nation. Yet it is beyond all doubt that the new middle class must be Magyar, and cannot be anything else![29]

The above quote from Kossuth is interesting on two levels. On the one hand, Kossuth emphasized that Hungary's bourgeoisie had to accept Magyar as its primary language. A nation-building middle class could not speak a language different from the rest of the nation, and

Glatz's recommendation that the German-speaking urban estate maintain its equal but distinct identity was not a functional solution. On the other hand, Kossuth believed that the Magyar nobility had to also undergo a metamorphosis. Essentially Kossuth is reiterating Johann Genersich's position that to combat backwardness, Hungary was in need of a strong central state, and one united language. Further, he was also in agreement with Genersich on the idea that Hungary's future is predicated on the merger of Magyar noble with German burgher. But while Genersich remained a staunch defender of the classic German Enlightenment ideal of the Weltbürger, Kossuth was a Magyar nationalist. Instead of trying to create Kant's Cosmopolitan Man, Kossuth had in mind the Magyarization of the bourgeoisie and the bourgeoisification of the nobility.

The idea, of course, to imbue the nobility with bourgeois values was first advanced by German pedagogues in the Uplands and Transylvania in the 1780s. Magyar intellectuals, with the rare exception of Berzeviczy and other Magyar Jacobins, raised this question only a generation later in the 1820s. The issue was rediscovered by Ferenc Kölcsey and Miklós Wesselényi, and promoted in the 1830s by political philosophers like Eötvös, Kossuth, and Széchenyi. The first generation of Magyar enlightened philosophers, like Bessenyei and Kazinczy, who had promoted the modernization of the Magyar vernacular held to the belief that the privileges of the Magyar nobility had to be maintained. They never developed a radical plan for the end of serfdom, nor any project to bourgeoisify the nobility. They limited the spread of Enlightenment values to defending as well as modernizing the Magyar language. In contrast, the generation that blossomed in the 1820s referred increasingly to the Enlightenment in stressing the importance of liberty and property, the redemption of feudal dues, the emancipation of the serfs, the abolishment of the tithes and manorial courts, as well as the taxation of the nobility. Hungary in the 1820s, therefore, produced its first substantial class of Magyar social scientists ready to explore the possibilities of social engineering.

Péter Hanák has shown that the renewed interest in the merger of Magyar noble and German burgher was not just an ideal in the 1840s. It could also boast a number of high profile success stories. By 1840 an influential segment of the aristocracy and nobility became involved in horticultural innovation, agricultural commercialization, the expansion of trade, road construction, and the establishment of credit institutions. István Széchenyi was the most glittering illustration of this trend, with his advocacy and investment in steamboat shipping on the

Danube, the creation of a national credit institution, as well as promoting improvements in agriculture and horticulture. But he was by no means alone. The Forgács family built a broadcloth factory at Gács, a number of noble families formed the Rimai Union (a large iron foundry), and there were—especially in the uplands—numerous nobles investing in glass manufacturing, paper-mills, forges, and potash kilns.[30] The growth of this segment of society was so noticeable that Kossuth coined the term "second estate" to describe it, and argued that without this new element Hungary could not go forward. Kossuth specifically wrote: "Without an independent, enfranchised second estate . . . our nation has no future."[31]

Leading up to the Revolution of 1848, there were signs that the "gentleman middle class" model proposed by political philosophers like Széchenyi, Eötvös, Deák, Wesselényi, and Kossuth would succeed. In towns such as Pest, Bratislava, Szeged, Košice, and Timişoara, a successful merger of German burghers with Magyar nobles had taken place. Nobles were becoming more bourgeois and the burghers were becoming increasingly Magyarized. The growing popularity of liberalism in the 1840s within the middle class was therefore no coincidence. A tectonic shift was occurring between town and country, as many nobles jumped on the bandwagon to end serfdom, and many German burghers threw their support behind the abolition of guilds. This great wave of optimism contributed significantly to the outbreak of the revolution.

Nevertheless, as Hanák also emphasized, there were "internal contradictions" to the plan of transforming the nobility into a Western styled bourgeoisie. The most critical obstacle for Hanák was the tendency among Magyar nobles (numbering over 300,000 in the 1840s) to balk at real and substantial reform. The urbanized nobles were not the problem here. It was the mass of nobles living in the villages, expressing their opinions and defending their privileges through their backward and provincial County Diets. The staunchest opposition to reform came precisely from these poor Magyar nobles as exemplified by the case of Kölcsey in 1834. A prominent reformer from Szatmár County, Kölcsey was one of the leading Magyar nobles advocating the end of serfdom. On November 10, 1834, the very day "that the Diet passed the redemption enabling serfs to acquire ownership of their land, Szatmár County reversed the liberal instructions it had given to its representative. Rather than act on the new instructions, Kölcsey left the Diet. It is less commonly known that his one-time friend, Zsigmond Kende, an enthusiastic supporter of reform in his youth, gradually went over to the conservative camp." And when the proposal for the nobility's sharing in the tax burden was advanced, he called on "God of the nation" to keep the Diet from accepting the proposal, to keep it "from framing a law . . . that would completely undermine the nobility."[32] Simply put, the Magyar nobles were unreliable leaders of liberalism.

An equally significant problem with the "gentleman middle class" project was the ambiguity behind what the concept of "mutual merger" truly entailed. For the liberals, as previously noted, the "gentleman middle class" would be created from the bourgeoisification of the nobles and the Magyarization of the German burghers. However, while the bourgeoisification of the nobility was more or less clear—that is, it meant imbuing the nobility with occidental economic rationalism—the exact meaning of the "Magyarization" of the bourgeoisie remained less well-defined. Since the Enlightenment, the movement to spread Magyar culture was intricately tied to Magyar noble culture. To be a Magyar meant to be a Magyar noble or aristocrat. In contrast to late nineteenth-century volkish peasant nationalism (of the Slovakian and Romanian type), Magyar nationalism in the 1830s was distinctly "noble." This of course presented tremendous difficulties for the success of the "gentleman middle class project," for it meant that the plan to Magyarize the Hungarian bourgeoisie was not simply about teaching them the Magyar language, but also signified—at times intentionally and consciously—the gentrification of German burgher habitus. The great Achilles' heal of the reform movement of the 1830s was, consequently, its promotion of Magyar noble culture, not only because it was pushing a backward-looking class forward, but also idealizing that class as a national savior.

The implications of the contradiction in the plan to Magyarize the bourgeoisie and bourgeoisiefy the nobility did not become apparent until the rise of Romantic Nationalism in the 1870s. The worst of all possibilities emerged. By the end of the nineteenth century, the bourgeoisie was becoming ennobled, while the embourgeoisiement of the nobility remained incomplete. This was eloquently expressed by János Vajda in 1862, the "last of the March Youths" of 1848 as Péter Hanák called him, when he sadly reflected back on the state of the Hungarian nobility: "I must confess" Vajda wrote, "I am horrified and fear for my nation when I see that mute, death-like apathy, which . . . sometimes creeps up on her lion-like being. The main precondition of our national existence is that we rise to the level of the European middle class. [But] the lazy indifference of our own middle landowners, and our predilection for looking down on the middle class . . . the will to rule among our lesser nobility, their cavalier shallowness, their desperate grabbing for the halo of the aristocracy . . . . Indolence, indifference: an antipathy to learning; an inclination to disorderliness, to wastefulness; to excess; very little inclination for self-sacrifice, and even less real civic-virtue; great self-satisfaction to go with a profound contempt for all that is foreign, and a tyrannical impatience; little industry and economy, and the old seigniorial airs in spite of a daily diminishing estate . . . all of which are very far from being in keeping with the spirit of modern civilization, but are, rather, genuine Asian mores."[33]

Vajda's concluding words of "Asian more" as an explanatory device for what was happening to the Magyar nobility, was misplaced. The Magyar nobility, when they turned against the values of the Enlightenment, progress, and liberty, were not following an Asian but instead a Central European trend, where the old elite remained in political power and was hostile to middle-class reform. Throughout Europe, but especially in Eastern Europe, the nobility at the end of the nineteenth century drifted back to its traditional elitism, and defense of feudal hierarchies. The radical politics of the 1840s were an aberration for this class. Few supported real and substantial land reform, they remained suspicious of the city and the German and Jewish entrepreneurs, and they did not want any further expansion of the franchise. Instead of calling for Westernization and the development of industry and capitalism, the Magyar nobility adopted the values of Romanticism. The new values that were idealized, indeed, were in direct opposition to the revolutionary slogans of the 1840s. The Magyar intellectuals of the 1870s and 1880s turned against liberalism, to adopt what can be called the "Southern plantation" or Junker Weltanschauung. Instead of Rousseau or Voltaire, the Magyar nobility produced their own literature, which idealized the life of the country nobles as being closer to the true meaning of life. Zsolt Beöthy's *Tragikum* (Tragedy) was especially popular in the 1880s. In this work Beöthy drew a distinction between the urban and the rural world and argued that a Magyar is one who lives in the countryside, finding ultimate gratification in the family and the home, and his book values romantic nationalism against the destructive effects of liberalism. Similar ideas were echoed in Károly Eötvös's popular *Utazás a Balaton körül* (Travels around Lake Balaton). "For Zsolt Beöthy and Károly Eötvös the home German and Jewish bourgeoisie aims at wealth, while the [real] Magyar aims at land: one has an apartment, the other a home; one is an integral part of a community, the other changes his alliances according to his business interest; one has a family, a past, honor and trust of people, the other is clever, has a business, likes money; one bases life on traditional values, carries tradition along, the other bases his values on individual success and business utility.[34]

The extent to which the merger of German-burghers with the Magyar nobility also represented the gentrification of the historic bourgeoisie, of course, varied from family to family. The overwhelming trend among those German burghers who joined with the Magyar road was to become part of the Hungarian *Bildungsbürgertum* and *Beamtenbürgertum*, and abandon careers in business. After all, it was an easy transition for many, often accompanied by a great deal of success. As A. C. Janos has evidenced, the growth of the Hungarian civil service between 1867 and 1900 presented vast opportunities. In 1867 there were an estimated 16,000 civil servants in Hungary, their numbers growing to 22,000 in 1872, and to 32,000 in 1875. Increasing even further, by 1890 civil servants accounted for 60,776 jobs and, in 1900, an estimated 97,835. As A. C. Janos put it: "The total number of public employees (including the salaried employees of the municipalities and the enterprises of the state) was 265,447 in 1904 and 387,922 in 1914 . . . . These figures represent roughly 3.5 percent of the active labor force. In terms of this ratio, Hungary was on par with, if not slightly ahead of, some of the most advanced industrial societies of the continent."[35] In other words, the urban estate, as it merged with the new Hungarian middle class, raised the university diploma as a way to maintain a barrier between itself and the poorer classes and retain its exclusive standing in society. This also happened in Western Europe, although the exclusivity of the urban estate was amplified in the Hungarian Kingdom. Instead of becoming transmitters of *jus civile*, or spreading the values of liberalism, the assimilating German burghers closed ranks and collapsed around occupations within the state administration (including education) and bureaucracy.

There were critics who disdained the course taken by the assimilating gentrified German burghers. The classic example of this can be found in Kálmán Mikszáth's novel *A Noszti fiú esete Tóth Marival* (The Young Noszti's Affair with Mária Tóth; 1906). The antagonist of Mikszáth's novel is Ferenc Noszti, who comes from a family of German Lutheran burghers that assimilated into Hungarian society in the 1840s. His father is an elected official of the County Diet, who hopes to find a political office for his son. But it is difficult to find

Ferenc Noszti a good job, because he is a degenerate, manipulative, womanizing, good-for-nothing, spoiled young man. In one part of the novel the hero, Mihály Tóth says to his wife after the young Noszti had seduced his daughter:

> Let us look at it in order. At the present my daughter's honor has been destroyed, but she still has youth, beauty and a dowry. That scoundrel will take that too. Slowly he will ruin her beauty, he will treat her badly, will probably beat her, because he is mean, spends money frivolously, because he is a lumpen, and then when she has nothing, no beauty, her youth gone, her body a ruin, and the money spent, he will leave her, if he does not leave her immediately after he has spent the money.[36]

Many Hungarian-Germans were able to identify with the tension that Mikszáth describes between Ferenc Noszti and Mihály Tóth. Those German burghers who remained closer to the tradition of their ancestors, from the 1870s onward, developed a definite distaste for their relatives who had become gentrified and entered bureaucratic careers in a perceived over-bloated state. They saw their relatives as squirrels trying to climb one of the great aristocratic trees, while abandoning their own flesh and blood. This antagonism toward those who mimicked noble-aristocratic habits and lifestyles can be seen in what Gyuri Verkovics, one of the main characters in Mikszáth's novel, says to his wife about whether their daughter should be allowed to marry her aristocratic suitor. Verkovics:

> I will not give my daughter to this lieutenant. Quiet! Stop your complaining and listen me out. I will not agree to the marriage, not because he is just a lieutenant, because even if he was a captain I would not give her to him. It is because he is a scoundrel. But even if he was not a scoundrel I would not give her to him, because he is Catholic, and I, in my Lutheran lifestyle would only give her to a Lutheran. But even if he was a Lutheran I would not give her to him, because he comes from an aristocratic background, and whoever goes there once, will not return, even to visit their family. You women think it is a sign of distinction to give one's daughter away to such a family, from which she thinks it is a disgrace to visit her own home. Well, I call that a burial. I would rather give my daughter to a big donkey than an important lord. Well my little daughter Rozali is not going to become a squirrel that will try to climb any big tree while I am alive.[37]

Mikszáth's novel was popular, but he was waging a losing battle. For the German burghers who assimilated by 1870, Magyarization no longer signified the ideals of Kossuth and Széchenyi, or Genersich and Liedemann, of the merger of the best elements of the German burghers with Magyar nobles. Magyarization signified gentrification, and an abandonment of liberal bourgeois values. The warnings of fathers to sons against marrying into a Magyar noble family, which Pukánszky highlighted, were no longer heeded but, instead, were followed with an eye on the advantage it would bring when entering a career in state administration. On the walls of the assimilated burghers a title of nobility would now be displayed, recently acquired through marriage or conveniently discovered in some ancestral lineage. A new chapter opened in the life of these families, and the new identity they adopted had little in common with their past. The gentleman middle-class project had succeeded in gentrifying the burghers, but failed in bringing the gentry closer to the middle class.

The Historical Urban Estate After 1848

Between 1850 and 1900 Hungary experienced sharp demographic growth and rapid industrialization. While in 1850 Hungary had a population of 11.6 million, by 1869 it grew to 13.6 million, by 1890 to 15.2 million, and by 1910 it reached 18.2 million. Most relevant for this study was that industrialization radically altered the role and ethnolinguistic composition of towns. In the context of Hungarian urban history, the most profound transformation took place in the city of Budapest, the name given to three towns—Pest, Buda, and Óbuda—consolidated in 1873. The combined population of these three towns grew from 145,000 in 1851 to 271,000 in 1869, 492,000 in 1890, and 880,371 by 1910. "While in 1870 Budapest was the seventeenth largest city in Europe, by 1900 it was the eighth. Only Berlin witnessed a similar rapid growth."[38] Further, by 1900 Budapest had a population larger than the 44 oldest royal free towns combined.

The demographic explosion in the second half of the nineteenth century was paralleled by an equally dramatic change in the ethnolinguistic composition of the new industrializing cities. In 1851—before the consolidation of Pest, Buda, and Óbuda had taken place—40 percent of the urban dwellers of Pest listed German as their mother tongue, 38.2 percent listed Magyar, and the remaining 20 percent was split along linguistic lines that spanned Slovakian, Croatian, Serbian, Romanian, Italian, and French. The distribution of the population of Buda in 1851 was 69.1 percent German, 20 percent Magyar, 4 percent Serbian, and 16 percent other, similar to the smaller linguistic groups also evident in

Pest.[39] Although German speakers represented a majority of Budapest's population in the 1850s, they comprised only 34.4 percent by the 1870s—markedly below the 56.6 percent of the city's residents who listed their mother tongue as Magyar. The latter increased to 79.5 percent, while the percentage of German speakers dwindled to 14.4 percent by 1900.[40] The evolution of Budapest was paralleled throughout the kingdom. While Elek Fényes estimated that in 1839 approximately 47 percent of the urban population of Hungary were Magyar speakers, by 1880 out of the 131 urban units classified as towns, 73 had a Magyar majority, and out of the estimated 2,144,000 urban dwellers, 64.5 percent claimed Magyar as their mother tongue, 18.2 percent German, 7.5 percent Slovak, 4.3 percent Serbian and Croatian, and 3.7 percent Romanian. The speed at which the Magyarization of towns was taking place can also be seen in the fact that in the decade between 1880 and 1890, the number of urban dwellers who claimed Magyar as their mother tongue increased from 1.4 million to 1.66 million, while those who claimed German as their mother tongue declined from 391,000 to 388,000, representing a decrease from 18.2 percent to 15.9 percent.[41]

Arguably one of the most important changes to take place during this period was the rise of the Jewish middle class. As the German burghers assimilated and traded their traditional place in the economic sector of the Hungarian social structure for a position within the Hungarian *Bildungsbürgertum* and *Beamtenbürgertum*, Jews took their place as the leaders of economic modernization. It is true that Jews were important economic modernizers already in the 1780s, but their role in Hungarian economic development was enhanced significantly after 1848. Noteworthy here is that while between 1870 and 1900 the estimated size of the Jewish population was little more than 5–6 percent of the total population, they nevertheless owned 60–70 percent of the modern banking institutions, and 85 percent of the independent credit institutions. Viktor Kárády has shown that 40–50 percent of the founders of modern industrial enterprises were Jews and in 1918 they represented approximately 60–65 percent of the wholesalers. They also made an important contribution to the establishment of the modern press as 50–60 percent of the new publishing houses in the Hungarian Kingdom, and 76 percent of those in Budapest, has been credited to them.[42]

The histories of Szeged and Timişoara are illustrative here. In 1910 Szeged had a population of 118,328, with 2,338 claiming to be of the Hebrew faith. Among the Jewish residents, 36 percent were employed in industry, 48.3 percent in commerce and banking, and only 0.8 percent in agriculture. More significantly, 61 percent of the doctors, 51 percent of the lawyers, 47 percent of the industrial managers, and 61 percent of those involved in commerce were Jews.[43] A similar picture emerges when examining the social stratification of Timişoara. In 1910 the population of Timişoara was 72,555. While only 2,413 claimed to be of the Hebrew faith, of this small Jewish community, 37.3 percent were employed in industry, 49.9 percent in commerce and banking, and only 1.1 percent in agriculture.[44]

Some pockets of traditional German Lutheran burgher culture survived the impact of Magyar nationalism and industrialization. These closed communities clinging to their traditional ways could best survive in the absence of the railroad. If the railroad did arrive, however, traditional German burgher culture came under the dual pressures of industrialization and the influx of non-Germans into the towns. The most notable German burgher enclave was in the Saxon towns of Transylvania. There too, an immigration of non-Germans transpired, but in at least the towns of Sibiu, Mediaş, and Sighişoara, the Germans were able to hold their ground. In Sibiu, for instance, in 1910 out of a total population of 33,489, 16,832 claimed their mother tongue to be German, while there were 8,824 Romanians, and 7,252 Magyars. In the same year in Sighişoara, out of a population of 11,587, 5,486 indicated German as their mother tongue, while there were 3,031 Romanians, and 2,687 Magyars. Mediaş, another famous Saxon city, had a population of 8,626 in 1910, of which 3,866 claimed their mother tongue as German, 2,729 Romanian, and 1,715 Magyar. The common characteristic of each of these towns is that in contrast to many of the historic towns of Hungary, German-speakers continued to be the major ethnic-linguistic group, and while they were no longer able to halt the influx of non-Germans, they resisted the temptation of assimilation and did not leave their hometowns.

Interestingly, in the 1880s, the Saxons of Transylvania continued to cling to the hope of being accepted as a distinct nationality in Hungary, and trusted that a Swiss Confederation compromise with the Hungarian government could be achieved. Yet the German burghers' aspiration to remain a distinct and separate group, as Glatz proposed almost a century before, seemed hopelessly idealistic. By the 1880s, few leaders supported the idea of making Hungary the Switzerland of Eastern Europe. The classic illustration of this is Prime Minister Kálmán Tisza's (1875–1890) declaration in 1875: "There can be only one viable nation within the frontiers of Hungary: that political nation is the Hungarian one. Hungary cannot become an eastern Switzerland because then it would cease to exist."[45] And when speaking of the Saxons specifically, Tisza claimed: "a Saxon nation does not exist." His successor, as the historian John Lukacs has pointed out, was even more hostile to the nationalities, and proclaimed that Hungary, "being a unified nation state, cannot tolerate political parties on the basis of nationality."[46]

A possible alternative to assimilation into Hungarian society was to turn to German nationalism. Prior to German unification in 1871, German nationalism had not played a significant role, and Magyar nationalism, as it gained momentum in the 1830s and 1840s, was significantly more advanced. From the 1870s, however, the strength of the idea of German nationalism did gain ground. As Béla Pukánszky wrote:

> [After the victory over France by Germany in 1870] the question emerged where the German Empire would stop? When the idea of an Austrian unification with the German Empire emerged, the German community [of Hungary] jumped on the bandwagon of the recreation of the Holy Roman Empire. The origin of this idea can be found in the popular belief that if Joseph II had had time, if two generations of enlightened rulers had followed the road of enlightened absolutism, the unification of Germandom—universal Germandom—would have been realized. It was a reflection back on the period of Joseph II, as a time of missed opportunities.[47]

Yet in the last decades of the nineteenth century, German nationalism and the idea of universal Germandom was rarely supported by the German burghers of Hungary. As Pál Hunfalvy, a Hungarian-German burgher born Paul Hunsdorfer, wrote in 1882 in *German*: "The soul [of the Hungarian-Germans] is so closely smelted with the soul of Hungary, that only the apocalypse could separate them."[48] Even in the Transylvanian towns, which had been disenchanted by the Parliament in Pest, academics writing from Germany, like Franz Löher and Frederich Rudolph Haine, could garner little support. Despite the fact that the Transylvanian Saxons rejected the Magyar gentry road, they looked to Vienna and not Berlin for protection.

In conclusion, using Gellner's model, the last three decades of the nineteenth century saw the urban estate fuse with Megalomanian culture. They adopted the language as well as the national identity of the Magyar nobility. Few of them became members of Ruritanian culture, or part of the Slovak and Romanian middle class. In the process of merging with Megalomania, the urban estate prospered by monopolizing special occupations within the administration of the emerging Hungarian nation-state. They remained, therefore, an exclusive estate. More inclusive than when they lived within the medieval walls of the towns, but exclusive enough to be distinguishable. Asboth's prophecy proved correct. In embracing the Magyar nation, the German burghers became one of the dominant groups within the professional middle class. Their only significant competition was from the rising Jewish middle class. They were able to fend off that threat, however, by embracing and promoting anti-Semitism, and excluding Jews from entering occupations in the state sector. Hungary, in other words, made an awkward if incomplete transition into modernity. The outbreak of World War I, followed by the violent interwar period, tested the fragile middle class, and in significant ways it could not live up to the challenge.

7

Conclusion: The Failed Bourgeoisie?

The idea of the Central and East European bourgeoisie following a separate, unique, and failed road into modernity first emerged in the works of disgruntled Central European liberals at the twilight of the nineteenth century. Born in the backdrop of the disappointing revolutions of 1848, the Austro-Hungarian Compromise of 1867, and the Unification of Germany by the Junkers in 1871, the aristocracy and nobility of Central Europe seemingly were able to survive the threat of the French Revolution to the detriment of middle-class values and institutions. Disillusioned by this course of events, liberals criticized what they perceived to be the lethargy and impotency of their respective national bourgeoisies. As Theodore Mommsen bitterly wrote at the end of his life in 1899: "Ein wirklicher Bürger zu sein, das sei in dieser Nation nicht möglich" (To be a true bourgeois is not possible in this nation).[1] A shortcoming leveled at the bourgeoisie of Central Europe was their tendency to become ennobled, and their abandonment of puritan values for the leisurely consumption lifestyles of the nobility. Werner Sombart noted in his 1903 work *Die Deutsch Volkswirtschaft im 19. Jahrhundert*: "the bourgeoisie who have become rich try to forget their origins as soon as possible, and to rise into the landed aristocracy or at least into the ranks of the feudal estate owners."[2] The notion that the Central European bourgeoisie was feudalized was also noted by Max Weber, who had mixed feelings about the political compromise the German bourgeoisie was forced to make when Prussia unified Germany. Weber wrote of the uneasy alliance:

> It is in keeping with the wisdom of the state ruling Prussia today, to reconcile the bourgeois purse with the minimal political influence of the

bourgeoisie by granting a kind of "second class right of admission at court," and in the interested circles nothing would be more unpopular than if difficulties were created for the "nobilitation" of capital acquired in commerce, in industry, in the stock exchange by their metamorphosis into the form of the landed estate.[3]

In contrast to the idea of bourgeois subordination and failure, Geoff Eley and David Blackbourn have argued that while some liberals were critical toward the road traveled by the Central European bourgeoisie, the majority of German liberals made peace with Bismarck and, as Eley noted, "reached an accommodation within the framework of the small-German, semi-constitutional Reich."[4] Furthermore, the oft-quoted criticism of the *Sonderweg* traveled by the German middle class (i.e., their supposed feudalization following German unification), was not understood as a negative by everyone before World War I. The German middle class may not have produced a wealthy merchant-industrial class like in England, or a politically successful bourgeoisie as in France, but they did give rise to a more developed *Bildungsbürgertum*, an educated and literary middle class superior to either their French or English counterparts. To this tradition belongs Nietzsche who referred to the English as that "not very philosophical people."[5] And Oswald Spengler, who wrote of the French Revolutionary leaders Dalton and Robespierre that "every revolution produces such men by the dozen," while the Germany of the 1800s was home to Beethoven, Kant, and Goethe. What other land could boast of such towering intellectuals? This positive portrayal of the German road was expressed in Friedrich Meinecke's 1915 epilogue to his important work, *Cosmopolitanism and the Nation State*. In the book, Meinecke highlighted some of the difficulties produced by German unification led by Prussia, but in the 1915 epilogue he expressed the hope that war would give rise to a new spirit of solidarity and a new identity able to bring the great German intellect and the best elements of the Prussian character together. Meinecke noted:

> If our military succeeds in completely synthesizing the citizens' army and the professional army, then our state will also succeed in completely synthesizing the political systems of Prussia and of the Reich, for there will then be no more need to protect Prussian individuality anxiously under all circumstances .... This war has shown in an overwhelming way how deeply and inseparably Prussia and Germany are intertwined with each other. The exchange of their intellectual characteristics will continue to become more intense. The best feature of the Prussian

character, its capacity for rigorous organization, has now become a general German characteristic.[6]

Following the rise to power of the Nazis, of course, few social scientists outside Germany wanted to praise the *Sonderweg* traveled by the German bourgeoisie, or extol the advantages of the merger of Prussian discipline with the intellectual prowess of the *Bildungsbürgertum*. A critical turn had taken place in 1933, and the dominant view among historians, sociologists, and political scientists was that the Central European bourgeoisie had failed. The feudalization of the bourgeoisie which Sombart and Weber had noted before World War I reemerged and became once more the leading point of criticism. As George G. Iggers wrote on postwar German historiography: "For liberal historians, such as Kohn, Holborn, Mosse, and Stern, and Marxists, such as Alexander Abusch and George Lukács, the failure of German liberalism was related to the failure of the bourgeoisie to gain effective political power in Germany in the nineteenth or twentieth century."[7] The victory of the Junkers in unifying Germany was understood as having played a decisive role in the defeat of bourgeois liberal democratic principles. "It brought about," Iggers noted: "a refeudalization of the solid bourgeoisie as well as of the lower middle class and the artisans (Winkler), and contributed according to Hans Rosenberg and H. J. Puhle to the emergence of pre-fascist, *völkish*, anti-Semitic attitudes, which, according to Dirk Stegmann, found their fulfillment in the Nazi state."[8] Interestingly, this shift after World War II was not lost on Friedrich Meinecke, who in his book *The German Catastrophe*, written in 1949, rejected his own views of 1915 and became critical of the Prussian influence on German middle-class development. Meinecke wrote:

> However, in the era when the Empire was founded, the aspect of Prussian militarism which were bad and dangerous for the general well-being were obscured by the imposing proof of its power and discipline in its service for national unity and in the construction of Bismarck's Empire. The military man now seemed to be a consecrated spirit—the lieutenant moved through the world as a young god and the civilian reserve lieutenant at least as a demigod. He had to rise to be reserve officer in order to exert his full influence in the upper-middle-class world and above all in the state administration. Thus militarism penetrated civilian life. Thus there developed a conventional Prussianism (*Borussismus*), a naïve self-admiration in Prussian character, and together with it a serious narrowing of intellectual and political outlook. Everything was dissolved into a rigid conventionalism.[9]

At the time Francis Carsten was formulating his ideas on medieval urban development in the 1940s, therefore, the position was gaining momentum that Central European bourgeois development was weak, incomplete, and most important, subordinate to the nobility. Carsten published his first major article in 1943 under the title, "Medieval Democracy in the Brandenburg Towns and its Defeat in the Fifteenth Century." The last sentence read: "Both the historical weakness of democracy in Germany and the formation of the Prussian State are intimately connected with the subjugation of the towns at the end of the middle ages."[10] Readers did not have to be reminded of what Carsten had in mind. His work was intended as a contribution to understanding the victory of National Socialism in Germany. Nineteen thirty three became the year that had to be explained, and throughout his life he remained committed to the idea that stunted urbanization in the sixteenth century was the root cause of the weakness of liberalism and the rise of dictatorships in the twentieth. In his influential work *The Origins of Prussia* in 1954, he wrote: "The most important factor in the social history of Brandenburg and Prussia, and of many other eastern European countries, was the decline of the towns and the subsequent rise of the nobility: it definitely separated the developments in the east from those in the west and created a boundary line between two different social systems."[11]

This work challenges the traditional view of early modern urban development in Eastern Europe by arguing that in the case of Hungary, there was no direct correlation between the seigniorial reaction and urban decline. While some towns declined, others grew. Among the most fundamental changes to take place, urban constitutions were modernized, the family and social organization of the communal brotherhood were reformed, and towns converted to Lutheranism. Many diverse factors exist to explain Hungary's widespread urban dynamism. Bratislava, for instance, with the Ottoman occupation of Buda, became the new political capital of the Independent Hungarian Kingdom. Trnava's population grew dynamically because many of the influential burghers from Buda and Pest decided to settle there. Cluj-Napoca during these centuries became an important city in Transylvania, as it emerged as the core of a particular type of Magyar Renaissance. Pécs expanded because it became an important Ottoman administration city and transshipment point between the West and the East. But even the less impressive town of Levoča experienced growth. Between 1555 and 1667, the number of houses increased from 440 to 700, while the population of the town rose from 3,162 to 4,867.[12] Further, the populations of Košice,

Bardejov, Prešov, and virtually all of the mining towns experienced a similar demographic and economic rise.[13] In urban centers small and large, town halls, public baths, schoolhouses, stone fortifications, and Renaissance style homes were constructed.

How does this evidence help in understanding East Central European historical developments? Hungarian historians have used the urban decline thesis, similar to Carsten, to explain the medieval origins of Hungary's later political backwardness: namely, the rise of right-wing dictatorship in the interwar period and communism after World War II. This was directly expressed by Jenő Szűcs in his influential work entitled *Outline of the Three Historical Regions of Europe*:

> The weakness of the development of a Western type of autonomous urban/civic society, should not be looked for in the fact that in the Hungarian Kingdom town dwellers were ethnically different from the Magyars, but in the fact that urbanization that did develop lasted only for a short time and produced but a handful of towns between 1200–1350; and when this early urbanization was interrupted [with the decline of the Levantine trade route], those that did exist were dwarfed by the economics of the dominant latifundium system.[14]

In light of the evidence presented in this work, it becomes difficult to accept Szűcs's proposition that Hungary's weakly developed urban/civic traditions can be traced to a stunted or interrupted urbanization in the medieval period. On this point, Geoff Eley's argument appears most convincing, arguing that in Germany (and here Eastern Europe broadly can be included), there is too great a reliance on the continuity from the medieval to the modern, and historians should try and "loosen the deterministic grip of the road to 1933."[15] This is not to discard the importance of the medieval; yet as Eley writes, "In the end both perspectives are necessary—the deep historical long-term structural one and the stress on the immediate crises. But we have to be clear about what exactly each of them may reasonably explain."[16]

The critical question remains: Was the Hungarian experience unique? Or, does there have to be a review of urban development across all of Central and Eastern Europe under second serfdom? Is there a need for a new meta-narrative?

Arguments for Hungary's distinctiveness could begin with the Ottoman occupation. Where the Ottomans consolidated their control, occidental feudalism and second serfdom were abolished. Further, even where second serfdom continued, namely the Uplands and Transylvania, the tense international military competition was far different from that of, for instance, Poland. One of the strengths of this argument is that after the Ottomans were expelled and the Habsburgs consolidated their rule over Hungary, many royal free towns stagnated. Arguments against Hungary's distinctiveness, in contrast, would stress broader European structural developments. As Robert Brenner argued, for instance, there were three possible solutions to the crisis of the manorial economy in late medieval Europe: (1) Lords could expel their serfs and transform the land into their private property; (2) peasants could expel their lords and establish a system of free peasant family farming; and (3) lords could chain their serfs to the land and establish second serfdom. The first option was followed in England, the second in France, and the third in Eastern Europe.[17]

Within this larger European context, the military success of the Ottomans over Hungary should be understood as a symptom of the rise of second serfdom, and not an end in itself. One of the structural flaws of the seigniorial reaction throughout Hungary and Poland-Lithuania was that it weakened first and foremost the king. When Conrad Sperfogel in the town of Levoča took the tax collector down to the wine cellar to get him drunk on the best wine to avoid paying taxes, just at the moment the Hungarian King desperately needed to raise money to defend the kingdom from the Ottomans, he followed a practice common to Ringbürger rule. A direct line can be drawn from the borders of today's Croatia, Hungary, Slovakia, Poland, and up to Lithuania, where a similar pattern was apparent: rise of lords, corruption in the towns, followed by declining authority of the king, contested sovereignty, and invasion. Interestingly, it was precisely during the period of contested sovereignty and the growing international military competition of the sixteenth and first half of the seventeenth century that towns flourished. The case of Zápolya is telling here. Zápolya, when he re-granted Kežmarok its autonomy and ennobled all the burghers of Buda, was trying to rise from landlord leading the manorial reaction to king of Hungary. Some Polish nobles with similar aspirations must also have realized the advantages of this strategy, such as Hieronymous and Albert Łasky. In other words, the moment sovereignty was being renegotiated following the initial imposition of second serfdom was a fortuitous one for towns, and some emerged with greater autonomy. This does not mean to imply that all towns developed under second serfdom. Sometimes towns negotiated badly, with the wrong partner, becoming little more than villages. But when they negotiated well, with a good partner, had fortune on their side, and escaped major fires and plagues, they emerged stronger.

Contrary to the traditional view, therefore, there is no natural correlation between the seigniorial reaction and urban decay. As is accepted today, the old textbook supposition that towns existed outside and were antithetical to feudalism is an exaggeration. Towns did not lead the way for the decline of feudalism in the West. Taking this into account, it must also be accepted that their decline did not seal the victory for the seigniorial reaction in the East. Towns and lords during feudalism could slug it out, snob one another or, what was most frequent, live in a symbiotic relationship. But towns were rarely the natural allies of unfree peasants, and the chant of *stadtluft macht frei* (city air makes free) was often reserved for the already privileged. Obviously some towns declined as a consequence of the seigniorial reaction, but many did not. The fate of towns often hinged on local factors, the course of negotiations, and fortune, but not on a set and immutable law linking second serfdom with urban decay.

If we accept the proposition that there was urban growth under second serfdom, the bigger problem emerges as to why the urban decline thesis remains part of both the international comparative as well as national historical meta-narratives. Why did historians of Hungary pay almost exclusive attention to the signs of decline in the towns, while largely ignoring the signs of growth? Eley's conclusion that historians of Central and Eastern Europe are overly teleological explains part of the problem, but not all. It is illuminating to reflect back on the first half of Szűcs's summation of the reasons for stunted urbanization. Szűcs wrote that, "the weakness of the development of a western type of autonomous urban/civic society, should not be looked for in the fact that in the Hungarian Kingdom town dwellers were ethnically different from the Magyars."[18] When Szűcs wrote these lines, he had in mind the ethnic frictions and conflicts engulfing the Interwar period and World War II Hungary. His intention was to dismiss the argument of Hungarian nationalist historians who stirred up ethnic passions by blaming the problems of Hungarian national as well as economic development on the non-native bourgeoisie. Specifically he had in mind Gyula Szekfű, who famously noted in his popular work, *Three Generations* (1922):

> Of the almost 600,000 urban-dwellers, that is of the most cultured and wealthiest elements [of the Hungarian Kingdom], half we cannot consider as a national class . . .[Because] for the most part they are German-speaking burghers, who only recently assimilated into the Hungarian nation.[19]

Szekfű wrote these lines from a deep-seated bitterness over the dissolution of the Austro-Hungarian Monarchy following the end of World War I, and the reduction of the Hungarian Kingdom to one-third its former size. He was convinced that Hungary had followed a different road because the urban dwellers had not fulfilled their nation-building role. This was for him the leading difference between Eastern Europe and the West.

Szekfű and Szűcs were unique because in their work they did focus considerable attention on the role of towns. They are exceptional figures in Hungarian historiography, which is dominated by a focus on the nobility and peasantry. Interestingly though, the tension between Szűcs who thought the ethnicity of the urban-dwellers played no role, and Szekfű who thought it played the most critical role, is an excellent illustration of the confusion surrounding the significance of German burghers in Hungary's national development. Both share as their central thesis the idea that Hungary's political as well as economic backwardness is reducible to the failure of towns and the historic bourgeoisie, although each understands the critical period as happening at entirely different times, caused by radically different reasons. Szűcs argued that the bourgeoisie failed in Eastern Europe because in the medieval period towns were subordinated to noble rule. Szekfű, in contrast, thought the grand failure to be in the nineteenth century, when the German burghers either assimilated too fast, or too slow and, in the process, abdicated their nation-building calling to the Hungarian nobility. Interestingly, despite these radically different approaches, Szűcs and Szekfű arrived at similar conclusions. Namely, the tragedy of Hungary in the twentieth century was that its home-bourgeoisie was small, weak, ineffective—and for Szekfű, foreign. Consequently, Hungary could not follow the path of Western liberal democratic capitalism.

The confusion surrounding the role of towns and the German bourgeoisie in Hungary is, therefore, intricately tied to the centrality of the Magyar nobility in the construction of Hungarian national history. Because the Magyar nobility emerged as the agent of nation-state building, the national historical meta-narrative was also constructed around that class. The emphasis in modern Hungarian historical meta-narratives thus fell on the achievements of great nobles and the world of the country. Assimilating German burghers often adopted this Magyar noble historical meta-narrative as their own, and the history of towns fell into neglect. Hungarian national history was understood as driven by the Magyar nobility, in which towns played only a minor role. This view of the role of towns in nation-building was, in turn, taken as a sign of stagnation or decline. The reverse of what took place in France, therefore, occurred. While in France after the French Revolution, the historical meta-narrative became compulsively fixated on the contribution made by towns and the bourgeoisie in the construction of the French nation, in Hungary it was obsessively concerned with the role played by the Magyar nobility and aristocracy.

Here, of course, Thomas Bender's criticism of the dominance of the nation-state in the teaching of history is very relevant. As Thomas Bender argued in the *American Historical Review*: "With the exception of the historians of France [and the United States]. . . histories of other modern nations seem to have had fewer doubts about the basic framing of a [national] narrative synthesis."[20] In the case of Hungarian towns, Bender's criticism rings especially true. Hungarian national meta-narratives, or those of the successor states like Slovakia and Romania, have not been successful in bridging the gap between the urban and rural histories, because they have not as yet broken from the centrality of the nation-state (and the ethnic majority which came to monopolize that state) as the leading actor of the historical dialectic. After all, who were the town-dwellers under the Ottoman occupation? In Pest, Buda, Pécs, and Szeged, they were Armenians, Greeks, Jews, and Turks. Buda in 1660 had three synagogues within the old town walls, more than at any other time in its history. In the Uplands and Transylvania there were towns with a Magyar majority, but out of the over thirty or more royal free towns in the seventeenth century, only seven had a Magyar-speaking majority.

The scholarly treatment, consequently, of urban development in the sixteenth and seventeenth centuries may be reduced to the dominance and influence of mono-ethnic historical meta-narratives. When Slovak, Romanian, Magyar, and Croatian historians pushed pen to paper at the end of the nineteenth century, they conceived of their calling as nation-builders and not professional historians. Underlying their research agenda, historians were also trying to make history. They shouted in the spirit of the French Revolution: "Vive la Nation!" Unfortunately, in their rush to build their own distinct national-ethnic meta-narratives, few stood up to argue that focusing on nation-building distorts historical reality. Furthermore, as István Deák has written, "even if inspired historians have used history not to inflame nationalistic passions but to illuminate errors and crimes of the past, a good part of the public has preferred to identify with those historians whose main goal has been to incite hostility toward outsiders, minorities, and aliens."[21]

Taking the above into consideration, the important question remains: was there anything unique about the road traveled by the Hungarian bourgeoisie? If there was no stunted urbanization in the fifteenth-sixteenth century, where exactly does the problem lie?

Over the past half century, questions about the role and significance of the bourgeoisie in the making of Western civilization have engaged historians and sociologists across Europe. Before addressing specifically the case of Hungary, it is important to review briefly these larger European debates. After World War II, the dominant view was that an ascending middle class had come to power in England and France, where they established liberal capitalist democracies. Furthermore, the rise of fascist regimes, followed by the establishment of communism in East Central Europe was understood as caused by the failure of the bourgeoisie east of the Elbe to assert their independence. The dichotomy contrasting a bourgeois West with an agrarian aristocratic East, from the beginning, had its critics and doubters, but with the rise of the Cold War in the 1950s, many thinkers found the model useful in describing the east-west division of Europe. A classic summary of this bipolar view of European development was made by Ralf Dahrendorf in his successful book *Society and Democracy in Germany*:

> Just as the economy of Imperial Germany became industrial, but not capitalist the German society of the time did not become bourgeois, but remained quasi-feudal. Industrialization in Germany failed to produce a self-confident bourgeoisie with its own political aspirations. In so far as a bourgeoisie emerged at all, it remained relatively small and, what is more, unsure of itself and dependent in its social and political standards. As a result, German society lacked the stratum that in England and America, and to a lesser extent even in France, had been the moving force of a development in the direction of greater modernity and liberalism.[22]

Interestingly, the attack on the Cold War dichotomy of a liberal, capitalist, civic, and bourgeois West versus an authoritarian, agrarian, militaristic, and aristocratic East first emerged in England. In 1953 H. R. Trevor-Roper published an article criticizing R. H. Tawney, who maintained that the Glorious Revolution in England had been led by a rising creditor (i.e., capitalist) class. Trevor-Roper, in his now classic *The Gentry 1540–1640*, argued that instead of an ascending capitalist class, the Glorious Revolution was actually driven by the declining gentry.[23] Trevor-Roper's article marked the first significant revisionist challenge to the classic understanding of bourgeois and middle-class development in Europe. The next major challenge emerged from France in the 1950s, with the publication of Alfred Cobban's famous article "The Myth of the French Revolution" (1954). This was followed by successive publications by François Furet and Denis Richet, who "dismissed any validity to the idea that a bourgeois revolution was set in motion in 1789, pointing to the lack of manufacturers or industrialists in the leading ranks of the Convention, and to the slow rates of French capitalist growth after the fall of the Monarchy."[24] An extreme expression of this school is Sarah Maza's recent book, *The Myth of the French Bourgeoisie* (2003). At the center of Maza's book lies the assertion that "the French bourgeoisie did not exist." Neither the French nor English revisionists have been able to declare victory, but they have certainly influenced the course of the debate.[25]

Ironically, revisionism in Germany has gone in the opposite direction to that of France and England. While English and French revisionism has dismissed the notion that either the Glorious or French Revolution was set off by an ascending bourgeoisie or capitalist class, German revisionism has set out to prove that there was nothing wrong with the Central European bourgeoisie prior to World War I. Turning against the thesis that the German bourgeoisie had been "feudalized" following German unification, the new view claims that the German middle class was stronger than ever in 1900. Or as David Blackbourn summarized the new view of German middle-class development: "It might be in fact more accurate to talk of the embourgeoisement of German society rather than the feudalization of the German bourgeoisie."[26] These views, as is well known, were first popularized in the English-speaking works by Eley and Blackbourn's path-breaking book, *The Peculiarities of German History*, and more recently in a collection of essays published by Blackbourn and Evans entitled *The German Bourgeoisie*. But the roots of German revisionism can be traced to Jürgen Kocka, the leading theorist of German middle-class development since the 1970s. Kocka concedes that there were elements of the feudalization thesis which merit attention. However, he also points to some serious inconsistencies. Namely, the feudalization thesis often interprets the failed revolution of 1848 and the unification of Germany by Prussia as bourgeois defeats. Kocka argues that this is an oversimplification, because it gives "insufficient consideration to the fact that there were also compromises between the bourgeois movements and the old powers in which both sides made concessions, achieved some gains and came closer to each other."[27] He also noted that the increasing intermingling between the nobility and the upper middle class was not a Central European peculiarity, but instead a pan-European phenomenon. The new view of German bourgeois development which Kocka champions can be narrowed down to three points: (1) In Central and Eastern Europe the nobility had significantly more political power than in Western Europe; (2) There was intermingling between the bourgeoisie and nobility in Western and Eastern Europe, but the English and French bourgeoisie were far more advanced than their Central European counterparts; and (3) there was less intermingling between the bourgeoisie and the nobility in Central Europe than is suggested by the feudalization thesis, and more intermingling between these classes in France and England. In short, instead of understanding the bourgeoisie as having been subsumed into the aristocratic world, and subordinated, the German bourgeoisie may have been more independent and even more bourgeois than either their English or French counterparts. As Kocka put it:

> The Bürgertum as a whole, however, in spite of its inner fragmentation and its lack of sharply defined boundaries, had a clearer shape in Germany than elsewhere. The feudalization thesis, in its traditional form, needs to be modified. The core of the *Sonderweg* thesis, however, survives. The relationship between the *Bürgertum* and the nobility manifested certain peculiarities which pointed to the former's weakness. Its relatively clear boundaries as a social formation corresponded to a relative weakness in its capacity to influence and integrate the rest of society . . . . The bureaucratic aspects of German Bürgerlichkeit were the product of its most critical limitations.[28]

Hungarian historiography on bourgeois development since World War II has followed the major contours of German historiography.[29] The leading historian of this school was Péter Hanák. However, Hanák also gave a more nuanced description of the Hungarian experience. Hungary shared with other Central European countries the "*Drang nach Beamter Leben*" (Drive for the Bureaucratic Life), or the flood of the historic bourgeoisie into the state bureaucracy, which, as Hanák argued, led to their feudalization. But at this precise moment a large number of Jews immigrated into Hungary and filled the vacuum created by the entry of the German burghers into white collar professions. Jews experienced unprecedented social mobility by becoming a "substitute middle class." This also happened in Germany, but the relative size of the Jewish population in Hungary was significantly larger. Hanák maintained that Jews were less likely to be feudalized, because the anti-Semitic Magyar political class excluded them from entering careers in the state. Middle-class development in Hungary, therefore, conforms more or less to the German pattern, except for the problem of ethnic fragmentation. The middle class in 1900 became subdivided into small caste-like exclusive groups, the Protestants, Catholics, and Jews, which obviously intersected at the professional level, but had little to do with one another at the private level. As A. C. Janos succinctly summarized the course of Hungarian bourgeois development, "The flight of the German bourgeoisie from commercial and industrial pursuits deepened the ethnic division of labor that had been taking shape in the pre-1848 period, for the Germans were replaced by Jewish immigrants whose numbers steadily increased."[30] Or as Mária Kovács wrote more recently: "Rather than gradually transforming the native agrarian elite into an indigenous commercial class, Hungary's rapid entry into the company of industrial nations resulted in an unusually sharp ethnic division of labor, with the majority of the business class coming from outside traditional society."[31]

Over the past two decades, Hungarian revisionists have also launched a challenge to the "feudalization" thesis. Led by Gábor Gyáni and György Kövér, Hungarian revisionism has raised objections regarding the significance of the ethnic fragmentation thesis within the middle class, and rejected the idea that at the turn of the twentieth century a dual society existed in Hungary: a backward, traditional, noble Christian feudalized middle class, versus a modern, progressive, Jewish middle class.[32] The most important work produced by this group was Gábor Gyáni's *Történészdiskurzusok* [Historical Discourses] (Budapest, 2002), which is a collection of essays that attempt to show how Magyar nobles were not all backward and traditional, and why not all Jews were as modern as is often assumed. Similar to Blackbourn, Eley, and Kocka, Hungarian revisionists highlight that those factors which are used to evidence the "feudalization" thesis, such as the predominance of dueling, the overabundance of former nobles in the political field, and the "*Drang nach Beamter Leben*," were not necessarily "feudal" characteristics at all.[33]

To summarize the debates on the role of the bourgeoisie in European history: while traditionally in the west liberal capitalist democracy was thought to have been a product of an ascending bourgeoisie, and the weakness of democracy and liberalism in Central Europe a sign of its failure, today these positions have reversed. In France revisionists argue that it was not the bourgeoisie which led the revolution, and even the existence of the class is now questioned. In England, revisionists posit that it was not an ascending capitalist middle class that led the way toward modernization of the state, but the declining gentry. Last and most importantly, Germany and Hungary, traditionally thought to have produced an incomplete bourgeoisie, are now argued to have possessed a more complete and autonomous middle class than either France or England. Which of these pictures is correct? Was Hungarian and German bourgeois development stronger than that of the French and English? Did earlier historians get it completely wrong? Was there no failed bourgeoisie in Central Europe?

In discussing the ways in which the Hungarian bourgeoisie failed, this work has concentrated on long-term historical processes and highlighted the differences between preindustrial and industrializing Hungary. It is critical to draw a distinction between these two separate periods, because urban dwellers both in Hungary and elsewhere understood their positions and options in radically different ways. Preindustrial society is dominated by peasants, lords, and monarchs. Industrial society, in contrast, brings with it an emerging proletariat, the shift from agriculture to industrial capital, as well as modern state building. In the first half of the book it was shown that during the period of second serfdom, a balance of power emerged in which towns, nobles, and monarchs shared power. Towns were not the natural allies of peasants, but instead allied with the king against lords, or the nobles against the king. The natural inclination of towns under the feudal political economy was not to be islands of modernity, growing incessantly larger and conquering the backward feudal countryside. Towns under late feudalism existed in a symbiotic relationship with the countryside, and lords and burghers lived within a system of shared values and norms.

A radical shift in the behavior of the historic bourgeoisie occurred following the rise of Enlightened Absolutism. Starting in the late seventeenth century and intensifying with Maria Theresa (1740–1780) and the rule of Joseph II (1780–1790) and Leopold II (1790–1792), the Habsburg state attempted to undermine the autonomy and independence of towns and nobles, thereby emerging as the single entity with a monopoly of "legitimate violence" in the Weberian sense. The state disarmed both nobles and towns, and under the short but radical rule of Joseph II abolished the privileges of guilds, the royal free standing of towns, and serfdom. Many of these reforms were overturned shortly thereafter, but they represented a trend which would dominate the relationship of state and society in the modern period. The late eighteenth century therefore represents the end of second serfdom and the beginnings of what can be called modern social development. The feudal division of labor, based on estates, privilege, and birth, was undergoing radical transformation toward a more flexible and open class-based system.

While change was inevitable, it is important to note that in the eighteenth century it remained confined to the realm of ideas. Peasants formed the bulk of the population, and within the towns the artisan worldview was far different from what would emerge under the conditions of industrial society. The transition from feudalism to capitalism was, therefore, first felt on the cultural front. Before the outbreak of the French Revolution, the Cultural Revolution sweeping across western Europe was also making a deep impression in the Hungarian Kingdom. Reformers in the towns began to articulate their calling as modernizers. Johann Schneider, Joseph Benczúr, Johann Genersich in the Upland towns, the Brukenthal family in the town of Sibiu, Martin Liedemann in the town of Timişoara, were implementing school reforms with the explicit aim of bringing the burghers and nobles closer together, and thereby giving birth to a new class which would be in the vanguard of change. When the revolution broke, however, the German burghers hesitated. A small fringe movement calling itself the Hungarian Jacobins did emerge, but as was evidenced, this revolutionary cell was recruited from the declining gentry and the upwardly mobile small holders. Towns and the historic bourgeoisie did not support the revolution, because they were opposed to allowing the mob into politics, and they were unprepared and unwilling to endorse change which would open the floodgates and allow for the mass immigration of non-Germans into the towns.

Failure in 1848 was, of course, not so much caused by the weakness of internal bourgeois development, as much as the overwhelming military superiority of the combined forces of the Habsburgs and Romanovs. The year 1848 was also different from the period of the French Revolution, because by that time towns did throw their support behind the cause of liberalism in John Stuart Mill's classic sense of the term. Although here again, it is noteworthy that the Saxons of Transylvania turned against the revolution, and remained loyal subjects of the Habsburg state. In part this was because the Saxons claimed they did not want to see a Magyar noble takeover of the Hungarian state. But it was also caused by internal pressures within the Saxon community, which opposed the abolition of guilds or the royal free standing and autonomy of towns. Saxon liberalism extended only so far as it did not infringe on their feudal privileges.

Nevertheless, in 1848 many of the towns and the historic bourgeoisie became supporters of change, and adopted overwhelmingly revolutionary slogans, such as liberty, individuality, and the abolition of feudal privileges. This was the last time in Hungarian history when the historic bourgeoisie would support revolution from below, and it was also the last preindustrial revolution.

Defeat in 1848 did not mean that the bourgeoisie was shortly thereafter re-feudalized. As economic development progressed, and Hungary began to industrialize, the goals and aspirations of the bourgeoisie simply changed. Blackbourn's conclusion, therefore, that late-nineteenth- century Germany was a period of embourgeoisement, rather than feudalization, is also true for Hungary. This is not to dismiss Péter Hanák's claim that the liberal reform movement stumbled in its goals to Magyarize the bourgeoisie and bourgeoisify the nobility.[34] When German burghers assimilated they did adopt overwhelmingly the Magyar gentry habitus, while the Magyar nobility assimilated few German burgher traits and traditions. But the Hungarian revisionist Gyáni is correct to claim that this cannot be called "feudalization." Indeed the use of the term feudalization is extremely misleading, because it harkens back to the period of second serfdom and the subjugation of towns by nobles. Not only is the traditional view of urban stagnation following the manorial reaction wrong, but the nineteenth century gentrification of the bourgeoisie resembled nothing out of the feudal period. Throughout Europe in the late nineteenth century there was a tendency within the historic bourgeoisie to adopt a lifestyle that concerned itself more with leisurely consumption than Protestant piety. As modern nation-state building gained momentum and industrialization transformed the relationship between town and country, the bourgeoisie stopped being a revolutionary force. A new alliance was forged where the historic bourgeoisie joined with the nobility, as practically all of the legal and institutional demands of 1848 were met by 1880. In assimilating into Hungarian society, the German burghers did adopt the Magyar noble historic imagined national identity, but this did not mean that they went back to the land and became landlords. They failed to grab state power in 1789 and in 1848, but after 1867 they succeeded without the need for revolution to enter the state.

Hungarian revisionism, however, underestimates the critical limitation ethnic fragmentation within the middle class had on the future course of events, as evidenced in the works of Hanák, Karády, Berend, Kovács, and many others.[35] There did emerge a "dual society" in Hungary, but the dynamic of that duality has been incorrectly interpreted.

The Jewish and Christian middle class did occupy different positions within the social structure, and after 1867 both groups seemed to have developed a tendency toward the monopolization of certain occupations. On this point, Kocka's analysis of the German case is especially poignant, when he noted that in Germany the bourgeoisie was more isolated from the rest of society than their French or English counterparts. In a similar way, in Hungary the assimilated Germans and Magyar gentry collapsed around occupations within the state sector, while Jews did so in the private sector. Lutherans may have played less of an important role in the upper echelons of political administration than Catholics, but the tendency was for the Christian middle class to swarm around positions within the expanding national railroad system, post offices, libraries, the tax offices, and the many other modern administrative offices, as well as the growing educational infrastructure. A. C. Janos has estimated that perhaps 70 percent of the new political bureaucracy "were members of the erstwhile German bourgeoisie which, with the few stubborn Saxon communities, was ready en mass to give up economics for public service." Furthermore, as Janos goes on to write: "The government in turn was ready to embrace them on condition that they renounce their language and ethnic identity."[36]

There were Jews who could also be found employed in the state, but far fewer. William McCagg had shown that between 1800 and 1918 approximately 346 wealthy Jewish families were ennobled, some converting to Christianity and having successful political careers. McCagg also argued in his influential book *Jewish Nobles and Geniuses* that it was from this exclusive group that a disproportionate number of Hungary's so-called geniuses came from, such as John von Neumann, Edward Teller, Albert Szent-György, Karl Mannheim, George Lukács, Karl Polányi, and his brother Michael Polányi.[37] But these 346 odd families were the exception. As Viktor Karády showed, the social contract governing the assimilation of Jews and Germans into Hungarian society was significantly different. Jews were tolerated, and were allowed to participate as equal citizens in the private sphere, but there was an understanding that they would not be allowed into the state bureaucracy.[38] There was consequently a duality to Hungary's middle class which also had an ethnic basis. But this duality between the Gentleman Christian middle class—as it was called—and the liberal Jewish middle class did not represent a struggle between a backward, feudal force on the one hand and a progressive, modernizing one on the other. Both segments of Hungary's ethnically fragmented bourgeoisie were modern, but they were traveling on very different trajectories.

Until the fall of the Austro-Hungarian Monarchy, the problems of ethnic fragmentation within the middle class were not clearly understood, or discussed in great detail. There were radicals around the journal *Huszadik Század* who wrote on the decay and inevitable fall of the bourgeoisie, but they were often enthusiastic young Communists convinced of the inevitability of world revolution. When Gyáni claims that there is little evidence for the crisis of middle-class culture in 1900, he is correct to point out that few within the middle class thought they were on the edge of disaster. After all, 1900 Hungary was beaming with filled cafés, casinos, lively restaurants, flourishing newspapers, journals, and magazines, mixed baths, and sport clubs. There were many places where the Jewish and Christian middle class intermingled. Intermarriage between the two groups increased after 1894/95 when parliament introduced the civic-marriage bill, allowing young couples to marry without the need of Church approval (i.e., conversion) and this trend increased until the 1930s. The single and most important early sign of problems to come was the rise of anti-Semitism from the mid-1870s. In newspapers, unflattering cartoons began to appear with growing frequency depicting the evil Jewish doctor, or the corrupt Jewish banker. And there was the famous Tisza-Eszlár Affair. On April 1, 1882, following the disappearance of a young Christian girl in the town of Tisza-Eszlár, accusations were made that she was killed as part of a ritual murder by Jews before Passover. The trial and the hysteria produced by the press led to numerous anti-Semitic demonstrations, as well as uprisings in Bratislava, Budapest, and other parts of Hungary after the accused were acquitted fifteen months later.[39] In 1883 Győző Istóczy founded an anti-Semitic party called *Országos Antiszemita Párt* (National Antisemitic Party), which had representatives in parliament from 1884 to 1892.[40] Some of these tensions were driven by traditional Christian anti-Semitism, but they were also a product of modern developments. Modernization, followed by industrialization in Hungary, advanced Jewish embourgeoisement, and this led to rising antagonism. In 1900, 25 percent of Budapest was estimated to be Jewish, which led the notorious anti-Semitic Mayor of Vienna, Karl Lueger, to disdainfully refer to the capital as Judapest. But before the actual fall of the Austro-Hungarian Monarchy, few were writing about the failure of the bourgeoisie.

Defeat in World War I, and the partition of the Hungarian Kingdom, deflated the optimism of 1900. Confronted by the legitimacy crisis of 1918, the Jewish and Christian middle classes were unable to forge a collective political voice. The short rule of the liberal republic of 1918 was replaced by the Communist Dictatorship of Béla Kun in 1919, followed by the counter-revolutionary White Terror of Admiral Miklós Horthy. During these violent revolutionary years, the schism between the Christian and Jewish middle class had become obvious. The Communist Revolution had a large Jewish bourgeois leadership, and the Counter-Revolution unleashed a round of anti-Semitic pogroms in which no one is quite sure how many were actually killed. It is telling that one of the defining features of the Counter-Revolutionary Regime was the enactment of the *Numerus Clausus* in 1920, prohibiting the percentage of Jews who could enter university to the relative size of the Jewish population in Hungary. These were the first twentieth-century Jewish Laws in Europe, and foreshadowed the politics of the Nazis after their seizure of power in 1933. First and foremost, Horthy passed the *Numerus Clausus* to satisfy the Christian middle class. It was designed to make it easier for Christian middle-class youths to enter careers in engineering, law, and medicine. The intra-class conflict between the Christian and Jewish middle classes became openly racist and blood-based. In the 1920s, official anti-Semitism was reeled back under the Bethlen ministry, but the middle class was forever torn into antagonistic camps, where the Christian middle class had the upper hand because of its monopoly of positions within the state. Or as A. C. Janos summarized: "Thus while the proportion of Jews in the first postwar decades did not much change in business and in the professions, it declined substantially in the ministries (from 4.9 percent to 1.5 percent), in the county bureaucracies (from 4.5 percent to 0.7 percent), and in the judiciary (from 5.0 to 1.7 percent). And if there were a dozen or so high officials in the government of Stephan Tisza, there was only one Jewish minister (Baron Korányi) in all of Bethlen's cabinets, and not more than a handful of Jewish deputies in his Unitary Party."[41]

Did the Hungarian bourgeoisie fail? Yes, if one were to look at their inability in comparison to the West to become the leading element of nation-building. But it did not fail because it was feudalized. The struggle between the Christian middle class and Jewish middle class was not about feudalism versus capitalism, stagnation versus progress, towns versus country, or agriculture versus industry. The struggle between these two forces relates to the distinct positions they held within modern Hungarian society. It was a conflict that was based very much in modern social structural evolution, and that is why the growing anti-Semitism of the second half of the nineteenth century is new and not simply a replay of medieval pogroms. In relation to this, it is important to remember that the notion of a failed bourgeoisie is a post–World War I construct. It became a tool for historians to explain why and how the Austro-Hungarian Monarchy collapsed, why Hungary was partitioned, why there was a weak liberal capitalist democratic tradition, why fascism was popular in the interwar period, and why Communism was established after World War II. The notion of the failed bourgeoisie, therefore, became the magic wand which historians waved in the air to explain the ills of Hungary's miserable experience in the twentieth century. When used in these terms, the bourgeoisie did not fail. There are plenty of examples in World History, in which the bourgeoisie did not support liberal democratic principles. The Hungarian example is one of these. The historic bourgeoisie, as it successfully entered the state in the late nineteenth century, did not feel a need to support liberalism. A gap emerged between state and society, as the modern bureaucracy looked down at the proletariat and peasantry. Instead of being agents that introduced the virtues of liberty, tolerance, meritocracy, democracy, and an open society, they became instead sympathetic to right wing politics and fascism in the 1930s. But this was all very modern and not feudal. The Jewish middle class had, of course, many more members sympathetic to liberal causes and socialism. They might have balanced out the right wing inclination of the Christian middle class. But they were excluded from state administration. If fault lies with Hungarian middle-class development, it was, therefore, a social structural one. Namely, as it evolved it was divided along ethnic lines. If the two sides could somehow have forged a common identity things might have turned out different. But they did not.

Appendix

Index of Town Names in Hungarian and German

Index of Royal Free Town Names in Hungarian

Bártfa: in Slovakia (Bardejov in Slovakian and Bartfeld in German).

Bazin: in Slovakia (Pezinok in Slovakian and Bösing in German).

Bakabánya: in Slovakia (Pukanec in Slovakian and Pukkanz in German).

Bélabánya: in Slovakia (Banská Belá in Slovakian and Dilln in German).

Beszterce: in Romania (Bistriţa in Romanian and Bistritz in German).

Besztercebánya: in Slovakia (Banská Bystrica in Slovakian and Neusohl in German).

Brassó: in Romania (Braşov in Romanian and Kronstadt in German).

Breznóbánya: in Slovakia (Brezno in Slovakian and Bries in German).

Eperjes: in Slovakia (Prešov in Slovakian and Preschau in German).

Esztergom: in Hungary (Gran in German).

Győr: in Hungary (Raab in German).

Gyulafehérvár: in Romania (Alba Iulia in Romanian and Karlsburg in German).

Felsőbánya: in Romania (Baia Sprie in Romanian and Mittelstadt in German).

Kassa: in Slovakia (Košice in Slovakian and Kaschau in German).

Késmárk: in Slovakia (Kežmarok in Slovakian and Käsmarkt in German).

Kismarton: in Austria (Eisenstadt in German).

Kis-Szeben: in Slovakia (Sabinov in Slovakian and Zeben in German).

Kolozsvár: in Romania (Cluj-Napoca in Romanian and Klausenburg in German).

Korpona: in Slovakia (Krupina in Slovakian and Karpfen in German).

Körmöczbánya: in Slovakia (Kremnica in Slovakian and Kremnitz in German).

Kőszeg: in Hungary (Günst in German).

Libetbánya: in Slovakia (L'ubietová in Slovakian and Libethen in German).

Lőcse: in Slovakia (Levoča in Slovakian and Leutschau in German).

Marosvásárhely: in Romania (Tîrgu Mureş in Romanian and Neumarkt in German).

Medgyes: in Romania (Mediaş in Romanian and Mediasch in German).

Modor: in Slovakia (Modra in Slovakian and Modern in German).

Nagybánya: in Romania (Baia Mare in Romanian and Neustadt in German).

Nagyszeben: in Romania (Sibiu in Romanian and Hermannstadt in German).

Nagyszombat: in Slovakia (Trnava in Slovakian and Tyrnau in German).

Pécs: in Hungary (Fünfkirchen in German).

Pozsony: in Slovakia (Bratislava in Slovakian and Pressburg in German).

Segesvár: in Romania (Sighişoara in Romanian and Schässburg in German).

Selmecbánya: in Slovakia (Banská Štiavnica in Slovakian and Schemnitz in German).

Sopron: in Hungary (Ödenburg in German).

Szakolcza: in Slovakia (Skalica in Slovakian and Skalitz in German).

Szatmár-Németi: in Romania (Satu Mare in Romanian and Sathmar in German).

Székesfehérvár: in Hungary (Stuhlweissenburg in German).

Szentgyörgy: in Slovakia (Svätÿ Jur in Slovakian and Sankt-Georgen in German).

Trencsén: in Slovakia (Trenčin in Slovakian and Trenschin in German).

Újbánya: in Slovakia (Nová Baňa in Slovakian and Königsberg in German).

Zólyom: in Slovakia (Zvolen in Slovakian and Altsohl in German).

Index of Royal Free Town Names in German

Altsohl: in Slovakia (Zólyom in Hungarian and Zvolen in Slovakian).

Bartfeld: in Slovakia (Bártfa in Hungarian and Bardejov in Slovakian).

Bistritz: in Romania (Beszterce in Hungarian and Bistriţa in Romanian).

Bösing: in Slovakia (Bazin in Hungarian and Pezinok in Slovakian).

Bries: in Slovakia (Breznóbánya in Hungarian and Brezno in Slovakian).

Dilln: in Slovakia (Bélabánya in Hungarian and Banská Belá in Slovakian).

Eisenstadt: in Austria (Kismarton in Hungarian).

Fünfkirchen: in Hungary (Pécs in Hungarian).

Gran: in Hungary (Esztergom in Hungarian).

Günst: in Hungarian (Kőszeg in Hungarian).

Hermannstadt: in Romania (Nagyszeben in Hungarian and Sibiu in Romanian).

Karpfen: in Slovakia (Korpona in Hungarian and Krupina in Slovakian).

Karlsburg: in Romania (Gyulafehérvár in Hungarian and Alba Iulia in Romanian).

Kaschau: in Slovakia (Kassa in Hungarian and Košice in Slovakian).

Käsmarkt: in Slovakia (Késmárk in Hungarian and Kežmarok in Slovakian).

Klausenburg: in Romania (Kolozsvár in Hungarian and Cluj-Napoca in Romanian).

Königsberg: in Slovakia (Újbánya in Hungarian and Nová Baňa in Slovakian).

Kremnitz: in Slovakia (Körmöczbánya in Hungarian and Kremnica in Slovakian).

Kronstadt: in Romania (Brassó in Hungarian and Braşov in Romanian).

Leutschau: in Slovakia (Lőcse in Hungarian and Levoča in Slovakian).

Libethen: in Slovakia (Libetbánya in Hungarian and L'ubietová in Slovakian).

Mediasch: in Romania (Medgyes in Hungarian and Mediaş in Romanian).

Mittelstadt: in Romania (Felsőbánya in Hungarian and Baia Sprie in Romanian).

Modern: in Slovakia (Modor in Hungarian and Modra in Slovakian).

Neumarkt: in Romania (Marosvásárhely in Hungarian and Tîrgu Mureş in Romanian).

Neusohl: in Slovakia (Besztercebánya in Hungarian and Banská Bystrica in Slovakian).

Neustadt: in Romania (Nagybánya in Hungarian and Baia Mare in Romanian).

Ödenburg: in Hungary (Sopron in Hungarian).

Preschau: in Slovakia (Eperjes in Hungarian and Prešov in Slovakian).

Pressburg: in Slovakia (Pozsony in Hungarian Bratislava in Slovakian).

Pukkanz: in Slovakia (Bakabánya in Hungarian and Pukanec in Slovakian).

Sankt-Georgen: in Slovakia (Szentgyörgy in Hungarian and Svätÿ Jur in Slovakian).

Sathmar: in Romania (Szatmár-Németi in Hungarian and Satu Mare in Romanian).

Schässburg: in Romania (Segesvár in Hungarian and Sighişoara in Romanian).

Schemnitz: in Slovakia (Selmecbánya in Hungarian and Banská Štiavnica in Slovakian).

Skalitz: in Slovakia (Szakolcza in Hungarian and Skalica in Slovakian).

Stuhlweissenburg: in Hungary (Székesfehérvár in Hungarian).

Trenschin: in Slovakia (Trencsén in Hungarian and Trenčin in Slovakian).

Tyrnau: in Slovakia (Nagyszombat in Hungarian and Trnava in Slovakian).

Zeben: in Slovakia (Kis-Szeben in Hungarian and Sabinov in Slovakian).

The Demography of Royal Free Towns between 1715/1720 and 1910

In 1715 and 1720, the Habsburg state commissioned two censuses in Hungary. In 1896 the Hungarian Royal Statistics Office published the results of the censuses in a special publication entitled *Magyarország népessége a Pragmatica Sanctio korában* (Hungary's Population during the time of the Pragmatic Sanction). The following list of towns contains information taken from the 1715–1720 censuses, as well as the censuses of 1784/1787, 1868, and 1910. Of course, the most unique and problematic data in the following index are those relating to the censuses of 1715 and 1720. While these early censuses note the number of artisans, merchants, and guilds in most towns, instead of providing an estimate of the total population, the census takers in 1715 and 1720 simply recorded the number of registered households. Further complicating the issue is that according to the Hungarian Royal Statistics Office in 1896, the number of households registered in the royal free towns in 1715 and 1720 was underreported by 20 percent, and in a number of towns the census takers simply got the figures wrong. In addition, there is no clear figure about the size of the Jewish population. The census takers noted the registered burghers of the towns, but not the Jews. Yet we know that some towns did have large Jewish settlements, such as Bratislava and Eisenstadt. Most towns, therefore, were probably larger than the figures given in this index, and where possible I have added the Jewish urban dwellers to the total population. Last but not least, I have tried to establish the ethnic composition of the towns by looking at the etymology of family names. Whenever possible, both raw numbers and percentages are reported. These percentages might add up to more or less than 100 percent because of rounding. Furthermore, because census takers in 1715 and 1720 produced uneven data, sometimes only percentages are given, while other times only the actual breakdown of households is presented.

In 1715–1720, there were 44 royal free towns in the Kingdom of Hungary and Transylvania; 36 were located in Hungary proper and 8 in Transylvania. The total population of Hungary in 1720 was an estimated 1.7 million, with an urban population of approximately 110,000 individuals (not including Győr, Komárom, and Pécs). Transylvania had an estimated total population of 806,221, with an urban population of 61,000. The following list contains 47 towns, because Győr, Komárom, and Pécs have been added. These three towns did not have royal free standing in 1715–1720, but were large enough to be included. In 1910, over 80 towns in Hungary claimed royal free standing, but the towns that were granted royal free standing after 1720, with the exception of Győr, Komárom, and Pécs, are not included here.

The following index also includes the year when towns were granted royal free privileges. There is a great deal of confusion that surrounds these data. The two Encyclopedias of Hungary, for instance, the Pallas and Révai, provide different years for many towns. In the following appendix, the year a town was granted royal free privileges is based on an 1869 publication by the Hungarian Royal Statistical Office.

A great deal of confusion surrounds the names of towns in the former Hungarian Kingdom, because each ethnonational group had their own version of a town's name. I have organized the following list according to the current name of the town to make it more accessible for future researchers.

Alba Iulia

(Romania) [Karlsburg or Weissenburg in German and Gyulafehérvár in Hungarian). Alba Iulia was an ancient Roman settlement, supposedly granted municipal privileges by Marcus Aurelius. After the arrival of the Magyars, it emerged as an important town at the crossroads of the Transylvania salt and gold mining and trade. In the sixteenth and seventeenth centuries Alba Iulia was one of the Magyar political and cultural centers of Transylvania which, between 1542 and 1690, was also the home of the Transylvanian Princes. Many Transylvanian Princes and leaders are buried there, including János Hunyadi, János Zápolya, István Bocskay, and Mihály Apaffy. The town reached its political-cultural zenith during the rule of Gábor Bethlen, when some of the most prominent buildings were built, and a printing house was established. However, it suffered heavily during the Decades of Revolt (1670–1711). In 1720, Alba Iulia had an estimated population of only 3,481, which increased to 4,917 by 1784/87. In 1720, there were approximately 211 households, out of which 115 had Magyar, 76 Romanian, and 20 German family names. In 1784/1787, 48 priests/ministers (it was one of the center of Magyar Calvinism), 26 nobles, and 24 officials lived in the town. In 1784/1787, there were also 172 peasant-households—one of the highest levels of any royal free town—and reflecting the difficulties the town was undergoing at the turn of the eighteenth century. Alba Iulia also had one of the larger Jewish settlements in 1784/1787, with as estimated 81 Jewish males above the age of 14 listed by the census takers.

During the nineteenth century, the town doubled its population, but the ethnic division that existed in 1784/1787 remained unchanged. In 1910, out of 11,616 urban dwellers, 5,226 claimed Magyar as their mother tongue, 5,170 Romanian, 792 German, and there were an estimated 287 whose mother tongue was Roma. In the nineteenth century, the town was an important administrative center, as it was the seat of the Transylvanian Catholic Bishopric, had a Royal Court of Appeals, a Royal Mining Court, and was an important center for the Hungarian Railroad.

Baia Mare

(Romania) [Neustadt in German and Nagybánya in Hungarian] was an important medieval (predominately German) mining town that was granted royal free privileges in 1347. By the turn of the eighteenth century, Baia Mare was strongly on the decline. In 1715, the census taker noted that the years of the expulsion of the Ottomans and the Rákóczi Revolt were particularly harmful to urban development, as the town came under siege several times from the troops of his Holy Roman Emperor, the Ottomans, and Rákóczi. His Holy Roman Emperor alone laid siege to the town four separate times. The fire of 1705 also caused a great deal of damage, and many buildings were not rebuilt. In 1720 the census taker wrote that Baia Mare resembled more a village than a town.

The period between 1715 and 1720 represented sharp decline. While in 1715, 343 households were registered, by 1720 this number dropped to only 296. The artisans' noteworthy grievance was that the Romanian peasants surrounding the town were self-sufficient and had no money to buy manufactured goods. In 1720, the population of the town was approximately 2,423. Wine production appeared to be the only source of income for the town, and many merchants complained about their poverty. It was an overwhelmingly Magyar town, and out of the 296 registered households, 98 percent had Magyar names, 1 percent German, and 10.35 percent Serbian-Croatian.

Baia Mare in 1784/1787 had an estimated population of only 4,078, with 19 priests/ministers, 58 nobles, and 30 officials. The nineteenth century saw urban growth and, by 1868, the population of Baia Mare increased to approximately 7,500, and to 12,877 by 1910, out of which 9,992 claimed Magyar as their mother tongue, 2,677 Romanian, and 175 German.

Baia Sprie

(Romania) [Mittelstadt in German and Felsőbánya in Hungarian] was a poor, predominantly Magyar mining town. In 1715, there were 217 registered households, out of which 78 were listed as burgher households and 139 as cottagers. Baia Sprie showed some early-eighteenth-century dynamism. Between 1715 and 1723, the urban population grew significantly. While in 1715, there were 217 registered households, this figure increased to 334 households in 1723, accounting for an estimated population of 1,803. In this overwhelmingly Magyar town, out of the 217 households in 1715, 202 had Magyar and 15 had Romanian names. Between 1723 and 1784/1787, the population of the town more than doubled to an estimated 3,873. In 1784/1787, there were 5 priests/ministers, 26 nobles, and 30 officials registered as living in the town.

Baia Sprie stumbled in the nineteenth century, and in 1868 had a population of only 6,100, which declined to 4,422 in 1910. It remained strongly Magyar, and in 1910, 4,149 claimed Magyar as their mother tongue and only 230 Romanian.

Banská Belá

(Slovakia), [Dilln in German and Bélabánya in Hungarian] was one of the very small royal free towns of the Hungarian Uplands. It was granted royal free privileges in 1468, and in 1720 had an estimated population of only 614. According to the etymology of family names, 44 percent had German names, 46 percent Slovak, 7 percent Magyar, and 2 percent Italian. The slight Slovak majority was formed between the years 1715 and 1720. In 1715, 40 families had German names, but this declined to 36 by 1720, while concurrently the number of those with Slovak names rose slightly from 36 to 37.

Historically, the town prospered through mining and manufacturing, but from the late seventeenth century a sharp depression gripped these sectors and the town never recovered. The census takers in 1720 also noted that the municipal government owned the mills, breweries, and taverns. In 1784/1787, Banská Belá had an estimated population of 1,592, with only one registered priest/minister, 8 nobles, and 10 officials. But the town saw virtually no growth in the nineteenth century and, in 1868, the population was estimated at 1,600. After Banská Belá merged with Banská Štiavnica in the 1870s, the combined population of the towns was 15,185 in 1910, out of which 8,341 claimed Slovak as their mother tongue, 6,340 Magyar, and 453 German.

Banská Bystrica

(Slovakia) [Neusohl in German and Besztercebánya in Hungarian] was granted royal free privileges in 1225, making it one of the oldest royal free towns in the Hungarian Kingdom. The town was famous in the sixteenth century because of the Thurzó-Fugger family mining enterprise, when it emerged as one of the world's leading centers of silver production. During the early eighteenth century, Banská Bystrica experienced a unique, albeit contradictory development. In 1715, only 231 heads of households were employed in manufacturing and trade, but this declined to 156 households in 1720. Between 1715 and 1720, 78 fewer families were paying taxes because they had either died out or moved out. Furthermore, between 1715 and 1720 the number of individual industrialists declined from 226 to 148. Concurrently, however, annual income from the manufacturing and commercial sectors more than doubled.

An area of the urban economy that experienced significant decline was beer production. The privilege to brew and distribute beer belonged to the ring burghers of the town. In 1720, there were 25 such elite burghers, but only 14 were practicing the trade. Because of the great debt of the town, an additional 27 individuals were granted the right to open a tavern, for which they paid a special tax to the municipal government. The town's debt was significant, totaling approximately 74,206 Denar in 1720. In 1715 and 1720, 14 and 16 noble families, respectively, were living in the town. The goldsmiths were the worst affected by the stagnation, while interestingly the butchers' guild prospered. Other profitable and influential branches of the economy included the smiths, hat-makers, boot-makers, button-makers, gingerbread-makers, and tanners. The merchants, whose traditional markets were in northern towns like Leipzig, or the Silesians towns, as well as Bratislava and Spiss County, while making profit, complained in 1720 about the growing competition represented by merchants from Kecskemét.

In 1720, Banská Bystrica remained one of the larger Hungarian royal free towns, with a population of 2,651. According to family names, the town's population can be divided into 10 percent Magyar, 40 percent German, and 50 percent Slovak. The Slovaks represented 50 percent in spite of the fact that the number of families with Slovak names declined from 211 in 1715 to 153 in 1720, and the number of those with German names increased from 97 to 123 during the same period. In 1784/1787, the town had an estimated population of 5,053, with 36 priests ministers, 92 nobles, and 40 officials. Among the working male population, 570 were listed as cottagers and 423 as burghers.

Banská Bystrica did not prosper in the modern period, and even declined during the second half of the nineteenth century, from 12,400 in 1868 to 10,776 in 1910. Magyar speakers represented a slight majority in 1910, with 5,261 claiming Magyar as their mother language, 4,388 Slovak, and 879 German.

Banská Štiavnica

(Slovakia) [Schemnitz in German and Selmecbánya in Hungarian] was granted royal free privileges in 1244. One of the most important mining towns in sixteenth-century Hungary, Banská Štiavnica experienced sharp decline between 1680 and 1710, as the Thököly and Rákóczi Revolts greatly disrupted its social and economic development. From the censuses of 1715 and 1720, two important trends are observable.

First, the urban economy, dominated by mining, was unable to make progress and declined during the five-year period. Second, German burghers left the town and Slovak cottagers moved in. In 1715, there were 814 registered households, out of which 789 were burgher households and 25 cottagers. From the 814 households, 424 had Slovak names, 360 German names, 22 Magyar, and 8 Italian. By the 1720s, the number of households had increased to 938, but in a stunning development households with German names declined from 360 in 1715 to only 87. Concurrently, the number of households with Slovak names increased from 424 to 819.

In 1720 Banská Štiavnica was one of the largest towns of the Hungarian Uplands with an estimated population of 6,953. In the eighteenth century it grew impressively, and between 1720 and 1784/1787 the population almost tripled to 18,839, with 26 priests/ministers, 67 nobles, and 77 officials. However, in contrast to the medieval and early modern past, when the town grew on the strength of mining and manufacturing, the eighteenth-century demographic growth was based on the cottage industry.

Banská Štiavnica did not make a successful transition into modernity, and declined during the nineteenth century. There was an attempt to transform the town into a center of higher education, and in 1848 the town was a place of student radicalism. But after World War I, the Universities established in the nineteenth century were transferred to Hungary. In 1868 it had an estimated population of only 14,800, and in 1910, after it had joined with its neighbor town of Banská Belá (also a royal free town), it had an estimated population of 15,185. The Slovaks continued to represent the majority of the urban dwellers, and in 1910, 8,341 claimed Slovak as their mother tongue, with 6,340 Magyar, and 453 German.

Bardejov

(Slovakia) [Bartfeld in German and Bártfa in Hungarian] was granted royal free privileges in 1324. The town prospered as a transshipment point of the Levantine trade between the Orient, Poland, and the Baltic. In the sixteenth and the first half of the seventeenth century, it experienced its zenith. Part of this impressive growth came from textile production, and it is claimed that in the 1660s, every household possessed a spinning wheel. The 1715 census also mentions 28 two-storey buildings in the center of town, the majority built in the first half of the seventeenth century. In 1680, however, Bardejov burnt to the ground while the troops of Thököly tried to seize the town. There was some urban dynamism between 1696 and 1720, but it was limited to construction (the rebuilding of destroyed houses). In 1696, 178 buildings were listed (106 within the town walls and 72 outside of the walls). This figure increased to 186 in 1715 and 207 in 1720. After the defeat of the Magyar rebels and the start of Habsburg reconstruction, Bardejov suffered stagnation, and its population barely grew between 1696 and 1720.

Wars were not the only cause of decline in textile production, as internal reasons also led to economic stagnation. In the second half of the seventeenth century, a struggle ensued within the textile manufacturing sector. When the municipal government clamped down and forbade the sale and production of textiles on a wholesale basis, the future of textile production suffered irreversibly. By 1696, only 6 weavers were listed on the census and in 1715, only 10. Added to the declining production was the import of textiles from Poland, which further reduced the profits of Bardejov's weavers. Besides the decline in textile manufacturing, the second important branch of the urban economy that experienced problems was beer production. In 1568, the town was given privileges positing that only burghers of the town could brew beer in a two-mile radius, and in 1696, 55 breweries existed in the town. The reasons behind the decline of the urban breweries are not entirely clear, but there was wide complaint about the sharp increases in production costs. By 1715, the census listed only 32 breweries, and a number of abandoned old breweries burnt out. Beer production then became concentrated in a handful of families.

In 1696, 108 masters of craft employed in 31 professions and 12 merchants are listed. The merchants were clearly the wealthiest stratum, with 12 merchants accounting for an income approximately three times the amount of all the artisans combined. However, the merchants and artisans experienced a sharp decline between 1715 and 1720. When the 1720 census was taken, the individual manufacturing branches were not even listed separately, and all that was noted in the records is that the manufacturers lived in a great deal of poverty. In 1696 and 1715, 190 and 219 burghers, respectively, paid taxes.

The population of the town in 1720 was approximately 1,578. It was predominantly a German-Lutheran town, and it is estimated that in 1720, 65 percent of the population was German, 23 percent Slovak, 10 percent Magyar, and a small 2 percent, Italian. Like Pukanec and other royal free towns of the Uplands, agriculture was not profitable because of the poor soil and weather (hail-storms are listed as causing great damage to the crops). Bardejov had an estimated population of

3,671 in 1784/1787, with 23 priests/ministers, 55 nobles, and 21 officials. Among the male population above the age of fourteen, 37 were "non-Christians," who were most probably Jews. In 1868, Bardejov had a population of 4,700 and grew to 6,578 in 1910. By 1910, the Slovaks had become the ethnic majority, with 2,571 claiming Slovak as their mother tongue, compared to 2,179 listing Magyar, and 1,617 German.

Bistriţa

(Romania) [Bistritz in German and Beszterce in Hungarian] was one of the old large German Saxon-dominated towns of Transylvania. In 1713, out of the 735 registered households, 410 had German names, 284 Magyar, 37 Romanian, 2 Slovakian/Ruthinian, and 2 Serbian/Croatian.

Bistriţa was one of the royal free towns that declined during Habsburg consolidation. In 1720, its population is estimated at 5,307, while in 1784/1787 it declined to an estimated 4,637, with 20 priests/ministers, 16 nobles, and 20 officials. During the nineteenth century, the town almost tripled its population to 13,236 by 1910. In 1910, the Germans represented the majority, with 5,835 claiming German as their mother tongue, 4,470 Romanian, and 2,824 Magyar.

Braşov

(Romania) [Kronstadt in German and Brassó in Hungarian]. Braşov was one of the most important and largest towns of Transylvania. It rose in the fourteenth century as a critical transshipment point between the Levant and Central Europe. Between the thirteenth and fourteenth centuries it was granted many staple rights and municipal and trading privileges. It also played a critical role in the spread of Protestantism in the sixteenth and seventeenth centuries. In the fifteenth century it has been estimated that its population was over 10,000. In 1713, Braşov was a multiethnic city with a slight German-speaking majority. Out of the 2,333 households in 1713, 955 had German names, 738 Romanian, 631 Magyar, and 9 Serbian-Croatian. The town situated at the border of Transylvania and the Ottoman Empire, thrived historically as a frontier town, but experienced minimal growth during the eighteenth century. While Braşov in 1720 was the largest town of Transylvania and Hungary proper, with an estimated population of 16,816, in 1784/1787 its population was only 17,792 (with 53 priests/ministers, 65 nobles, and 39 officials). In 1910

Braşov had an estimated population of 41,056, with 17,831 claiming Magyar as their mother tongue, 11,786 Romanian, 10,841 German, and the rest claiming Czech, Slovak, and Roma.

Bratislava

(Slovakia) [Pressburg in German and Pozsony in Hungarian] was granted royal free privileges in 1291. These were reaffirmed again in 1436. After the Ottoman occupation, Bratislava was made the capital of the Hungarian Kingdom, and remained the political capital until the late nineteenth century. The 1720 census takers were strongly reprimanded by officials in Vienna for their report on Bratislava. Every town tried to portray itself as poor when the census takers arrived because of the fear that higher taxes would be levied if prosperity was shown. However, the length to which the census takers were trying to describe the poverty of Bratislava went beyond what the most tolerant of officials at Court were willing to accept. What most perturbed officials in Vienna was the census takers' report that tavern keepers could not make a profit and no mention was made of the income produced by the restaurants. But in Vienna—only about 100 kilometers away—it was well known that Bratislava had many breweries and restaurants that were often full, because the town was frequently visited by free-spending Magyar nobles and aristocrats.

In 1720, there were 814 registered households, with an estimated population of 7,943 (including 770 unregistered Jews). Out of the 814 households, 158 were nobles, making Bratislava one of the most noble-dominated towns in the kingdom. It was also strongly German, and from the 814 registered households, 685 had German names (84 percent), 80 had Magyar names (10 percent), 44 Slovak (5 percent), and 5 had French names (0.61 percent). Bratislava was one of the most dynamic towns of eighteenth-century Central Europe, and its population increased to 28,707 by 1784/1787. The rule of Joseph II and Leopold II was arguably one of the most prosperous times in its history. In 1784/1787 there were 528 nobles, 236 priests/ministers, and 117 heads of households registered as officials. After Komárom's 797, Bratislava had the largest urbanized noble layer of any town in Hungary, followed closely by Cluj-Napoca with 511.

In 1868, Bratislava had a population of approximately 43,600, and in 1910 a population of 78,223, out of which 32,790 claimed German as their mother tongue, 31,705 Magyar, 11,673 Slovak, 1,242 Czech, 351 Croatian, and 115 Polish.

Brezno

(Slovakia) [Bries in German and Breznóbánya in Hungarian] was one
of the small royal free mining towns of Hungary, which was granted
its privileges in 1650. It was by all accounts one of the poorest royal
free towns of the kingdom. The houses in 1720 were mostly made of
wood and, with the exception of the public buildings, none were two-
storey high. It was also the most Slovakian of all the towns. In 1720,
the urban population was approximately 1,154. According to the etymology of the family names, 75 percent were Slovak, 17 percent
German, 4 percent Serbian-Croatian, and 4 percent Magyar. The
municipal government's debt was estimated at 70,000 Denars. In
1720, there were 47 craftsmen in the town, but only 38 practiced their
trade. In 1784/1787, Brezno had an estimated population of 2,675,
with 12 priests/ministers, 79 nobles, and 8 officials living in the town.
Brezno belongs to that group of Upland mining towns that never
became a big city. In 1910, it had a population of approximately
4,179, out of which 3,081 claimed Slovak as their mother tongue and
1,010, Magyar.

Buda

(Hungary) was granted royal free privileges in 1244. The town became
the commercial and political center of Hungary by the fifteenth century,
and experienced the early renaissance under the rule of the famous
medieval Hungarian King Matthias Corvinus, when many Italians
lived in the city. Buda fell under Ottoman administration between
1540 and 1686. This 150-year period represented hardship, devastation, as well as some prosperity and growth. The many sieges, of
course, had a devastating effect. But there was urban development
under Ottoman administration. Buda became a leading transshipment
point between the Ottoman Empire and the Holy Roman Empire. In
the mid-seventeenth century, there were three Synagogues within the
town walls, the most it would have in its entire history. When the
Christian forces retook Buda in 1686, however, there was a mass execution of all those who lived there and were not Christians.

During the 1715 and 1720 censuses, Buda still bore the scars of the
reoccupation of Hungary. The vast majority of buildings constructed
during the Ottoman period, the Mosques, Synagogues, as well as
everyday homes, were destroyed. In 1720, the urban population was
estimated at 12,324 (including 156 unregistered Jews). According to
the etymology of family names, Germans represented the majority of

town dwellers at 57 percent, followed by Serbian-Croatians at 38 percent, and Italians and Slovaks at less than 1 percent. Interestingly, in 1720 only 5 percent of registered burghers had Magyar names. The unregistered poor lived in the surrounding hills, which were covered with shanties.

In 1715–1720, Buda was divided into 6 quarters. Two of these were named after the ethnic groups that lived in them: *Horvátváros* (meaning Croatian-town) and *Ráczváros* (meaning Serbian town). Out of the 706 registered households listed on the 1715 census relating to the Serbian quarters, 668 had Serbian or Croatians names, while in the Croatian quarter, 50 percent had Croatian names and the other 50 percent, German. The south Slav quarters were the poorest, and the houses in the Croatian quarter stood on 1/16, 1/32, or even as small as 1/64 plots of land. Affluent and well to do Germans lived in what today is called the old district, and in the quarter called Watertown at the foot of the Buda Castle. A sign of hard times was that in 1720 few of the houses were listed as first or second-class quality. Twenty-two houses were labeled first-class, meaning they had multiple rooms, faced the street, and most importantly had both a stall and a special building for the wagon. Sixty houses were labeled "second class" homes, meaning that each house had up to 3–4 rooms but no stalls. The remaining 600 (approximately), however, were collectively classified as third-class, meaning that they were very small, and according to the census takers "not even worth calling houses."

Viniculture was critical for the urban economy, but there was also a budding miller industry and, in 1720, there were 20 millers working in the town. The merchants complained to the census takers that since the capture of Belgrade and Timişoara (Transylvania-Romania today) from the Ottomans, their trade routes had been disrupted because merchants from the Ottoman Empire sold their goods in the new border towns and no longer traveled to Buda. In spite of this, both the number of merchants and manufacturers tripled between 1715 and 1720, and their incomes improved sixfold. The largest guilds were the butcher, tailor, cooper, locksmith, baker, skinner, and tavern-keeper. The tailor's guild had the largest membership with 38 members, followed by the butcher's guild with 28 members, but the butchers accounted for three times more income.

In 1784/1787, Buda had an estimated population of 23,919, with 151 priests/ministers, 489 nobles, and 225 officials. It made a successful transition into modernity and had an estimated population of 54,800 in 1868. In 1873, Buda united with Óbuda and Pest to form Budapest.

Cluj-Napoca

(Romania) [Klausenburg in German and Kolozsvár in Hungarian] was one of the important royal free towns of Transylvania. The town supposedly was granted municipal privileges by the Roman Emperor Hadrian, and became the capital of the province *Dacia Porolissensis*. The birthplace of the famous Hungarian King, Matthias Corvinus, it was a leading political, cultural, and economic center from the late fourteenth century. When Hungary was partitioned following the Ottoman invasion, Cluj emerged as the capital of Magyar culture in Transylvania. In 1720, there were approximately 1,095 households, with an estimated population of 10,472, which increased to 13,928 by 1784/1787. In 1784/1787, 146 priests/ministers (many Calvinist ministers), 511 nobles, and 17 officials lived in the town. After Komárom's 797, and Bratislava's 528, Cluj had the largest number of nobles of any town. Ethnically, it was divided between Magyars and Germans during the time of Matthias Corvinus but, in the sixteenth century, the Magyars emerged as the majority. In the nineteenth century, some Romanians immigrated into the town, but Cluj remained the center of Magyar culture in Transylvania and, in 1910, out of the 60,808 urban-dwellers, 50,704 claimed Magyar as their mother tongue, 7,562 Romanian, 1,676 German, 371 Roma, 124 Czech, and 107 Slovak.

Debrecen

(Hungary) was one of the greatest agricultural towns of the Carpathian Plains, and granted royal free privileges in 1715. During the Ottoman period, Debrecen converted to Calvinism, and paid taxes to the Sultan but remained a free town. Debrecen suffered greatly during the Rákóczi Revolt, and in 1720 the census takers noted that the houses in the town had been built in better times, and the town resembled more a village than a royal free town. It was also written that many vagabonds lived at the end of the main street. They were so poor that they lived in the holes they dug in the ground. Their exact numbers are difficult to establish because many were agricultural migrant workers.

In 1715, there were 922 households in Debrecen, and this grew to 1,070 by 1720. The largest increase came from burgher households, which grew from 658 to 905. The rise in burgher households probably came from the elevation and granting full burgher rights to cottager families. There was a decline in the number of noble households from 72 in 1715 to 42 in 1720. Officially, the population of Debrecen in 1720 was approximately 8,208. However, because of the large number of vagabonds, the urban population was probably closer to 10,000.

Debrecen was one of the most important centers of horticulture as well as processed foods in the Hungarian Kingdom. Yet besides cattle, pigs, and goats, Debrecen also had one of the largest concentrations of artisans and merchants in the kingdom. The number of artisans and merchants increased sharply between 1715 and 1720, from 445 to 687. Out of this 687, 140 were tailors, 53 shoemakers, 41 millers, and 39 furriers. Despite being one of the most successful urban centers, the merchants complained under oath, however, that the predominance of Greeks, Serbians, Armenians, Jews, and Turks in commerce was detrimental to their profits.

Between 1720 and 1784/1787, Debrecen tripled its population to an estimated 30,064, with 31 priests/ministers, 207 nobles, and 32 officials. There were also 20 peasants listed as living in the town. The town's demographic growth continued throughout the nineteenth century, and in 1868 it had a population of approximately 46,800, and in 1910 a population of 92,792. Debrecen was a Magyar town throughout its history and out of the 92,729 urban dwellers in 1910 a significant 91,305 claimed Magyar as their mother tongue, followed by 695 Germans, and 286 Romanians.

Eisenstadt

(Austria) [Kismarton in Hungarian] was granted royal free privileges in 1648, and was one of the small wine growing towns of western Hungary. In 1720, it had an estimated population of 1,520 (including 600 unregistered Jews). Eisenstadt was supposedly the most Jewish town of the kingdom in the eighteenth century. Unfortunately, the census only recorded the professions of the Christian burghers. Viniculture played the dominant part in the urban economy and, in 1720, while approximately 596 hectares were cultivated for grains, 675 hectares were for grapes.

Eisenstadt was an overwhelmingly German town, and out of the 106 registered households, 104 had German names, and, in 1720, only two had Magyar names. Eisenstadt's population more than doubled between 1720 and 1784/1787 to an estimated 2,271. In 1784/1787, there were 18 priests/ministers, 32 nobles, and 19 officials living in the town. It remained a small town throughout the nineteenth century, and in 1868 its population was only 3,700, and in 1910 it was 3,073. Eisenstadt remained German-dominated, and in 1910, 2,074 claimed German as their mother tongue, compared to 834 Magyars, and 101 Croatians.

Esztergom

(Hungary) [Gran in German] played a prominent role as a center of the Roman Catholic Church in Hungary. It was granted royal free privileges late (1708), because it was an ecclesiastic city. During the Ottoman occupation it came under Ottoman rule, and was retaken by the Christian forces in 1683. However, shortly afterwards, during the Rákóczi Revolt it suffered significantly.

In 1715, Esztergom had 304 registered households. By 1720, the number of households increased to 332, but the increase came from the rise of cottager households from 50 to 75, and not from an increase in burgher households. Esztergom's economy declined slightly between 1715 and 1720, as the number of households involved in manufacturing and commerce declined between 1715 and 1720 from 72 to 63. In 1720, the estimated population of Esztergom was 2,399. Magyars represented the largest ethnic group, and out of 332 total households, 286 had Magyar-sounding family names, 32 German, 10 Slovak, 3 Serbian-Croatian, and one family had a French name. Between 1720 and 1784/1787, the town more than doubled in size to 5,492, with 37 priests/ministers, 46 nobles, and 14 officials living in the town. By 1868, Esztergom's population increased to approximately 8,700, and in 1910 to 17,881. Magyars remained the overwhelming majority, with 16,675 claiming Magyar as their mother tongue, 719 German, and 309 Slovak.

Győr

(Hungary) [Raab in German, and during Ottoman rule it was called Janik] was granted royal free privileges in 1743. During the Ottoman occupation of Hungary, Győr was one of the military border castle-towns separating the Ottoman and Habsburg Empires. After the expulsion of the Ottomans, the town continued to play a militarily strategic role, as the Habsburgs stationed a large army in the city. The existence of this large stationary army had a detrimental effect on urban development, and was a source of great frustration for the burghers and municipal government. At the time of the 1720 census, anger at the soldiers was particularly acute because in that year seventy new soldier families moved into the town and occupied the houses of the poor burghers. Besides the problems of disorderly conduct and confiscation of houses without reparations, the burghers complained that soldiers were participating in the urban economy without heeding the authority of the guilds or the municipal government. The soldier families countered these complaints by claiming that they were forced to become merchants because their military pay was not enough to support a family. According to the 1720 census takers, the soldiers enjoyed a monopoly over the sale of wine in the town. The town showed robust growth between 1715 and 1720. In 1715, there were little more than 300 households participating in the urban economy, but by 1720 there were over 380.

Despite the fact that Győr did not receive royal free standing until 1743, in 1720 it was already a large town with a population of approximately 7,308. According to the etymology of family names, in 1720 out of the 808 registered households, 542 (67 percent) had Magyar, 221 (27 percent) German, and 45 (5 percent) Serbian-Croatian family names. The town experienced steady demographic growth in the eighteenth century and in 1784/87 it had an estimated population of 13,421. There were 109 priests/ministers, 517 nobles, and 51 officials living in the town. Next to Bratislava, Cluj-Napoca, and Komárom, Győr had one of the largest urbanized noble populations in the kingdom. It was also one of the most dynamic urban centers, and its population grew from 19,200 in 1868 to 44,300 by 1910. Magyars played a prominent role and, in 1910, over 90 percent (or 42,039) claimed Magyar as their mother tongue. Beside the large Magyar population, in 1910, 1,167 claimed German as their mother tongue, compared to 579 Slovaks, 246 Czechs, and 107 Croatians.

Kežmarok

(Slovakia) [Käsmarkt in German and Késmárk in Hungarian] was one of the Zipser Lutheran towns of northeastern Hungary at the foot of the Tatra Mountains. It was granted royal free privileges in 1380, lost them during the fifteenth century, and was newly re-granted them in 1650. Kežmarok with Brezno, Prešov, Košice, and Levoča, suffered extensively during the Thököly and Rákóczi Revolts. Home to the Thököly family, it was one of the focal points of opposition to Habsburg rule in the seventeenth century. During the Rákóczi Revolt, 64 houses were destroyed in the town. Hardship and misfortune characterized the early eighteenth century as a fire in 1717 destroyed

18 houses and 36 were ruined during the fire of 1720. Despite these hardships, Kežmarok evidenced contradictory tendencies between 1715 and 1720. On the one hand, urban decline seems to have increased between 1715 and 1720, as 23 houses stood unoccupied in 1715, and by 1720 this number increased to 36. Furthermore, in 1720 Kežmarok had one of the largest municipal debts of the kingdom, estimated at 90,000 Denars. On the other hand, Kežmarok also experienced demographic growth between 1715 and 1720. In 1715 there were 322 households, out of which 11 were nobles, 310 burghers, and 1 cottager. By 1720, the number of households increased to 378, out of which 18 were nobles, 357 burghers, and 3 cottagers.

In 1720, the population of Kežmarok was approximately 2,976. Out of the 372 registered household family names in 1720, 298 (80 percent) were German, 40 (11 percent) Slovak, and 34 (9 percent) Magyar. By 1784/1787, the population of the town increased to an estimated 4,487, with 8 priests/ministers, 107 nobles, and 25 officials. In the nineteenth century, however, Kežmarok's population declined and in 1868 it had an estimated population of only 3,500. During the last decades of the nineteenth century, the decline was reversed, and by 1910 the town's population was 6,317 strong, out of which 3,242 claimed German as their mother tongue, 1,606 Slovak, and 1,314 Magyar. A large part of this demographic increase came from the immigration into the town of both rural Slovaks as well as many Jews.

Komárom

(Hungary) [Komorn in German and Komárno in Slovak] is a town with a strong Catholic tradition that lies on the Danube between Bratislava and Budapest. It was granted royal free privileges by Maria Theresa in 1745. In the census of 1720, it was written that the town's houses did not resemble those of other royal free towns, but instead a village. It was further noted that 40 houses in the town collectively had the value of one good house in a proper royal free town. Many houses in Komárom, it was written, were constructed from bamboo and were, therefore, unstable. In 1720, out of the 932 households, 197 were nobles and 172 soldiers. Komárom with Győr, Bratislava, and Cluj had a very large noble population. Ethnically it was strongly Magyar, as 777 (83 percent) of the registered households had Magyar names, 93 (10 percent) German, 43 (5 percent) Slovak, 17 (2 percent) Serbian, and there were two households with Italian family names.

Interestingly, while the income from the handicraft sector increased between 1715 and 1720, the income from the commercial sector declined during the same period. The commercial sector stagnated despite the fact that the number of merchants increased from 53 to 58. A large cottage workforce supported manufacturing and, in 1715, 270 cottage households were listed on the census. Fishery played a noteworthy role in the urban economy, and the Fishers' Guild had 38 members.

The population of the town was approximately 8,321 in 1720. In 1784/1787, Komárom had a population of approximately 11,970, out of which 61 were priests/nobles, and 21 were officials. One of Komárom's distinct features was that it had 797 nobles living in the town in 1784/1787, the largest number of urbanized nobles in the kingdom. However, the town remained poor and during the nineteenth century grew slowly, with an estimated population of 12,800 in 1868. The last decades of the nineteenth century saw improvement, and by 1910 the urban population was approximately 22,337, out of which 19,924 claimed Magyar as their mother tongue, 1,248 German, and 768 Slovak.

Košice

(Slovakia) [Kaschau in German and Kassa in Hungarian] was granted royal free privileges in 1244 and again in 1380. Similar to towns like Győr and Prešov, in 1720 Košice had a large occupying army causing a great deal of problems for burghers of the town. The most frequent complaint was the tax burden the troops of his Emperor produced, and the fact that some houses were confiscated without compensation by the soldiers.

Between 1715 and 1720, Košice experienced demographic decline. In 1715, 306 households were registered, out of which 205 had Magyar names, 62 German, and 39 Slovak. In 1720, however, there were only 272 households registered, out of which 194 had Magyar names, 53 German, and 25 Slovak. The population of the town in 1720 was estimated at 4,000. (Officially Košice in 1720 had a population of only 1,961, but that number reflects the fact that the census takers did not include the cottage households.) In the eighteenth century, the town grew slowly and in 1784/1787 the urban population was estimated at 7,590, with 113 priests/ministers, 128 nobles, and 57 officials. From the late nineteenth century, Košice experienced a demographic explosion as it industrialized. Between 1868 and 1910, the population increased from 16,800 to 44,211, thereafter establishing its importance in the twentieth century. It was historically an ethnically mixed town, although Magyar speakers did represent the majority. Out of 44,211 urban-dwellers in 1910, for instance, 33,350 claimed Magyar as their mother tongue, while 6,547 claimed Slovak, 3,189 German, 453 Polish, and 227 Czech. *Kőszey* (Hungary) [Günst in German] was granted royal free privileges in 1649. A large fire in 1720 destroyed 157 houses in the town, including the town hall and the school. However, because the urban economy was based on viniculture, the annual income of the town did not slip extensively. There were 438 registered households in 1720, with an estimated population of 3,164, including 367 burgher and 71 cottager households. It was a predominantly German town, and out of the 438 households, 299 (68 percent) had German names, 98 (22 percent) Magyar, 35 (8 percent) Serbian-Croatian, and the rest, Italian. In 1784/87, Kőszeg had a population of 5,326, with 21 priests/ministers, 128 nobles, and 17 officials. The town grew slowly in the second half of the nineteenth century, from 7,100 in 1868 to 8,423 in 1910. Further, while it was a German-dominated town in 1720, by 1910 Magyar speakers represented the majority, although German speakers continued to play a large role. Out of the 8,432 urban dwellers in 1910, 5,134 claimed Magyar as their mother tongue, 3,066 German, and 137 Croatian.

Kremnica

(Slovakia) [Kremnitz in German and Körmöczbánya in Hungarian] was granted royal free privileges in 1100, making it one of the oldest royal free towns of the Hungarian Kingdom. Historically, it was one of the largest mining towns in the Hungarian Kingdom, but experienced sharp decline from the late seventeenth century. Decay continued during the early part of the eighteenth century, and between 1715 and 1720 the number of registered households fell from 667 to 619. A noteworthy aspect of the decline between 1715 and 1720 was that while the number of burgher households fell from 474 to 364, the number of cottager households rose from 193 to 255. The fading of burgher and strengthening of cottager households also represented a change in the ethnic composition of the town, as Slovak households were on the rise, and those of Germans decreasing. In 1715, 584 households had German names, but by 1720 their numbers decreased to 500. Further, during the same period the number of household with Slovak names increased from 55 to 96. However, Kremnica continued to be predominantly German, with 81 percent of the population in 1720 having German names, 16 percent Slovak, 4 percent Magyar, and the rest Italian.

The population of the town in 1720 was estimated at 5,257, making it one of the largest towns of the Hungarian Uplands in the early eighteenth century. Like Baia Mare and Bistriţa, the population of Kremnica declined in the eighteenth century, and in 1784/1787 its population is estimated at only 5,185, with 47 priests/ministers, 106 nobles, and 18 officials. Kremnica never regained the influence it had in the medieval period, and experienced a sharp decline between 1868 and 1910, when the urban population declined from 8,500 to 4,515. During this late nineteenth-century urban contraction, the town also underwent an important ethnic change. While in 1720, it was a predominantly German town, by 1910 Germans, Magyars, and Slovaks balanced each other out. In 1910, of the 4,515 urban dwellers, 1,514 claimed German as their mother tongue, 1,501 Magyar, and 1,482 Slovak.

Krupina

(Slovakia) [Karpfen in German and Korpona in Hungarian] was granted royal free privileges in 1244. It was one of the five mining and royal free towns of Zvolen (Zólyom) County. Similar to its neighboring mining towns of Banská Bystrica, Brezno, Ľubietová, and Zvolen, Krupina suffered a great deal during the Thököly and Rákóczi Revolts. The five mining towns of Zvolen County followed a similar path. They were important mining centers in the medieval period, having reached their zenith between 1450 and 1650. Their sharp decline set in simultaneous to the outbreak of the Decades of Revolt (1670–1711). By 1720, these five towns also experienced a similar ethnic metamorphosis. Instead of German mining towns, they became centers of Slovak handicraft and the cottage industry, home to craftsmen, weavers, and tailors, but not foreign merchants and early modern mining entrepreneurs. When the census takers arrived in 1715 and 1720, they wrote that the town had seen better days, and besides the homes owned by the nobility, the other houses resembled hovels rather than burgher homes. Adding to the misfortune were the fires of 1708 and 1716, whose destructive effects were unmistakable in 1720.

Despite hardship in the second half of the seventeenth century, Krupina in the first three decades of the eighteenth century underwent an impressive demographic rejuvenation. While in 1715, 164 households were registered, by 1720 their numbers increased to 209. Krupina had a large cottage economy, and out of the 209 households in 1720, 106 were burgher households while 103 were cottage households. The impressive growth in the number of households between 1715 and 1720 was due to the entry of Germans into the town, reversing a pattern of several decades, when German burghers left and were replaced by Slovaks. The number of households with German family names increased from 17 to 55 between 1715 and 1720. Yet, in 1720 Slovaks remained the major ethnic group, as 40 percent of the urban population had Slovak names, 29 percent Magyar, 26 percent German, and 5 percent Croatian.

In 1720 Krupina had an estimated population of 1,503, by 1784/1787 it grew to 2,981, with 12 priests/ministers, 59 nobles, and 8 officials. The population increased only slightly during the nineteenth century and in 1868, Krupina was home to only 3,500 residents. In 1910, the town had an estimated population of 4,016, out of which 3,460 claimed Slovak as their mother tongue, and 484 Magyar.

Levoča

(Slovakia) [Leutschau in German and Lőcse in Hungarian] was the capital of the Zipser Germans who lived at the foot of the Tatra Mountains. The town was granted royal free privileges in 1242, and reached its political, cultural, and economic zenith in the sixteenth and first half of the seventeenth centuries. The town, with Prešov, Košice, Bardejov, and Kežmarok, had suffered tremendous demographic loss during the Rákóczi Revolt. While in the 1670s, over 700 houses were occupied in the town, by 1715 there were only 429, and in 1720, only 410. The greatest damage was caused by the outbreak of cholera in 1710, reducing the size of the population by almost 50 percent. The census takers of 1715 noted that 171 houses stood in rubble. Adding to the misfortune was the large 107,553 Denar municipal debt, making Levoča one of the most indebted towns of the Hungarian Kingdom relative to its size.

Despite many signs of decline, between 1715 and 1720 the number of households increased slightly from 432 to 439. However, even this modest gain had a downside. The number of burgher households actually decreased from 411 to 398 between 1715 and 1720. The growth in the number of households came from the increase of cottager families from 1 to 15, and noble households from 11 to 17. Levoča was becoming poorer and social differentiation was on the rise. In 1720, the town's population was approximately 3,162, which was well below its 1670s estimated level of over 7,000. When the census takers arrived in 1720, the merchants of the town complained a great deal.

There were five first-class merchants, but four of them were widows. Out of the six second-class merchants, one was in poverty, another claimed bankruptcy, and the remaining four had died.

Between 1720 and 1784/1787, Levoča increased its population to 5,062, with 40 priests/ministers, 61 nobles, and 20 officials. By 1868, Levoča had an estimated population of 6,100. While in 1720, the town was predominantly German, by 1910 Slovaks represented the majority, and out of a population of 7,528 in 1910, 3,094 claimed Slovak as their mother tongue, 2,410 Magyar, 1,377 German, 201 Ukrainian, and 197 Romanian.

L'ubietová

(Slovakia) [Libethen in German and Libetbánya in Hungarian] was granted royal free privileges in 1379. It was a mining town that prospered in the fifteenth and sixteenth centuries, but similar to other Upland mining towns, was undergoing economic decline in the eighteenth century. Adding to the problems of the urban economy was the presence of a stationary army. There was a slight decline in the urban population between 1715 and 1720 from 113 households to 102 and in 1720 the estimated population of the town was 745. Out of the 103 households, 51 percent had Slovakian names, 45 percent German, and 4 percent Magyar. Between 1720 and 1784/1787, L'ubietová's population grew to 1,255, with 2 priests/ministers, 3 nobles, and 9 officials. The town never made the transition into becoming a modern city, and during the last decades of the nineteenth century the urban population even declined, from 1,900 in 1868 to 1,813 in 1910. In 1910, all of the urban dwellers claimed Slovak as their mother tongue.

Mediaş

(Romania) [Mediasch in German and Medgyes in Hungarian] was one of the important Saxon towns of Transylvania. In 1720, it had an estimated population of 4,328, which increased slightly to 4,586 by 1784/1787, out of whom 30 priests/ministers (mostly Lutheran ministers), 13 nobles, and 21 officials were living in the town. Ethnically the town had a German majority, although the German proportion declined during the late nineteenth century, and in 1910 out of the 8,626 urban dwellers, 3,866 claimed German as their mother tongue, 2,729 Romanian, and 1,715 Magyar.

Modra

(Slovakia) [Modern in German and Modor in Hungarian] was granted royal free privileges in 1607. It was one of the poorest towns in 1720, and the census takers noted that only 105 buildings could be considered "houses." Much of the town was in great disorder and many houses were built from bamboo, mud, and straw. Despite these dire conditions, Modra's population grew between 1715 and 1720 from 211 households to 308, with the number of noble households increasing from 15 to 22, and that of burgher households, from 186 to 286. The growth in the number of households was due to the immigration of Slovaks into the town. Between 1715 and 1720, the number of households with Slovak names rose from 32 to 114. The most important source of capital for the town was viniculture.

Modra experienced strong demographic growth between 1720 and 1784/1787, as it grew from an estimated population of 2,299 to 4,740, with 8 priests/ministers, 34 nobles, and 5 officials. During the nineteenth century, however, urban growth slowed and in 1868 Modra had an estimated population of only 4,600, slightly above the 1784/1787 level. The ethnic complexion of the town changed between 1720 and 1910, from being strongly German to Slovak. In 1720, out of the 308 registered households, 57 percent had German names, 37 percent Slovakian, and 7 percent Magyar. By 1910 the town's population had increased to 5,009, with 4,124 claiming Slovak as their mother tongue, 525 German, and 347 Magyar.

Nová Baňa

(Slovakia) [Königsberg in German and Újbánya in Hungarian] was granted royal free privileges in 1345. One of the important medieval mining towns of the Uplands, between 1715 and 1720 Nová Baňa was experiencing demographic decline, as the number of households fell from 225 to 208. A change also transpired in the ethnic composition of the town, characterized by the exit of German burghers and the entry of Slovak cottagers. Households with German names declined from 201 to 134, while those with Slovak names increased from 10 to 62. The largest guilds were those of the shoemakers and the boot-makers.

Nová Baňa's estimated population doubled between 1720 and 1784/1787, from 1,497 to 2,958. In 1784/1787, 3 priests/ministers, 4 nobles, and 8 officials lived in the town. While the town's population again doubled between 1784/1787 and 1868, to reach an estimated 5,100, it declined to 4,813 by 1910. Nová Baňa belongs to that group of Upland towns which, in the course of the eighteenth and nineteenth centuries, lost their German-speaking population and became Slovak-dominated. While in 1720, out of the registered households, 64 percent had German names, 30 percent Slovak, and 6 percent Magyar, by 1910 out of the estimated urban population of 4,813, 4,256 claimed Slovak as their mother tongue and 470 Magyar.

Pécs

(Hungary) [Fünfkirchen in German] was granted royal free privileges in 1780. Pécs had experienced a unique development under Ottoman rule, and some eyewitness accounts described it as the most magnificent town of seventeenth century Hungary. When it was retaken, however, virtually the whole town was destroyed and little of its sixteenth or seventeenth century glamour survived. Pécs belongs to those towns in the Carpathian basin—like Buda, Szeged, and Pest—that, though destroyed during the expulsion of the Ottomans, experienced fast growth during the eighteenth and nineteenth centuries. In 1720, the estimated population of the town was 2,310, increasing to 8,853 by 1784/1787, to 20,000 in 1868, and 49,822 by 1910. In 1784/1787, there were 133 priests/ministers, 48 officials, and 117 nobles living in the town.

After the expulsion of the Ottomans from Pécs, Magyars, German-Swabians, Croatians, and Serbians settled in the town. In 1720, out of the 320 registered households, 138 had Magyar names, 127 Serbian-Croatian, 52 German, and 3 Slovak. By 1910, the Magyars were clearly the largest ethnic group, but the Germans continued to play a significant role. Out of the town's population of 49,822 in 1910, 41,628 claimed Magyar as their mother tongue, while 6,356 claimed German, 688 Croatian, 521 Czech, 162 Slovak, 125 Serbian, and 119 Roma.

Pest

(Hungary) was originally granted royal free privileges in 1291, which it lost during the Ottoman occupation, and was then re-granted in 1703. While the town was retaken in 1686 from the Ottomans, the first years of reconstruction were difficult. Rákóczi did not succeed in subduing Pest during his revolt, but his sieges caused considerable damage. In 1710, Pest did not look like the city that would become the leading urban center of the Hungarian Kingdom in the modern period. Nevertheless, urban dynamism was evident during the years 1715 and

1720, when it experienced the most impressive demographic growth of any town in the Hungarian Kingdom. In 1715, there were 184 households, increasing to 376 by 1720. The sharp growth was primarily due to the immigration of Germans (the so-called Swabians) into the city. In 1715, 150 households had German names, but by 1720, their numbers reached 244. The number of households with Magyar names also increased, from 25 to 78 and the number of noble households rose slightly from 12 to 17. Mirroring the impressive demographic growth was an equally strong expansion on the economic front, which grew fivefold. Yet despite these gains, the census taker noted in 1720 that Pest was a poor town, and out of the 375 houses, 200 were built from bamboo, mud, or straw, and inhabited by day laborers.

Between 1720 and 1784/87, no town grew at a faster rate than Pest. While in 1720, it had an estimated population of 2,713, by 1784/87 this increased to 20,704. In 1784/87 there were 131 priests/ministers, 83 officials, and 410 nobles living in the town. By 1868, the population of Pest had grown to an estimated 144,400, making it the largest city of the kingdom. In 1873, it merged with Buda and Óbuda to form Budapest.

The ethnic composition of the city changed significantly between 1720 and 1910. In 1720, it was a German-dominated city, and out of the 376 households, 244 had German names, 78 Magyar, 34 Serbian-Croatian, and 20 Slovak. However, by 1910, Budapest was overwhelmingly Magyar. From its estimated population of 880,371, 756,070 claimed Magyar as their mother tongue, 78,882 German, 20,359 Slovak, 5,782 Polish, 5,003 Czech, 3,972 Serbian, 2,922 Croatian, 2,777 Romanian, 921 Italian, 866 French, and 608 Bulgarian.

Pezinok

(Slovakia) [Bösing in German and Bazin in Hungarian] was granted royal free privileges in 1647. The town was dependent on viniculture and, at the turn of the seventeenth century, was in a deep economic recession. Typical for wine-growing towns, Pezinok had many urbanized nobles and, in 1720, besides the 367 registered burgher households, there were 53 noble households as well. Between 1720 and 1784/1787, the town experienced stagnation, and the urban population grew from 3,290 to only 4,443. In 1784/87, there were 25 priests/ministers, 11 officials and 68 nobles living in the town.

Between 1784/1787 and 1868, Pezinok's population increased by only 257, to an estimated 4,700 and in 1910 its population was 4,809.

Pezinok belongs to that group of royal free towns in the Uplands that ethnically had a German majority at the end of the seventeenth century, but by the turn of the twentieth century, turned overwhelmingly Slovak. In 1720, out of the 420 registered households, 64 percent had German names, 22 percent Slovak names, 14 percent Magyar, and 1 percent Italian. By 1910, out of the 4,809 urban dwellers, 2,642 claimed Slovak as their mother tongue, 1,558 German, and 575 Magyar.

Prešov

(Slovakia) [Preschau in German and Eperjes in Hungarian] was granted royal free privileges in 1324. The town experienced its most impressive growth in the first half of the seventeenth century, but suffered tremendously during the Thököly and Rákóczi Revolts. In 1715, there were 284 houses in the town, out of which 109 were two storeys high, a reminder of its once affluent past. By 1715, however, the census taker noted, many burgher homes stood in rubble. Adding to the difficulties was that—like Győr and Košice—Prešov had a large occupying army, deterring many burghers from rebuilding. The burghers claimed that since soldiers occupied any house with more than three rooms, there was no reason to rebuild. The situation deteriorated in 1720, when a fire destroyed 32 additional houses and 2 churches. The burghers further complained about urban decline in 1720, and the census taker noted that only those selling wine to the occupying troops were able to make a profit. Between 1715 and 1720, the number of households fell from 309 to 282, with noble households declining from 28 to 20, and burgher households from 281 to 262.

Prešov never regained the glamour it enjoyed in the seventeenth century, but the eighteenth century saw improvement in the urban economy. From 1720 to 1784/1787, the urban population almost tripled from an estimated 2,033 to 6,019. In 1784/1787 there were 59 priests/ministers (it was strongly Lutheran at the time), 87 nobles, and 23 officials living in the town. Prešov made a relatively successful transition into the nineteenth century, and in 1868 the town had an estimated population of 9,900, increasing to 16,323 by 1910. Ethnically, Prešov was German-dominated in 1720, but by 1910 Magyar speakers had come to form the largest linguistic group. In 1720, out of the 282 households, 134 had German names, 72 Slovak, 69 Magyar, and 7 Italian names. By 1910, however, out of the 16,323 urban dwellers, 7,976 claimed Magyar as their mother tongue, 6,494 Slovak, 1,404 German, and 170 Romanian.

Pukanec

(Slovakia) [Pukkanz in German and Bakabánya in Hungarian] was granted royal free privileges in 1686. Pukanec grew as a mining town in the medieval period, but declined in the early modern times. It was one of the smallest royal free towns of the kingdom and, from the seventeenth century, had a Slovak majority. In 1715, a major fire destroyed many houses, leaving 29 families homeless. The main source of income was manufacturing but, between 1715 and 1720, that sector was experiencing a deep recession. Lying at the foot of a mountain, the town's soil was not ideal for grain harvesting. In addition, hailstorms often damaged the crops.

Pukanec experienced growth between 1720 and 1784/1787, as its estimated population increased from 698 to 2,280. In 1784/1787, the town had 2 priests/ministers, 31 nobles, and 6 officials. However, during the nineteenth century the town experienced stagnation and decline. In 1868, the urban population was estimated at 3,700, but by 1910 it had fallen to 3,141.

Pukanec was one of the Slovak-dominated royal free towns of the Hungarian Kingdom. In 1720, out of the 97 registered households, 72 percent had Slovak names, 19 percent Magyar, 8 percent German, and 1 percent Italian. In 1910, of the 3,141 urban dwellers, 2,935 claimed their mother tongue to be Slovak and 107 Magyar.

Rust

(Austria) [Ruszt in Hungarian] was granted royal free privileges in 1681. As one of the smallest royal free towns, in 1720 only 63 houses and 121 households were registered. Rust was a poor town and, in many houses, 3 or 4 families were living together. The urban economy was dominated by viniculture. Out of the 4,009 cultivated hectares, 3,395, or 85 percent of the land, were used for grape harvesting.

Rust never became an important city. Industry failed to develop and no demographic explosion occurred. Between 1720 and 1784/1787, the population increased only from 956 to 1,055. In 1784/1787, there were 4 priests/ministers, 5 nobles, and 8 officials living in the town. The urban population increased only slightly during the nineteenth century, from approximately 1,500 in 1868 to 1,535 in 1910. Ethnically, Rust was a strongly German town. In 1715, all of the 103 households had German-sounding names. In 1910, of the 1,535 urban-dwellers, 1,290 claimed German as their mother tongue and 218 claimed Magyar.

Sabinov

(Slovakia) [Zeben in German and Kis-Szeben in Hungarian] was granted royal free privileges in 1534. Sabinov was one of the poorest and smallest royal free towns in the kingdom. According to the census taker in 1715, out of the 111 registered houses, 32 made from brick were standing, 36 made from wood were barely standing, 35 made from brick and wood were only half standing, and 8 houses were in rubble.

Sabinov's population doubled during the eighteenth century. In 1720, the town had an estimated population of 1,040 and by 1784/1787 it grew to 2,163. In 1784/1787 there were 14 priests/ministers, 22 nobles, and 14 officials living in the town. The population growth continued throughout the nineteenth century and in 1868, Sabinov had around 2,700 residents, increasing to 3,288 by 1910.

In the seventeenth century, Sabinov was a German-dominated city, but when the decline set in from the 1680s, Slovaks moved in and became the majority. In 1720, out of the 113 registered households, 52 had Slovak names, 42 German, and 17 Magyar. Between 1720 and 1910, a surprising change occurred in the town's ethnic composition, characterized by a strong growth in the number of Magyars. While in 1720, only 15 percent of the urban population had Magyar-sounding names, by 1910 out of the 3,288 urban dwellers, 1,640 claimed Slovak as their mother tongue, 1,168 Magyar, and only 341 German. The growth in the Magyar element was most probably due to the assimilation of Slovaks and Germans, rather than the immigration of Magyars into the town.

Satu Mare

(Romania) [Sathmar in German and Szatmár-Németi in Hungarian] represents the unification of two towns, Szatmár and Németi, in 1715. That same year, Satu Mare was also granted royal free privileges. Originally a German town, by the seventeenth century it was over-whelmingly Magyar. Few towns suffered as much as Satu Mare during the Rákóczi Revolt. In 1674, there were 1,427 buildings in the town, but by 1715 it is estimated that the population was only a quarter or two-fifths of its 1674 level. In 1715, there were 282 registered house-holds, out of which 49 were nobles, 201 burghers, and 32 cottagers. One bright spot for the urban economy was a sharp increase in the number of households between 1715 and 1720 from 282 to 352. This growth also mirrored a noticeable improvement in the handicraft sector. While in 1715, 126 artisans and merchants were registered in the town, out of which 104 were artisans, by 1720 there were 151 artisans and merchants. The largest guild was that of the tailors, with 21 members in 1720, followed by the tanners with 15 members. However, there was one downside to the demographic developments between 1715 and 1720. While the number of households increased from 282 to 352, the greatest increase was for cottager households, rising from 32 in 1715 to 101 in 1720. The number of burgher households increased, but only from 201 to 251. These demographic trends indicate that wealthy burghers were moving out of the town, their place taken by poor artisans and landless peasants.

Throughout the eighteenth century, Satu Mare experienced impressive demographic growth. From 1720 to 1784/1787, the urban population increased from an estimated 2,554 to 8,378. In 1784/1787, 9 priests/ministers, 4 officials, and 186 nobles were registered. Satu Mare continued the trend of strong growth in the second half of the nineteenth century and, while in 1868, the urban population rose to 16,400, by 1910 it jumped to 34,892. From the late seventeenth century, it was a predominantly Magyar town, and in 1720 out of the 352 households, 320 had Magyar names. This continued in the nineteenth century and, in 1910, out of the 34,892 urban dwellers, 33,094 claimed Magyar as their mother tongue, 986 Romanian, and 629 German.

Sibiu

(Romania) [Hermannstadt in German and Nagyszeben in Hungarian] was the capital of the Saxons in Transylvania. In 1720, it had an estimated population of 10,116, which increased to 14,066 by 1784/1787. In 1784/1787, 56 priests/ministers (the majority, Lutheran ministers), 233 nobles, and 197 officials were living in the town. After Buda's 225, Sibiu had the highest number of officials of any town in the kingdom (Bratislava having—surprisingly—only 117). Historically a German town, in 1910 out of the 33,489 urban-dwellers, 16,832 claimed German as their mother tongue, 8,824 Romanian, 7,252 Magyar, 134 Czech, and 116 Roma.

Sighişoara

(Romania) [Schässburg in German and Segesvár in Hungarian] was one of the Saxon royal free towns of Transylvania. In 1720, the town had an estimated population of 5,579, which declined to 5,517 by

1784/1787. In 1784/1787, 17 priests/ministers (mostly Lutheran ministers), 4 nobles, and 18 officials were living in the town. The problems of urbanization in the eighteenth century can be evidenced by the large number of peasants (145 households) living within the town walls in 1784/1787. Historically, Sighişoara was a German town and while the German population was proportionally in decline throughout the nineteenth century, they maintained their majority into the twentieth century and, in 1910, out of the 11,587 urban-dwellers, 5,486 claimed German as their mother tongue, 3,031 Romanian, and 2,687 Magyar.

Skalica

(Slovakia) [Skalitz in German and Szakolcza in Hungarian] was granted royal free privileges in 1141, making it the second oldest town with such privileges (Kremnica received royal free standing in 1100). Within the handicraft sector in 1720, 27 households were employed as croppers (Posztónyíró), 18 as tailors, and rounding out the three biggest handicraft sectors was the Boot-Makers' Guild with 15 members.

Skalica experienced slow growth between 1720 and 1784/1787. In 1720, it had an estimated population of 4,006, increasing to 5,690 by 1784/1787, when 60 priests/ministers, 47 nobles, and 20 officials lived in the town. During the second half of the nineteenth century, however, Skalica experienced difficulties maintaining urban growth. Its population reached approximately 7,500 in 1868, but then declined to 5,018 in 1910.

Ethnically a Slovak-dominated town, in 1720 out of the 448 burgher households, 418 (93 percent) had Slovak names, 23 Magyar (5 percent), and 7 German (2 percent). This trend continued throughout the nineteenth century and, in 1910, out of the 5,018 urban dwellers, 4,155 claimed Slovak as their mother tongue, 505 Magyar, and 259 German.

Sopron

(Hungary) [Ödenburg in German] was one of the oldest settlements in the Hungarian Kingdom, its name deriving from Celtic origin (Scarban). It was granted royal free privileges in 1342. Besides Bratislava, Sopron attracted the most illustrious aristocratic families of the kingdom. In 1720, Count József Eszterházy, General Ebergényi, Counts György and Zsigmond Széchenyi, Count Hohenfeld, Count Mandorff, Baron Brank, Baron Mandorff, and Count Adam Szelestey lived in Sopron. The town had a wide artisan base, but the urban economy was strongly dependent on viniculture and, as noted by an iron merchant in 1720, the town was not able to sell any products other than wine.

Situated in the far west corner of Hungary, the Ottomans never occupied the town and neither the Thököly nor the Rákóczi Revolt caused significant damage. Sopron was clearly one of the most fortunate towns of seventeenth century Hungary, as it escaped the ravages of both international and civil war. Between 1715 and 1720, Sopron also experienced impressive demographic growth, as the number of registered households grew from 692 to 760. In 1720 it had an estimated population of 5,486, which increased to 12,639 by 1784/1787, out of which were 74 priests/ministers, 175 nobles, and 36 officials.

Sopron continued to grow during the nineteenth century. In 1868, it had an estimated population of 19,200, and this increased to 33,932 by 1910. For most of its history, it was a German cultural center, and in 1715 out of the 692 registered households, 639 (92 percent) had German names, 35 Magyar (5 percent), 16 Slovak (2 percent), and 2 Serbian-Croatian. During the second half of the nineteenth century, the German influence was challenged by the rise of the Magyar-speaking population, or more specifically the assimilation of German burghers into Hungarian society. In 1910, out of the 33,932 urban dwellers, 17,318 claimed German as their mother tongue, 15,022 Magyar, 781 Croatian, 409 Czech, and 184 Slovak.

Szeged

(Hungary) [Szegedin in German] was granted royal free privileges in 1200, lost them during the Ottoman occupation, and regained them in 1715. Like Buda, Pest, and Pécs, the town was completely destroyed during the re-conquest, and when the census takers arrived in 1715 and 1720, it was in the process of rebuilding. In 1720, the burghers of Szeged complained bitterly about the 500 soldiers stationed in the town. Their grievances were many and varied. Some complained that the soldiers' horses grazed on the commons, while others noted that the soldiers had razed 90 burgher houses without compensation to strengthen the urban fortifications. Yet others were concerned about soldiers that opened taverns in the city, but refused to pay taxes. The merchants, on their part, raised their voices against Croatian soldiers who, participating in commerce and trade, paid no heed to either guild regulations or municipal laws. Szeged's economy was dominated by animal husbandry.

Similar to Pécs, Pest, and Buda, Szeged experienced rapid demographic growth in the eighteenth century. In 1720, it had an estimated population of 4,949 and this increased to 20,947 by 1784/1787, when 61 priests/ministers, 113 nobles, and 29 officials lived in the town. Szeged made a successful transition into modernity, and in 1868 it had an estimated population of 74,000 and 118,328 in 1910. The town's ethnic composition was dominated by Magyars. In 1720, there were 404 households and 95 percent of the population had Magyar names and 5 percent had Serbian names. In 1910, this trend continued and out of 118,328 urban dwellers, 113,380 claimed Magyar as their mother tongue, 2,554 German, 1,152 Serbian, 619 Romanian, 221 Slovakian, and 109 Czech.

Székesfehérvár

(Hungary) [Stuhlweissenburg in German] was an ancient Roman settlement, called Cimbrian, Antian, and sometimes Florian. It was also probably an ancient Celtic site. Székesfehérvár was founded by King St. Stephan who, according to legend, wanted to build his capital on the spot where Árpad set up his tent and consolidated his rule over the Carpathian basin. In the time of King St. Stephan, the town became the capital of the Hungarian Kingdom, where the crown was kept and the kings buried. It is difficult to establish, however, when the town gained royal free standing, because the early documents relating to the town have been lost. What can be established with certainty is that, in the early medieval period, the burghers of the town enjoyed trading privileges and elected their own judge. But the first royal free town privileges date from only 1541, which were again reissued in 1681 by Leopold I.

Similar to Győr, Székesfehérvár was a military border town during the Ottoman occupation of the Carpathian basin. After the expulsion of the Ottomans, its reconstruction was strongly influenced by the stationing of soldier families within the town walls. Like other towns of the early eighteenth century with a large stationary army—Győr, Pécs, Szeged, Prešov,—the soldiers participated in trade and manufacturing (to subsidize their small military incomes), but were not under the political administration of either the guilds or the municipal government. In 1720, the burghers of Székesfehérvár were particularly upset that after moving in, the soldiers occupied the best houses without compensation. Despite these limitations, between 1715 and 1720 there was some demographic growth as the number of households increased from 394 to 434.

In the eighteenth century, Székesfehérvár's population almost quadrupled, from 3,132 in 1720 to 11,816 in 1784/1787, with 91 priests/ministers, 195 nobles, and 13 officials. Székesfehérvár's population continued to grow in the nineteenth century, although not as fast as in the eighteenth. In 1868, it had an estimated population of 27,200 and this grew to 36,625 by 1910. The ethnic composition of the town experienced strong fluctuations. Between 1715 and 1720, for instance, when the total number of registered households increased from 394 to 434, households with Magyar names decreased from 296 to 225, while those with German names increased from 81 to 172 households, and households with South Slav names grew from 17 to 37. By 1910, however, Magyar speakers were dominant, and out of the 36,625 urban-dwellers, 35,354 claimed Magyar as their mother tongue, 538 German, 239 Croatian, and 222 Serbian.

Svätÿ Jur

(Slovakia) [Sankt-Georgen in German and Szentgyörgy in Hungarian] was granted royal free privileges in 1647. It was one of the small wine producing royal free towns of Hungary. In 1715, out of the 6,649 cultivated hectares, 6,212.5 hectares (or 92 percent) were for grape harvesting. Between 1715 and 1720, Svätÿ Jur experienced tremendous demographic fluctuations. While in 1715, 194 households were registered, in 1720 there were only 139. The decline was sharpest among those households with Slovak names. In 1715, there were 44 Slovak households, but by 1720 only 24. Svätÿ Jur never became a big city. In 1720, it had an estimated population of 1,402, and this increased to 2,360 by 1784/1787, with 20 priests/ministers, 20 nobles, and 5 officials. During the second half of the nineteenth century, the town's population grew, from 2,700 in 1868 to 3,458 in 1910. In 1720, Svätÿ Jur was overwhelmingly German, but by 1910 had a Slovakian majority. In 1720, out of the 139 registered households, 103 had German names, 24 Slovak, and 12 Magyar. In 1910, however, out of the 3,458 urban dwellers, 1,897 claimed Slovak as their mother tongue, 916 German, and 641 Magyar.

Tîrgu Mureş

(Romania) [Neumarkt in German and Marosvásárhely in Hungarian] was one of the royal free towns of Transylvania. In 1720, it had an estimated population of 5,041, and this rose slightly to 5,934 by 1784/1787. In 1784/1787, there were 36 priests/ministers (many of whom were

Calvinist ministers), 40 nobles, and 33 officials. Tîrgu Mureş was historically a Magyar town, and this trend continued into the twentieth century. In 1910, out of the 25,517 urban-dwellers, 22,790 claimed Magyar as their mother tongue, 1,717 Romanian, and 606 German.

Trenčin

(Slovakia) [Trenschin in German and Trencsén in Hungarian] was granted royal free privileges in 1412. A Slovak-dominated royal free town, Trenčin suffered a great deal during the Rákóczi Revolt. In 1720, half of the houses around the town square had no roof, and in the outer district—the census takers noted—many houses were in rubble. Between 1720 and 1784/1787, Trenčin recovered significantly, and the urban population grew from an estimated 1,756 to 3,222. In 1784/1787 there were 20 priests/ministers, 82 nobles, and 6 officials living in the town. While the town grew slowly during the first half of the nineteenth century, it developed rapidly from 1868 to1910 as the population increased from 3,500 to 7,805.

Historically, Trenčin had a Slovak majority. In 1720 out of the 230 registered households, 185 had Slovak names, 27 German, 11 Magyar, and 7 Italian. There was also a relatively large Jewish population, accounting for 98 unregistered households in 1720, and there were 178 Jewish males above the age of 14 in 1784/1787. In the second half of the nineteenth century, Magyar speakers emerged as an important part of the urban demography, and in 1910 out of the 7,805 urban dwellers, 3,676 claimed Slovak as their mother tongue, 2,997 Magyar, and 925 German.

Trnava

(Slovakia) [Tyrnau in German and Nagyszombat in Hungarian] was granted royal free privileges in 1238, making it one of the oldest royal free towns in the kingdom. Trnava experienced decline between 1715 and 1720. In 1715, there were 378 households, but by 1720, only 342. This demographic drop was interesting for two reasons. On the one hand, while the overall number of households declined, the number of noble households actually increased from 49 to 63. On the other hand, Trnava was becoming more German. In 1715, out of the 378 households, 170 had Magyar names, 114 Slovak, and 94 German. In 1720, out of the 342 households, only 104 had Magyar names, while 107 had German names, and 128 households had Slovak names.

Trnava's population increased between 1720 and 1784/1787 from an estimated 2,857 to 7,002. In 1784/1787, there were 103 priests/ministers, 251 nobles, and 15 officials living in the town. During the first half of the nineteenth century, the town stagnated, but between 1868 and 1910 the urban population grew rapidly from approximately 8,500 to 15,163. Historically, Trnava experienced large fluctuations in its ethnic composition. While in the medieval period, it was a German town, in the sixteenth century it became Magyar-dominated, and in 1720 the Slovaks had a slight majority. By 1910, however, the Slovaks had clearly become the largest ethnic group, and out of the 15,163 urban dwellers, 8,032 claimed Slovak as their mother tongue, 4,593 Magyar, and 2,280 German.

Zvolen

(Slovakia) [Altsohl in German and Zólyom in Hungarian] was granted royal free privileges in 1342. Zvolen was one of the small royal free towns in the Hungarian Kingdom. In 1715, the town registered 122 households but, in 1720, only 113. Despite this slight drop, the urban economy recorded growth between 1715 and 1720. Interestingly, the economic growth between 1715 and 1720 occurred simultaneously to the declining influence of guilds. In 1715, all of the artisans in the town belonged to a guild, but by 1720 only the butchers, tailors, hatters, shoemakers, and fullers did so. Those outside the guilds apparently earned more money than guild members because, as the census takers noted in 1720, many guild members were forced to subsidize their income by agricultural work.

Zvolen's population grew at a steady pace in the eighteenth century and, between 1720 and 1784/1787, it increased from an estimated 980 to 1,690. In 1784/1787, 4 priests/ministers, 49 nobles, and three officials lived in the town. Like many Upland towns, during the first half of the nineteenth century, urbanization stagnated. In the second half of the nineteenth century, however, Zvolen's urban population experienced phenomenal growth between 1868 and 1910, as it increased from 1,900 to 8,799. The town's ethnic composition changed from being dominated by Slovaks in 1720, to a Magyar-speaking majority at the turn of the twentieth century. In 1720, out of 113 households, 81 percent had Slovak, 18 percent Magyar, and 14 percent German family names. By 1910, however, out of the 8,799 urban-dwellers, 4,973 claimed Magyar as their mother tongue, 3,579 Slovak, and 209 German.

Notes

I Introduction

1. Francis L. Carsten, "The Origins of the Junkers," *The English Historical Review* 62, no. 243 (April, 1947): 145–178, see 164.
2. Francis L. Carsten, "Medieval Democracy in the Brandenburg Towns and Its Defeat in the Fifteenth Century," *Transaction of the Royal Historical Society*, 4th ser. (London, 1943): 73–92, see 90.
3. Francis L. Carsten, *Origins of Prussia* (Oxford: Clarendon Press, 1954), 135.
4. Jerome Blum, "The Rise of Serfdom in Eastern Europe," *American Historical Review* 62 (July 1957): 807–836, see 833.
5. Often the criticism is leveled specifically at G. F. Knapp's famous work, *Die Bauernbefreiung und der Urprung der Landarbeiter in den älteren Theilen Preussens* (München: Duncker & Humblot, 1927), which formed one pillar of Carsten and Rosenberg's criticism of the Junkers. William Hagen, "Seventh-century Crisis in Brandenburg: The Thirty Years' War, the Destabilization of Serfdom and the Rise of Absolutism," *American Historical Review* 94 (April, 1989): 302–335; also see Hagen, *Ordinary Prussians* (New York: Cambridge University Press, 2002); Hagen, "How mighty the Junkers? Peasant Rents and Seigniorial Profits in Sixteenth Century Brandenburg," *Past and Present*, no. 108 (1985): 80–116; Peter Kriedte, *Peasants, Landlords and Merchants: Europe and the World Economy 1500–1800* (Cambridge [Cambridgeshire]; New York: Cambridge University Press, 1983); also by Kriedte, "Spätmittelalterische Agrarkrise oder Krise des Feudalismus?" *Geschichte und Gesselschaft* 7 (1981): 42–67; Edgar Melton, "Gutsherrschaft in East Elbian Germany and Livonia, 1500–1800: A Critique of the Model," *Central European History* 21(December, 1988): 315–349; Jan Peters ed., *Konflikt und Kontrolle in Gutsherrschaftsgesellschaften* (Göttingen: Vandenhoeck & Ruprecht, 1995); Tom Scott, *Freiburg and the Breisgau* (Oxford [Oxfordshire]; New York: Clarendon Press, 1986); Heidi Wunder, "Serfdom in Later Medieval and Early Modern Germany," in T. S. Aston ed., *Social Relations and Ideas* (Cambridge [Cambridgeshire]; New York: Cambridge University Press, 1983), 273–294.
6. William Hagen, "Seventeenth Century Crisis in Brandenburg," 311.
7. Edgar Melton, "Gutsherrschaft in East Elbian Germany and Livonia," 326.

8. William Hagen, "Seventeenth Century Crisis in Brandenburg," 313.
9. R. J. W. Evans, *The Making of the Habsburg Monarchy 1550–1700* (Oxford: Clarendon Press; New York: Oxford University Press, 1979), 84–85.
10. John Merrington, "Town and Country in the Transition to Capitalism," in Paul Sweezy ed., *The Transition from Feudalism to Capitalism* (London: NLB; Atlantic Highlands [N.J.]: Humanities Press, 1976), 170–195, see 170.
11. As John Merrington put it: "According to Pirenne's enormously influential studies of medieval towns and commerce, the closing of the Mediterranean trade routes was the key to the substitution of an agrarian economy in the seventh to ninth centuries: 'For an economy of exchange was substituted with an economy of consumption. Each demesne . . . constituted from this time on a little world of its own . . . a closed domestic economy . . . of no markets. They did not sell because they could not sell, because markets were wanting;' " (John Merrington, 1976, 173). Merrington is quoting from Pirenne's *Medieval Cities: Their Origins and the Revival of Trade*, Frank D. Halsey translation (Princeton, NJ: Princeton University Press, 1925).
12. Henri Pirenne, *Belgian Democracy, Its Early History*, J. V. Saunders trans. (Manchester: The University press; London, New York [etc.] Longmans, Green & co., 1915); also see Pirenne, *Early democracies in the Low Countries: Urban Society and Political Conflict in the Middle Ages and the Renaissance*, J. V. Saunders translation (New York: Harper & Row, 1963).
13. Oswald Spengler, *Decline of the West*, Charles F. Atkinson translation, 2 vols. in 1 (New York: A.A. Knopf, 1934), 2: 95.
14. Henri Pirenne, *A History of Europe from the Invasions to the XVI Century* (London: G. Allen & Unwin, 1939), 534.
15. On the Hungarian literature look to: Zsigmond Pál Pach, *Die ungarische Agrarentwicklung im 16–17. Jahrhundert; Abbiegung vom westeuropäischen Entwicklungsgang* (Budapest: Akadémiai Kiadó, 1964); Sándor Gyimesi, "Frühkapitalistische Entwicklung und Spätfeudalismus in 16. und 17 Jh. in Ungarn," *Jahrbuch für Wirtschaftgeschichte* 2 (1987): 51–64; Iván Berend, "The Historical Evolution of Eastern Europe as a Region," in Ellen Comisso and Laura D'Andrea Tyson eds., *Power, Purpose, and Collective Choice* (Ithaca, NY: Cornell University Press, 1986), 153–170; Jenő Szűcs, *Vázlat Európa három történeti régiójáról* [The three regions of Europe] (Budapest: Magvető, 1983); György Granasztói, *A középkori magyar város* [The medieval Hungarian town] (Budapest: Gondolat, 1980).
16. Zsigmond Pál Pach, "Sixteenth-Century Hungary: Commercial Activity and Market Production by the Nobles," in Peter Burke, ed., *Economy and Society in Early Modern Europe: Essays from Annales* (New York: Harper & Row, 1972): 113–133, see 114.
17. Pál Zsigmond Pach, "The Shifting of International Trade Routes in the 15th–17th Centuries," *Acta Historica Academiae Scientiarum Hungaricae* 14 (Budapest, 1968): 287–319, see 287, see also printed in Pach, *Hungary and the European Economy in the Early Modern Times* (Aldershot, Hampshire; Brookfield, Vt.: Variorum, 1994).
18. Zsigmond Pál Pach, "The Role of East Central Europe in International Trade," in: Pach, *Hungary and the European Economy*, 259.

19. Zsigmond Pál Pach, "Sixteenth-Century Hungary," 114.
20. Adriaan Verhulst, "The Origins of Towns in the Low Countries," 32.
21. A. B. Hibbert, "The Origins of the Medieval Town Patriciate" *Past and Present*, no. 3 (February 1953): 15–27, see 17.
22. Robert Brenner, "Agrarian Class Structure and Economic Development in Pre-Industrial Europe," *Past and Present* no. 70 (February, 1976): 30–74, see 54–55.
23. Brenner, "Agrarian Class Structure," 59–60.
24. R. H. Hilton, "Capitalism—What's in a Name?" *Past and Present* no. 1 (February, 1952): 32–43, see 41.
25. Maurice Dobb, "A Reply," in Hilton, *Transition from Feudalism to Capitalism*, 57–67, see 61.
26. Alba Iulia (Weissenberg/Gyulafehérvár), Baia Mare (Neustadt/Nagybánya), Baia Sprie (Mittelstadt/Felsőbánya), Cluj-Napoca (Klausenburg/Kolozsvár), Esztergom (Gran), Košice (Kaschau/Kassa), Tîrgu Mureş (Neumarkt/ Marosvásárhely).
27. Francis L. Carsten, "Medieval Democracy in the Brandenburg Towns and Its Defeat in the Fifteenth Century," *Transaction of the Royal Historical Society*, 4th ser. (London, 1943): 73–92, see 90.
28. Ivan T. Berend, *History Derailed* (Berkeley: University of California Press, 2003), 115.

2   Urban Development in the Hungarian Kingdom between the Thirteenth and Sixteenth Centuries

1. On Buda's medieval population look at Martyn C. Rady, *Medieval Buda: A Study of Municipal Government and Jurisdiction in the Kingdom of Hungary* (Boulder, CO: East European Monographs, 1985), 41; see also Jenő Szűcs, *Városok és kézművesség a XV. századi Magyarországon* [Towns and handicraft production in sixteenth century Hungary] (Budapest: Tudományos és Ismeretterjesztő Kiadó, 1955), 44.
2. Jenő Szűcs, *Városok és kézművesség a XV. századi Magyarországon*, 44.
3. Erik Fügedi, *Koldulό barátok, polgárok, nemesek* [Begging friars, burghers, nobles] (Budapest: Magvető, 1981).
4. Both the conservative interwar period historian Gyula Szekfű and the Marxist sociologist Ferenc Erdei are in agreement on this point. See, Gyula Szekfű, *Három nemzedék* [Three generations] (Budapest: Királyi Magyar Nyomda, 1922); Ferenc Erdei, "A Magyar társadalom a két világháború között," [Hungarian society in the interwar period], *Valóság*, no. 4 (1976), 23–53, and no. 5 (1976), 36–58.
5. Hóman and Szekfű, *Magyar történet* [History of Hungary] 5 vols. (Budapest: Királyi Magyar Egyetemi Nyomda, 1935–1936), 3: 97–101.
6. Henri Pirenne, *Early Democracies in the Low Countries*, (New York: Harper and Row, 1963), 168.

7. Sándor Domanovszky, *A szepesi városok árumegállító joga: Lőcse és Késmárk küzdelme az árumegállításért, 1358–1570* [The staple rights of the Zipser towns: The conflict between Levoča and Kežmarok to stop merchandise, 1358–1570] (Budapest: Magyar Tudományos Akadémia, 1922).

8. Pál Engel, *Királyi hatalom és arisztokrácia viszonya a Zsigmond-korban: 1387–1437* [The relationship of royal authority to the aristocracy during the reign of Sigismund: 1387–1437] (Budapest: Akadémiai Kiadó, 1977).

9. Vera Bácskai, *Magyar mezővárosok a XV. században* [Magyar agrarian towns in the fifteenth century] (Budapest: Akadémiai Kiadó, 1965), 18–19.

10. Adorján Divéky, *A Lengyelországnak elzálogosított XVI szepesi város viszszacsatolása 1770-ben* [The 1770 reunification of the XVI Scepius towns mortgaged previously to Poland] (Budapest: Szepesi Szövetség, 1929).

11. The best work on the topic is by Christian Genersich, *Merkwürdigkeit der königlichen Freystadt Käisermarkt* (Kaschau: Franz Lederer, 1804).

12. Granasztói, *A középkori magyar város*, 170.

13. Domanovszky, *A szepesi városok*. Braşov (Kronstadt/Brassó) and Sibiu (Hermannstadt/Nagyszeben) also lived in a virtual state of war in the early sixteenth century. Look to: Friedrich Teutsch, *Die Siebenbürger Sachsen in vergangenheit und gegenwart* (Leipzig: K. F. Koehler, 1916), 79.

14. Andrei Kertész, *Hermannstadt in Siebenbürgen* (Sibiu: Verlag Terra Incognita, 1999), 43–44.

15. Ibid.

16. Gernot Nussbächer, *Johannes Benkner* (Bucureşti: Kriterion 1988), 22–23.

17. Ibid.

18. Genersich, *Merkwürdigkeit der königlichen Freystadt Käisermarkt*; see also Ivan Chalupecký, *Kežmarok* (Košice: Východoslov. vydav., 1968); Nora Baráthová, *Kezmarský hrad* (Martin: Osveta, 1989).

19. Genersich, *Merkwürdigkeit der königlichen Freystadt*.

20. István Sinkovics, "Útkeresés Mohács után. Az ország három részre szakadása 1526–1541" [The search for order after Mohács. The partition of the kingdom into three parts 1526–1541], in: Zsigmond Pál Pach ed., *Magyarország története 152–1686*, 2 vols. [History of Hungary 1526–1686] (Budapest: Akadémiai Kiadó, 1987), 1: 147–222. 180–190. Also look at Gábor Barta ed., *Két tárgyalás Sztambulban: Hyeronimus Łaski tárgyalása a töröknél János király nevében, Habardanecz János jelentése 1528. nyári sztambuli tárgyalásairól* [Two conferences in Istanbul: Hyeronimus Łaski's meeting with the Turks in the name of King János; and János Habardanecz's report of his Istanbul conference in the summer of 1528] (Budapest: Balassi, 1996).

21. Christian Genersich, *Merkwürdigkeit der königlichen Freystadt*. Zápolya granting estate to Łaski can be found, MOL (Hungarian National Archive), Neo-regestrata acta, E 148. 59/20. Some of H. Łaski's correspondences can also be found in the Sibiu Branch of the National Archive of Romania, under the Brukenthal Index. Kežmarok's town book covering most of the fifteenth and sixteenth centuries is in the Poprad District Archive (Slovakia) and in excellent condition.

22. In 1493 the burghers of Cracow were also ennobled, and similar ennoblements took place among the burghers of Lwów (Ukraine) in 1658, and Wilno

in 1568. Maria Bogucka has noted that: "In practice also the largest Prussian towns, Gdańsk, Toruń, and Erbląg, had the status of the nobility." See Maria Bogucka, *The Lost World of the Sarmatians* (Warszawa: Polish Academy of Sciences, Institute of History, 1996), 32; András Kubinyi, "Budapest története a későbbi középkorban Buda elestéig 1541-ben" [The history of Budapest from the late medieval period to Buda's fall in 1541]; László Gerevich ed., *Budapest története a későbbi középkorban és a török hódoltság idején* [History of Budapest in the late medieval period and the Turkish occupation) (Budapest: Budapest Főváros Tanácsa, 1973), 210–212.

23. István Rácz, *Városlakó nemesek az Alföldön 1541–1848 között* [Urbanized nobles of the Plains between 1541–1848] (Budapest: Akadémiai Kiadó, 1988), 17–19.

24. Hóman and Szekfű, *Magyar történet*, 3: 554.

25. Rácz, *Városlakó nemesek az Alföldön*, 30.

26. Hóman and Szekfű, *Magyar történet*, 3: 555–556.

27. Ibid.

28. Erik Molnár, *A Magyar társadalom története az Árpádkortól Mohácsig* [The history of Hungarian society from the rule of the Árpáds to Mohács] (Budapest: Szikra Kiadó, 1949), 154–158.

29. Hóman and Szekfű, *Magyar történet*, 3: 558.

30. László Makkai, *A magyar városfejlődés és városépítés történeti vázlata* [A historical outline of Hungarian town development and town building] (Budapest: Tankönyvkiadó, 1963), 68.

31. Rácz, *Városlakó nemesek az Alföldön*, 27.

32. László Makkai, *A magyar városfejlődés és városépítés*, 62.

33. László Kürti, "The Ungaresca and Heyduck Music and Dance Tradition of Renaissance Europe," *Sixteenth Century Journal* 14, no. 1 (1983): 63–104, 83.

34. Rácz, *Városlakó nemesek az Alföldön*, 27–28.

35. Makkai, *A magyar városfejlődés*, 70.

36. Ferenc Szakály, *Magyar adóztatás a török hódoltságban* [Hungarian taxation during Ottoman occupation] (Budapest: Akadémiai Kiadó, 1981).

37. Rácz, *Városlakó nemesek az Alföldön*, 85–86.

38. Makkai, *A magyar városfejlődés*.

39. On soldiers and urban development in sixteenth century military border towns of Hungary, see István H. Németh, "Végvárak, városok, hadseregszállítók, 1526–1593," [Border castles, towns, and the transporters of troops, 1526–1593] *Történelmi Szemle* 3–4 (2000), 203–244.

3   The New Burghers

1. Max Weber, *The City*. The term "middle burghers" is often associated with the fast-rising group between the old patriciate and the traditional artisan classes in the royal free towns of the western Holy Roman Empire, dating to the mid-fourteenth century. See Steven Ozmant, *The Bürgermeister's Daughter* (New York: Harper Perennial, 1997), 12.

2. Friedrich Teutsch, *Die Siebenbürger Sachsen in Vergangenheit und Gegenwart*. Leipzig: K. F. Koehler, 1916.

3. Gernot Nussbächer, *Johannes Honterus: sein Leben und Werk im Bild* (Bukarest: Kriterion, 1978); Maja Philippi, *Kronstadt: historische Betrachtungen über eine Stadt in Siebenbürgen* (Bukarest: Kriterion-Verlag; Heidelberg: Arbeitskreis für Siebenbürgische Landeskunde Heidelberg, 1996), 126–127; also see Oskar Wittstock, *Johannes Honterus, der Siebenbürger Humanist und Reformator. Der Mann, das Werk, die Zeit* (Göttingen: Vandenhoeck u. Ruprecht, 1970).

4. Henri Pirenne, *Early Democracies in the Low Countries*, 53.

5. Maria Bogucka, *Nicholas Copernicus*, Leon Szwajcer translation (Wrocław: Ossoliński State Publishing House, 1973), 50; see also the Central Archives of Historical Records in Warsaw (AGAD): Collection of Parchment Records no. 5632. The laws were printed by Jan Haller and for his printing services he was given tax exemption for the remainder of his printing career (AGAD, Metryka Koronna, vol. 21, leaf 361).

6. Christian Genersich, *Merkwürdigkeit der königlichen Freystadt Käisermarkt*; on the history of the Sonntag family see Daniel Szontágh, *Iglói és Zabari Szontágh nemzetség származási története és oklevelei* [The history and documentation of the Spišska Nová Ves and Zabar Sonntag family] (Budapest: Emich Nyomda, 1864); see also Johann Lipták, *Alchimisten, Gottsucher, und Schatzgräber in der Zips* (Kesmark: P. Sauter, 1938), 28–31.

7. Sándor Domanovszky, *A szepesi városok árumegállító joga Lőcse és Késmárk*.

8. Béla Iványi, "Késmárkt város lakói és azoknak vagyoni viszonyai 1541-ben" [The social composition and wealth of the population of Kežmarok in 1541] *Közlemények Szepes Vármegye Múltjából* (1916): 68–86.

9. György Bruckner, "Késmárk és a Thököly család" [Kežmarok and the Thököly family], *Közlemények Szepes Vármegye Múltjából* (1909): 23–76; see also V. Greschik, "Die Belagerung Käsmarkt durch Emmericus Thököly" [The siege of Kežmarok by Thököly] *Közlemények Szepes Vármegye Múltjából*. (1923): 123–140.

10. John Dee, *A True and Faithful Relation of What Passed for Many Years Between Dr. John Dee and Some Spirits* (London: Printed by D. Maxwell for T. Garthwait, 1659); see also Deborah E. Harkness, "Shows in the Showstone: A Theater of Alchemy and Apocalypse in the Angel Conversations of John Dee (1527–1608/9)," *Renaissance Quarterly*, vol. 49, no. 4 (Winter, 1996): 707–737; Walter I. Trattner, "God and Expansion in Elizabethan England: John Dee, 1527–1583," *Journal of the History of Ideas*, vol. 25, no. 1 (Jan–Mar., 1964): 17–34.

11. Johann Lipták, *Alchimisten, Gottsucher, und Schatzgräber in der Zips* (Kesmark: P. Sauter, 1938), 28–31.

12. Dee, *A True and Faithful Relation of What Passed for Many Years Between Dr. John Dee and Some Spirits*.

13. Here an important qualification is in order. As R. J. W. Evans has observed, while in Dee's diary Kelley is said to have died in 1595, a great deal of ambiguity surrounds his death, and according to Evans he might well have been

alive in 1598. See R. J. W. Evans, *Rudolph and his World* (Oxford: Clarendon Press; New York: Oxford University Press, 1984, ca.1973.), 227.

14. George Hunston Williams, *Radical Reformation* (Philadelphia, PA: Westminster Press, 1962); Marian Hillar with Claire S. Allen, *Michael Servetus: Intellectual Giant, Humanist, and Martyr* (Lanham, MD: University Press of America, 2002).

15. This was the famous Henckel family, known as the Henkels in America. On the American branch of the family see Albert Sydney Edmonds, "The Henkels, Early Printers in New Market, Virginia, with a Bibliography," *William and Mary College Quarterly Historical Magazine*, 2nd Ser., vol. 18, no. 2 (April, 1938): 174–195.

16. Daniel Liechty, *Andreas Fischer and the Sabbatarian Anabaptists* (Scottdale, PA.: Herald Press, 1988), 88 and 93.

17. Liechty, *Andreas Fischer*, 76.

18. Ibid. 77.

19. Ibid. 79.

20. György Bruckner, *A reformáció és ellenreformáció története a Szepességben. 1520–1745* [The history of the reformation and counter-reformation in Scepius County 1520–1745] (Budapest: Szepességi Szövetség, 1922).

21. Oszkár Paulinyi, *A középkori magyar réztermelés gazdasági jelentősége* [The economic significance of medieval Hungarian copper production] (Budapest: Sárkány Nyomda, 1933).

22. The Hungarian historian Erik Molnár argued that Hungarian gold represented 42 percent and silver, 30 percent of world production between 1350 and 1450, while Jean Bérenger has put the figure at 33 percent for gold and 25 percent for silver. See Molnár, *A Magyar társadalom története*, 171; Jean Bérenger, *The History of the Habsburg Empire*, C.A. Simpson translation (London; New York: Longman, 1994), 78. Bérenger also noted the impact of South American mining, especially the Potosí mines: "Their annual production in the period 1560–1580, was 151 tons to which were added 50 tons from the Mexican mines. Annually, between 1581 and 1600, Spanish America supplied a total of 330 tons of silver. Peruvian silver, which was excavated with cheap slave labor provided by the *mita*, also profited from the process of amalgamation with mercury, with the result that its price became markedly lower than that of Central European silver. This inability to compete with American exports was the main reason why the Augsburg bankers were ruined and the Central European mines were left with only regional significance." See, Jean Bérenger, *The History of the Habsburg Empire*, 199.

23. Molnár, *A Magyar társadalom*, 176, 180.

24. Jean Bérenger, *The History of the Habsburg Empire*, 198.

25. Jean Bérenger, *The History of the Habsburg Empire*, 198; Günther V. Probszt, *Die alten 7 niederungarischen Bergstädte im Slowakischen Erzgebirge* (Wien: Montan-Verlag, 1960); Götz Freiherr von Pölnitz, *Anton Fugger* 3 volumes (Tübingen: Mohr 1958–1986); also by Pölnitz, *Die Fugger* (Frankfurt am Main: H. Scheffler, 1960).

26. Fernand Braudel, *Civilization and Capitalism 15th–18th century: The Wheels of Commerce* (London: Fontana Press, 1985), 323.

27. Ágnes Várkonyi, "Gazdaság és társadalom a 17. század második felében (1648–1686)" [Economy and society during the second half of the seventeenth century] in Zsigmond Pál Pach ed., *Magyarország története 1526–1686* [The history of Hungary, 1526–1686] 2 vols. (Budapest: Akadémiai Kiadó, 1987), 2: 1290.

4   The Difficult Victory of Habsburg Absolutism

1. Kálmán Mikszáth, *A Fekete Város* [The Black City] (Budapest: Franklin, 1910). This popular novel by Mikszáth was a fictional account of the history of Levoča during the Thököly revolt in the seventeenth century.

2. Martin Femée, seigneur de Genillé et de Marly-le Châtel, (1540? –1590?), *The Historie of the Ttrovbles of Hvngarie* (London: F. Kyngston, 1600), 131. Library of Congress Rare Books Collection. This 356-page work, written originally in French sometime between 1570 and 1580, is arguably the best sixteenth-century account of the state of Hungary and the Battle of Mohács as well as the civil war between Zápolya and Ferdinand.

3. Martin Femée, seigneur de Genillé et de Marly-le Châtel, *The Historie of the Trovbles of Hvngarie*, 131.

4. Ibid., 131.

5. Sebastian Műnster (1489–1552), *Cosmographey oder beschreibung aller länder herschaftenn vnd fürnemesten stetten des gantzen erdbodens* (Getruckt zu Basel, 1588).The Hungarian Simplicissimus appeared in print in 1683 and was an imitation of Grimmelshausen's work. Its author's identity remains a mystery. Some have attributed it to the Silesian born Daniel Speer. He was born in Wrocłav (Breslau) in 1635. However, linguists have questioned this assumption and there remains no definite answer to the author's true identity. Look to József Turóczi-Trostler eds., *Magyar Simplicissimus* (Budapest: Tudományos Ismeretterjesztő Könyvkiadó, 1956), 226.

6. Henri Pirenne, "The Stages in the Social History of Capitalism." *The American Historical Review*, vol. 19, no. 3 (April, 1914), 494–515. 512.

7. János Barta, *Miért halt meg Zrínyi Péter? A Wesselényi-összeesküvés története* [Why did Péter Zrínyi die? The history of the Wesselényi conspiracy] (Budapest: Móra, 1986); Gyula Pauler, *Wesselényi Ferencz Nádor és társainak összeesküvése, 1664–1671* [Palatine Ferencz Wesselényi and his co-conspirators 1664–1671] (Budapest: Magyar Tudományos Akadémia Könyvkiadó-Hivatalában, 1876); Ágnes R. Várkonyi, *Erdélyi változások: az erdélyi fejedelemség a török kiűzésének korában, 1660–1711* [Changes in Transylvania: Transylvania during the expulsion of the Ottomans, 1660–1711] (Budapest: Magvető, 1984).

8. *A Brief Narrative of the State of the Protestants in Hungary and the Sufferings and Persecutions of the Ministers of Christ for Religion in that Kingdom*, (London: Printed for T. Parkhurst, 1677) 3. This pamphlet described the machinations of the Jesuits in the following manner: "When the Prelates and Jesuits of that Nation saw no way, in many years, of overturning the Protestant Religion there, but by persecution: they still sought pretext, to

ingage [engage] the King, the Emperor of Germany, to persecute the Protestants, and especially the ministers thereof. In the year therefore 1670 when a Rebellion brake out, though the Heads thereof were known, such as Zereny [Zrínyi] Prince of Croatia, Earl Nadasdi [Nádasdy]; Judge of the Hungarian Court, Earl Frangepan [Frangepán], Prince Rakoczy [Rákóczi] (son to him of Transylvania and Zereny's [Zrinyi] son in law), and the two Barkoczys (who since, having made peace with the Emperor became great Persecutors of the Protestants) with divers [different] others, Noblemen and Gentlemen; and the Contests merely about Civil matters and nothing relating to Religion; yet the Popish Clergy indeavors [endeavors] to asperse as guilt thereof, or to be least complices [accomplices] therein."

9. *A Brief Narrative of the State of the Protestants in Hungary*, 4. On the reformation in Hungary, see also David P. Daniel, "Hungary," in Andrew Pettegree ed., *The Early Reformation in Europe*, (Cambridge [England]; New York: Cambridge University Press, 1992), 49–69; also by same author, "Calvinism in Hungary: The Theological and Ecclesiastic Transition to the Reformed Faith," in Andrew Pettegree, Alastair Duke, and Gillian Lewis eds., *Calvinism in Europe* (Cambridge; New York: Cambridge University Press, 1994), 205–231; Katalin Peter, "Hungary," in Bob Scribner, Roy Porter, and Mikuláš Teich, *The Reformation in National Context* (Cambridge; New York: Cambridge University Press, 1994), 155–169.

10. *A Brief Narrative of the State of the Protestants in Hungary*, 5.

11. László Benczédi, "Rendi szervezkedés és a kuruc mozgalom" [Feudal conspiracy and the Kuruc movement]. In: Zsigmond Pál Pach ed., *Magyarország története 1526–1686* [History of Hungary, 1526–1686] 2 vols. (Budapest: Akadémiai Kiadó, 1987), 2: 1210. Bálint Hóman and Gyula Szekfű, *Magyar történet* [History of Hungary], 5 vols. Budapest: Királyi Magyar Egyetemi Nyomda, 4: 190–191; György János Bauhofer, *History of the Protestant Church in Hungary, from the Beginning of the Rreformation to 1850* (Boston: Phillips, Sampson, and company; New York: J. C. Derby, 1854).

12. *A Brief Narrative of the State of the Protestants in Hungary*, 5.

13. The Kuruc name originated from the Latin word *cruciatus*, meaning torture and related in religious terminology to the cross and the crucifixion. Famous for their ballads and poetry, the Kuruc initially stressed the need for religious freedom and later turned to lyrics with growing national and political overtones.

14. *The declaration of the Hungarian War / lately set out by the most illustrious Michael Apafi, Prince of Transilvania, against the Emperour's S. Majesty* (according to the Transylvanian copy, anno 1682) (London: Printed for Francis Smith, 1682), 9.

15. Ibid., 9

16. Ibid., 11.

17. In Apafi's work there is also listed the "Compact and Conditions, betwixt the Emperor of the Turks and the Hungarian Male-coontents:" This in effect highlights how the Magyars would be allowed a semi-autonomous status. The work states: "The great Emperor of the Turks, upon the following conditions constitute, and to be performed on both Parts, hath received in protection, the

Hungarians, who have suffered extream violence. If the Kingdom of Hungary, rent from the House of Austria, shall become Tributary, shall yearly pay the same too, and ever continue in Faith and Obedience toward the Ottoman Port [or Court] which the Hungarians oblige themselves to perform, Hostages being yearly to be sent to the foresaid Port, for the ratification of the same. The Emperor of the Turks hath bound himself by Oath, to restore all the Hungarians to former Liberty by strong hands, to repell all violence which may be carried on against them by others, and to protect them. Above all, that he shall exact no tribute from the Hungarians, until the affairs of Hungary be reduced to good condition, all Tumults being appeased. That he shall draw to himself no Town or Fortress of the Hungarians; that he shall disturb none of their Liberty Ecclesiastick nor Pollitick; that he shall allow unto all, the free Exercise of their Religion; that he shall give Power to erect and repair Churches, Schools, and Parioches [Perishes]; and to choose a Prince of their own Nation, whom they shall judge sufficient, the suffrages of the Nations Inhabitants agreeing thereto, no Forrain [foreign], being to be forcible obtruded." *The declaration of the Hungarian War*, 14–15.

18. The rise of the Thököly family represents one of the more intriguing stories of Hungarian history. The founder of the family, Sebastian Thököly, started his career in the 1540s as a horse trader. By 1560, however, he was so successful that he became an important financier to notable Magyar families as well as—in a minor capacity—the Habsburg court. The title of noble, then baron, was quick to come in an age rife with mismanaged state finances. The family, therefore, rose to power through entrepreneurial skill and hard work and not by glorious victories on the battlefield. Sebastian Thököly's grand acquisition in the sixteenth century was the castle of Kežmarok. At the beginning of the sixteenth century, the castle belonged to the Zápolya family, who then passed it on to Hieronimus Łasky. The castle brought the leaseholder some taxes from the town. Its main attraction, however, was that Kežmarok lay at an important transshipment point between southern Hungary and Poland, in a territory where horse and wine trade flourished in the sixteenth and seventeenth centuries. Sebastian Thököly was able to gain control of the castle when Hieronimus Łasky's son, Albert, fell in debt to him. When Thököly took control of the town, he did not treat it as a separate entity but as his own private possession, and in 1582 issued an order demanding that: (a) His guests lodge for free, (b) The town must sell a set number of barrels of his wines a year, (c) The town must provide military assistance in case of war, (d) Provide craftsmen to repair the castle for free, (e) Allow Thököly unlimited use of the pasture land (for his horse trade), and (f) Support the Thököly family's choice of two candidates from whom the burghers could select the town judge. In sum, Sebastian Thököly had a remarkable career. Born the child of a peasant-burgher, he rose to be a baron and interacted with a royal free town as a Master.

It is important to point out that the relationship between the Thököly family and the town was never as one-sided as it may appear, and the Thökölys were never able to gain absolute control of Kežmarok. Guilds continued to function and control everyday life, and the House of Plebs remained a feisty institution that regularly expressed its independent opinion. One of the difficulties standing in the way of absolute control was the ambiguous legal status of Kežmarok. In the fourteenth century the town enjoyed royal free standing; a privilege the Zápolya family first withdrew and then re-granted. When in 1610 the Thököly family won the formal right of inheriting the castle "fief" of Kežmarok, the town kept sending ambassadors to represent itself as the "Republic of Kežmarok" to the Parliament in Bratislava and at the Court of the Habsburg Emperor. Throughout the Thököly family tenure, a number of serious rebellions rocked manorial rule. The most serious of these came in 1648, when Sebastian Thököly's son, István Thököly (1623–1670), used a force of 800 mercenaries to subdue the burgher revolt.

Until 1650, Kežmarok had difficulties defending its interests. On several occasions in the early part of the seventeenth century, ambassadors were sent by the town council with money for the king to buy back their privileges, but each time they were ambushed on the way and could not even secure an audience with the king. However, at one fortuitous moment, ambassadors in 1650 were able to meet with the king. At this meeting Leopold I agreed that for 160,000 Forints, the town would be re-granted the privileges of royal free standing with the condition that three burgher houses would be demolished and a Catholic church built on the site. Having deposited 20,000 Forints, the ambassadors left with the agreement of annual payments to pay off the deficit.

Understanding that he was losing the battle on the judicial front, István Thököly (1623–1670) made a gesture of good faith toward the town. In recognition of the 50,000 Forints from the House of Plebs in 1650, he returned the keys of the town armory to the municipality. Thököly's changing attitude about Kežmarok developed simultaneously to the town reevaluating its position toward its castle lord. Although a concordance was never fully reached, in time, the two sides started to grow closer and a mutually beneficial symbiotic relationship unfolded. At its most basic level, the town artisans began to enjoy the benefits a rich noble merchant family can bring to an urban economy. While nowhere close to the example of the Medici in Florence, within its East Central European context the Thököly family advanced the humanities, arts, and crafts in the town. The family remained committed to Lutheranism, and donations for scholarships and study trips abroad were regularly forthcoming to the town Lyceum. Jewelers also prospered, because of the demand from the noble ladies around Thököly's private court. Further, Thököly's horse-trading brigade and mercenaries also expanded the demand for belt, boot, glove, saddle, and travel pack production. As Gábor Bethlen won the loyalty of Levoča to his cause by requisitioning the boots for his soldiers from the town, so too had Thököly's court won converts within the craft guilds of Kežmarok by its positive influence on the handicraft sector of the urban economy.

Imre Thököly (1657–1705) was born at a critical time in both the history of the town and that of his family. His father had reached a compromise with the municipal government and no longer opposed the town's attempt to establish royal free standing. The relationship between the town and its castle lords had never been better. Yet just as the town's life had normalized, the world was turned upside down. István Thököly, the father of Imre, became involved in a conspiracy leading Magyar noble families against the Habsburg court. Before the plans could be put into action, Leopold I discovered the plot, and arrested the ringleaders. István Thököly was never caught, as he died in 1670 in his Arva County castle while under siege by the forces of Leopold I. All other leaders of this conspiracy were beheaded. Imre Thököly was therefore orphaned at the age of 13, having lost his mother when he was still an infant. At this point the young Thököly came under the protection of Mihály Apafi, the Prince of Transylvania. Apafi had grand hopes for the young Thököly and, even before the death of his father, had appointed him the Count of Máramaros County. After the death of his father, Imre Thököly emerged as the natural leader of the disgruntled Magyar nobility. He won converts by fiery speeches in the name of freedom, and led his first attack in 1678, the year Leopold I suspended the key elements of the Hungarian Constitution. Apafi continued to be the Prince of Transylvania, but Thököly was expected to be crowned king of Hungary in the event of his victory over the Habsburgs.

An interesting seventeenth-century account of Thököly is by Jean Le Clerk, *Memoirs of Emeric Count Teckely . . . Wherein are related all the most considerable transactions in Hungary and the Ottoman Empire, from his birth, anno 1656, till after the battel of Salankement, in the 1691,* (Translated from French) (London: T. Goodwin, 1693). On the Thököly family look to: Dávid Angyal, *Késmárki Thököly Imre, 1657–1705* (Emmerich Thököly 1657–1705, from Kežmarok) 2 vols. (Budapest: Mühner V., 1888–1889); Győző Bruckner, "Késmárk és a Thököly család" (Kežmarok and the Thököly family), *Közlemények Szepes Vármegye Múltjából,* (1909): 23–76;

19. *The Seat of the War in Hungary Between the Emperor and the Turks; being an historical and geographical account of the ancient Kingdom of Hungary, and provinces adjoining to it, viz. Croatia, Sclavonia, Transilvania, Moldavia, Walachia, Servia, and Bulgaria,* (London: Printed for A. Bettesworth, 1717). For a first hand account of the retaking of Buda, see *An historical description of the glorious conquest of the city of Buda: the capital city of the kingdom of Hungary, by the victorious arms of the thrice illustrious and invincible Emperor Leopold I. Under the conduct of His Most Serene Highness, the Duke of Lorraine, and the Elector of Bavaria,* (Licensed, October 1st 1686, R. L'Estrange; London: Printed for Robert Clavell, 1686). Another eyewitness account in English is: *A true and exact relation of the imperial expedition in Hungaria, in the year 1684. Wherein is contained an impartial and full account of the siege and defence of the city of Buda. As also, the most remarkable actions from day to day of the Elector of Bavaria* (Collected and brought together with great care by a chief military officer there; London: Printed for R. Taylor, 1685). Another interesting seventeenth-century account in English is by John Shirley (1680–1702), *The History of the Wars of Hungary* (London: Printed by T. M. for W. Whitwood, 1685).

20. *The seat of the war in Hungary between the Emperor and the Turks,* 190–208.

21. Ibid., 218–224.

22. This argument is made by Ágnes R. Várkonyi in *Historical Personality, Crisis and Progress in 17th Century Hungary* (Budapest: Akadémiai Kiadó, 1970). Várkonyi, of course, is not alone. Hungarian historiography is filled with the potentials that never became reality. But in the work Várkonyi aggressively tries to argue that Rákóczi understood all the necessities of modern state building, and it was the Habsburgs that derailed the natural progression of Hungary's historical evolution. I am not sure if the problem here is an underestimation of the importance of individuals like Locke, and the uniqueness of English development, or an overestimation of individuals like Ferenc Rákóczi II. Maybe a little bit of both. Also look to: Béla Köpeczi, *Függetlenség és haladás: politikai gondolkodás a régi magyar függetlenségi harcok századaiban* [Battle for independence and progress: the political thoughts of the old Magyar independence wars] (Budapest: Szépirod. Kiadó, 1977). Béla Köpeczi, *II. Rákóczi Ferenc az államférfi és az író* [Ferenc Rákóczi, the statesman and writer] (Budapest: Magvető, 1976). For the counterpoint argument, look at Gyula Szekfű *Mit vétettem én? Ki gyalázza Rákóczit?* (Budapest: Dick M. [19]) This work argues that Ferenc Rákóczi II did not understand all that was involved in modern state-building.

23. Perry Anderson, *Lineages of the Absolutist State*, (London: New Left Books, 1974), 195.

24. *Magyarország népessége a Pragmatica Sanctio korában 1720–21* [Hungary's population during the time of the Pragmatic Sanction] (Budapest: Magyar Királyi Statisztikai Hivatal, 1896).

25. The eight royal free towns of Transylvania with their estimated population in parenthesis in 1720 were: Alba Iulia (3,481), Braşov (16,816), Bistriţa (5,307), Cluj-Napoca (10,472), Madiaş (4,328), Sibiu (10,116), Sighişoara (5,579), and Tîrgu Mureş (5,041).

26. In Hont County it was the towns of Banská Belá, Banská Štiavnica and Pukanec, and in Zvolen County it was the towns of Banská Bystrica, Brezno, Korpona, L'ubietová, and Zvolen.

27. Rácz, István. *Városlakó nemesek az Alföldön 1514–1848 között* [Urbanized nobles of the plains between 1514–1848]. (Budapest: Akadémiai Kiadó, 1988), 85–86.

28. Ibid., 188.

29. Ibid., 175.

30. Ibid., 191.

31. Ibid., 247.

32. For the 1720's statistics look at *Magyarország népessége a Pragmatica Sanctio Korában, 1720–21* and for the statistics after 1780, look at *Az Első Magyarországi Népszámlálás 1784–1787* [The first Hungarian census 1784–1787] (Budapest: Statisztikai Hivatal, 1960).

33. Henrik Marczali, *Magyarország története II. József korában* [The history of Hungary in the age of Joseph II] 3 vols. (Budapest: Magyar Tudományos Akadémia Könyvkiadó-Hivatal, 1882–1888), 1: 193; see also Éva H. Balázs, *Hungary and the Habsburgs 1765–1800* (Budapest: CEU Press, 1997), 125.

34. Martin Schwartner, *Statistik des Königreichs Ungarn* (Pest: Gedruckt bey M. Trattner, 1798).

35. Kálmán Benda, "Az udvar és uralkodó osztály szövetsége a forradalom ellen 1795–1812," [The Court and the ruling classes' alliance against the revolution 1795–1812], in Gyula Mérei eds., *Magyarország története 1790–1848* [History of Hungary 1790–1848] (Budapest: Akadémiai Kiadó, 1980), 425–472: see 435–436.
36. Look to K. Benda, "A magyar nemesi mozgalom 1790–1792," [The Magyar noble movement 1790–1792], in Gyula Mérei eds., *Magyarország története 1790–1848*, 71; Domokos Kosáry, *Művelődés a XVIII. századi Magyarországon* [Culture and society in eighteenth-century Hungary] (Budapest: Akadémiai Kiadó, 1996).

5 Enlightenment from the Towns

1. Hóman, Balint and Gyula Szekfű, *Magyar történet* [History of Hungary]. 5 vols. (Budapest: Királyi Magyar Egyetemi Nyomda, 1935–1936), 5: 24–25.
2. Ibid.
3. Ibid., 26.
4. Norbert Elias did not think that the court everywhere played a similar role. In Prussia, with its younger and less established court, the Civilizing Process worked distinctly different than in France and the Habsburg Monarchy, which housed the two most illustrious courts of Europe in Versailles and Vienna, respectively. See Norbert Elias "Excurses on some differences in the paths of development of Britain, France and Germany," in Norbert Elias, *The Civilizing Process*, Edmund Jephcott translation (Oxford [England]; Cambridge, MA: Blackwell, ca.1994), 339–345. See also Norbert Elias, "Dueling and membership of the imperial ruling class: Demanding and giving satisfaction," in N. Elias, *The Germans*, (New York: Columbia University Press, 1996); George Barany, "Hoping against hope: The Enlightenment age in Hungary," in American Historical Review, no. 2 (1971), 319–357. Éva H. Balázs, *Berzeviczy Gergely. A reformpolitikus 1763–1795* [Gergely Berzeviczy, the reform politician] (Budapest: Akadémiai Kiadó, 1967); Moritz Csáky, *Von der Aufklärung zum Liberalismus: Studien zum Frühliberalismus in Ungarn* (Wien: Verlag der Österreichischen Akademie der Wissenschaften, 1981); Domokos Kosáry, *Művelődés a XVIII. századi Magyarországon* [Culture and society in eighteenth century Hungary] (Budapest: Akadémiai Kiadó, 1996).
   Or as Robert Kann noted, historians should be critical toward how progressive the Habsburg court really was. Kann wrote:
   "The identification of Josephine trends of thought with liberalism is a clear distortion of historical truths, however unintentional. Neither its deeds nor, what is more important, its objectives show any major trends in Josephinism indicating a greater concern with the interest of the individual as such or with even very modest steps in the direction of self-government. Quite the reverse. Josephine reforms, with their glorification of the state, its power, and its expansion, implicitly exclude respect for individual interests as a primary objective of government . . . even more clearly than [under] Maria Theresa's

regime, genuine Josephinism stood for unlimited absolutism and against the very poor kind of existing representative institutions."

Robert Kann was referring specifically to J. Bibl's right-wing work in praise of Joseph II published in 1943 (Vienna) under the title *Kaiser Joseph II: Ein Vorkämpfer der deutschen Idee*—and concludes by stating: "Thus it is no wonder that modern totalitarianism from both the right and the left has claimed a deeply rooted relationship with Josephinism. While the Communist left cautiously praises Joseph as a kind of forerunner of the idea of 'people's democracy,' National Socialism is far more outspoken in this respect and considers Joseph as a veritable party member." Robert Kann, *A study in Austrian Intellectual History* (New York: Frederick A. Praeger, 1960), 143.

5. Károly Vörös, "A magyaroszági társadalom 1790–1848" [Hungarian society 1790–1848] in Gyula Mérei and Károly Vörös eds., *Magyarország története 1790–1848* [History of Hungary 1790–1848] 2 vols. (Budapest: Akadémiai Kiadó, 1980), 1: 486.

6. Vörös, "A magyaroszági társadalom," 487–491; the best work on this topic is István Rácz's *Városlakó nemesek az Alföldön 1541–1848 között*, [Urbanized nobles of the Plains between 1541–1848] (Budapest: Akadémiai Kiadó, 1988).

7. These are my estimates based on work I did in the Hungarian National Statistics Bureau.

8. Karl Mannheim, *Ideologie und utopie* (Bonn: F. Cohen, 1929).

9. Benda, "A magyar nemesi mozgalom 1790–1791," Gyula Mérei and Károly Vörös eds., *Magyarország története 1790–1848* [History of Hungary 1790–1848] 2 vols. (Budapest: Akadémiai Kiadó, 1980), 1: 65.

10. Mention should here be made of Matthias Bél, who was a colleague of Benczúr and also played a critical role in the spread of the Enlightenment. The Slovak historian Eva Kowalska is currently working on his much anticipated biography.

11. Kosáry, *Művelődés a XVIII. századi Magyarországon*, 296; Balázs, *Berzeviczy Gergely*, 44–46.

12. City Archive of Košice, KK Schneider 1–3. 1586–1675.

13. György Kerekes, *A kassai kereskedők életéről 1687–1913* [The life of the Košice merchants] (Budapest: Felsőmagyarországi Nyomda, 1913); see also Kerekes, *Bepillantás Kassa régi céhéletébe 1597–1647* [A look at the history of the early Merchant's Guild of Košice, 1597–1647] (Budapest: Lampel Franklin, 1912).

14. Municipal Archive of Prešov. Auditorium Mathias Bongat Judicy, June 27, 1687.

15. "Okolicsányi Family," in Iván Nagy, *Magyarország családai*, [Encyclopedia of Hungarian families] 12 vols. (Pest: Kiadja I. Friebeisz, 1857–1865).

16. Hóman and Szekfű, *Magyar történet* [History of Hungary]. 5 vols. (Budapest: Királyi Magyar Egyetemi Nymoda, 1985), 4: 226.

17. Johann Schneider, *Definitiones propositiones Wolffinae*, (Lomnicz, 1769).

18. Balázs, *Berzeviczy Gergely. A reformpolitikus 1763–1795*.

19. Balázs, *Hungary and the Habsburgs 1765–1800*, 23.

20. Kálmán Demkó, *Lőcse története* [History of Levoča] (Lőcse: Reiss Nyomda, 1897).

21. Ödön Szelényi, "Johann Genersich 1761–1823. Egy szepesi pedagógus" [Johann Genersich 1761–1823. A Zipser pedagogue], *Közlemények Szepes Vármegye Múltjából* (1914), 1–74; and 113–140.

22. Ibid.

23. Benda, "A magyar nemesi mozgalom 1790–1791," 59.

24. Johann Lipták, *Geschichte des evangelische Lyceum in Käsmarkt* (Käsmarkt: Lyzealpatronat, 1933). István Palcsó, *A késmárki ágostai hitvallású evangélikus kerületi Lyceum története* [History of the Lutheran Lyceum in Kežmarok] (Késmárk: Sauter Nyomda, 1898). The leading expert on this question today is Eva Kowalská. Look to E. Kowalská, "Das volkschulwesen und die Gestaltung der Bildung in den Städten der Slowakei im 18. Jahrhundert," *Studia Historica Slovaca* XVII (1990), 125–152.

25. Ödön Szelényi, "Johann Genersich 1761–1823: Egy szepesi pedagógus", 1–74, 113–140.

26. Johann Bernhard Basedow (1720–1790) died in Magdenburg, where he remained a radical to the end. In the 1780s, he proposed to Frederick the Great the idea that the State should nationalize the baking of bread, and on different days bread should be baked in the form of different letters of the alphabet. In this way, at the cheapest expense the state could familiarize the lower classes with the alphabet and help them develop literacy skills.

27. Ödön Szelényi, "Johann Genersich 1761–1823."

28. Ibid.

29. District Archive of Levoča. Sz Podzupan Koresp. Horváth Stansith. Liedemann Martin 1795–1798.

30. Benedict Anderson, *Imagined Communities: Reflections on the Origin and Spread of Nationalism* (London: Verso, 1983); Ernest Gellner, *Nations and Nationalism* (Ithaca, NY: Cornell University Press, 1983).

31. Vera Bácskai, *A vállalkozók előfutárai* [Early entrepreneurs] (Budapest: Magvető, 1989), 62–64.

32. Jakab Pólya, *A pesti polgári kereskedelmi testület* [The Pest burgher commercial association] (Budapest: 1896).

33. Ibid., 215.

34. Benda, "A magyar nemesi mozgalom 1790–1792," 71.

35. Alexis de Tocqueville, *The Old Régime and the French Revolution*, Stuart Gilbert translation (New York: Doubleday, 1983), 1.

36. *Babel. Fragmente über die jetzigen politischen Angelegenheiten in Ungarn* (1790); *Ninive. Fortgesetzte Fragmente über die dermaligen politischen Angelegenheiten in Ungarn* (1790); see also Kálmán Benda, "A magyar nemesi mozgalom 1790–1791," 65.

37. Ernst Wangermann, *From Joseph II to the Jacobin Trials* (London: Oxford University Press, 1969), 87.

38. "A parasztság az uralkodóhoz fog folyamodni, hogy a következő országgyűlésen saját követei révén adhassa elő jogos sérelmeit. Nem kétséges hogy a király teljesiteni fogja ezt a szerény kérést." Benda, "A magyar nemesi mozgalom 1790–1791," 69.

39. Benda, "A magyar nemesi mozgalom (1790–1792)," 110.

40. Wangermann, *From Joseph II to the Jacobin Trials*, 89.

41. Walter Consuelo Langsam, "Emperor Francis II and the Austrian Jacobins, 1792–1796," *American History Review* 50 (April, 1945): 471–490.

42. Wangermann, *From Joseph II to the Jacobin Trials*, 111.

43. Langsam, "Emperor Francis II and the Austrian Jacobins, 1792–1796," 471.

44. The exception being Serbian and Croatian nationalism, both of which advanced quickly from the academic nationalism of the 1760s into a militant nationalism by 1790.

45. Martinovics's Testimony under interrogation can be found in the appendix of: Vilmos Fraknói, *Martinovics Élete* [The life of Martinovics] (Budapest: Athenaeum, 1921), specifically 245–281. As Martinovics explained under interrogation in 1794, he was a professor in Lviv (Lemberg/Lwów) in 1791, after which time he moved to Vienna and met with Leopold II: "In Lwów I was appointed Professor of Physics and Engineering at the University, a post I held until 1791. I then moved to Vienna, where I applied for the position, newly made available, of advisor to mining in Banská Štiavnica (Schemnitz/Selmecbánya). It was at this time that my fellow countryman Gotthardi, government minister, arranged for a meeting with Emperor Leopold II, who had in the meantime heard of my reputation as a chemist through a Cannon from Volta Mantua (who happened to be in Vienna in 1791) and Born, an advisor at court. Leopold shortly thereafter awarded me a stipend of 2,000 Forints and title of court chemist. This office brought me into frequent contact with his Emperor, who inquired—because I had traveled in Italy, France and England—about my acquaintances abroad, and whether or not I would be interested in writing to them, and collecting information on the functioning of secret societies in foreign lands as well as in Austria. I reported that I was a member of Learned Societies in Paris, Dijon, Dublin, Haarlem, St. Petersburg, and Munich. Further, I was in correspondence with Marquis Condorce, the Dublin Chemistry Professor De Morbeau—who at that time was a member of the National Convent under the pseudonym Guiton—the philosopher Pristley in Birmingham, and with Sir Landriani in London. At this point his Emperor requested that I gather as much information as I can on political questions, and to portray myself as a democrat."

46. Ignác Martinovics, "An Open letter to the Emperor and King of Hungary." (1792), translated by Margaret C. Ives, and printed in Margaret Ives, *Enlightenment and National Revival* (University Microfilms International, Ann Arbor, 1979), 235–245. I translate Martinovics's word "nyílt" as "public" instead of the more direct translation of "open" used by Dr. Ives. Instead of the "Open Letter," therefore, I use the phrase "Public Letter."

47. Ives, *Enlightenment and National Revival*, 244–245.

48. Henrik Marczali, *Az 1790/1 országgyűlés* [National Diet of 1790/91] (Budapest: Magyar Tudományos Akadémia, 1907).

49. Szekfű, *Magyar történet*, 5: 33; Kosáry, *Művelődés*, 302; see also Lajos Némedi, "Bessenyei György és a magyar művelődés," [György Bessenyei and Hungarian culture] *Valóság*, (1958), 60–78.

50. György Bessenyei, "Magyar Országnak Törvényes Állása" [The legal-administrative position of Hungary] (1804), in *Bessenyei György: Prózai Munkák* (Budapest: Akadémiai Kiadó, 1986), 292.

51. Bessenyei, *Bessenyei György: Prózai Munkák*, 270.
52. Fraknói, *Martinovics Élete*, 256. Martinovics made this clear under interrogation in 1794. According to his testimony of August 13th, Martinovics claimed: "I came to the conclusion, that in order to reform the state, Hungary must become independent. To accomplish this goal I went about organizing two secret societies, the purpose of which was to prepare the public for a revolution. In the first, called the Society of Reformers, membership was limited to nobles and poorer magnates. The second was called the Society of Equality and Liberty. In the summer of last year [1793] the leader of the Society of Reformers was the economic professor Gyurkovics. In May of last year [1793] I became the leader of the Society of Equality and Liberty. After the death of Gyurkovics, I became the leader of both groups. The goal of the Society of Reformers was to establish a two chamber parliamentary republic. The Society of Equality and Liberty was to support this endeavor. We hoped that the Society of Reformers would attract the county civil servants with the promise that they could keep their titles of nobility. All those in the Society of Equality and Liberty could become members of the Society of Reformers, but those who were members of the Society of Reformers were forbidden to know of the existence of the Society of Equality and Liberty."

During his testimony Martinovics also confessed to the reasons that compelled him to become a revolutionary: "My reasons are the following. When I became an advisor to the late emperor Leopold II, and worked my hardest to secure the interests of the state, his Excellency promised that I would be appointed a proper cabinet secretary position in the royal ministry. This was important to me because I had become accustomed to life at court, of influencing public policy and working for the prosperity and well being of the state. I tried to win favor with the new emperor when he came to power, and hoped the post promised to me by his emperor Leopold II would be given to me. However, I had no success. I was further disappointed when his Excellency [Francis I], misled by new advisors, began discussions once more about my possible expulsion from the Church. This issue had already been discussed and dismissed by Joseph II, but was again brought up. Not only did the new emperor stop paying my retirement, but he also unleashed the Magyar clerics who again began their persecution of me. Upon my request the issue was taken to the highest court, which judged in my favor. His Excellency then promised that my endowment from the Szászváry Abbey would be given to me gratis. Yet even though his Excellency signaled his intension three times, I had to pay a 500 Forint fine, and I was completely broke. Later his Excellency promised to pay me 1,000 Forints for my services to the state. But 500 Forints he paid through the Lwow (Lemberg) Camera cashier, which produced the impression that I collected this money through some scrupulous work. It damaged my dignity. [. . .] Count Pergen, the Police Commissioner to whom I had sent my reports, intervened and submitted a proposal recommending me for employment. But this endeavor drifted nowhere. The idea arose in me then, especially in relation to the clergy and state bureaucracy, to bring about a reform of the government." Fraknói, *Martinovics Élete*, 255.

53. Kálmán Benda, *A Magyar Jakobinusok iratai* [The Writings of the Hungarian Jacobins] 3 vols. (Budapest: Akadémiai Kiadó, 1952) 2: 67.
54. Benda, "A magyar Jakobinus mozgalom [The Hungarian Jacobin Movement], in Mérei and Vörös eds., *Magyarország története 1790–1848*, 1: 194–195.
55. The historian Paul Bernard summarized Hebenstreit's planned revolution in Vienna, as reported by Degen to Police Commissioner Pergen, the following way: "[Hebenstreit claimed that] what was required was a coup d'éclat in Vienna, and possibly in Prague. Those prepared to carry this out—some thirty-five hundred men would be needed— must be recruited among the craft journeymen and day laborers in the capital's various cheap taverns and dives. Such folk, when presented with a dilemma, had only one reaction, smashing in heads, and this must be taken advantage of by the students and theoreticians. As for what needed to be done, [Hebenstreit] was of the opinion that one must begin by burying sharpened iron bars, spears, scythes and pitchforks in various locations around the capital. Some evening, acting upon an agreed signal, the revolutionary army would unearth these weapons, massacre the night watch, prevent the troops stationed in the city from coming out of the garrisons (the cavalry and artillery units, Hebenstreit added, would in all probability support the uprising in any case), lay their hands on various government treasuries, kill some three hundred aristocrats along with their entire retinues, and physically take hold of the emperor, who would be forced to put his signature on several dozen cartes blanches, to be used in implementing various revolutionary aims, after which he would also be . . . Only then should one proceed to set up a provisional government and appeal to the provinces. Such an appeal would have to be made in the name of the emperor, and the peasantry would have to be deluded into thinking that they were following his orders. Before they could be disabused of this notion, they were to be won over to the cause of the revolution by the abolition of all manorial dues and work obligations. Anyone continuing to demand the performance of the robot was to be impaled forthwith. In order to break the habit of automatic obedience to their overlords, any peasant continuing to perform such obligations would be burned at the stake." Paul P. Bernard, *From Enlightenment to the Police State: The Public Life of Johann Anton Pergen*, (Chicago: University of Illinois Press, 1991), 213.
56. Béla Pukánszky, *Német polgárság magyar földön* [German burghers on Hungarian land] (Budapest: Franklin-Társulat, 1940), 5.

6   The Challenges of Ethnic Nationalism

1. Kálmán Benda, "Az udvar és az uralkodó osztály szövetsége a forradalom ellen" [The alliance of the court and ruling classes against the revolution] in Gyula Mérei and Károly Vörös eds., *Magyarország története 1790–1848* [History of Hungary 1790–1848] 2 vols. (Budapest: Akadémiai Kiadó, 1980), 1: 439.
2. László Katus, "A népesedés és a társadalmiszerkezet változásai," [Population and social structural transformation] in Endre Kovács and László Katus eds.,

Magyarország története 1848–1890, [History of Hungary 1848–1890] 2 vols. (Budapest: Akadémiai Kiadó, 1987), 2: 1149.

3. George Barany, *Stephen Széchenyi and the Awakening of Hungarian Nationalism 1791–1841* (Princeton, NJ: Princeton University Press, 1968), 157.

4. Ernest Gellner, *Nations and Nationalism*, (Ithaca, NY: Cornell Univerity Press, 1983).

5. Ibid., 61.

6. Benedict Anderson, *Imagined communities* (New York: Verso, 1991).

7. Hungarian National Library, Manuscript Collection, Letters of Karl Rumy.

8. Pukánszky, *Német polgárság magyar földön* [German burghers on Hungarian land] (Budapest: Franklin-Társulat, 1940), 22.

9. George Barany, "Hoping against Hope: The Enlightened Age in Hungary," *American Historical Review*, 76, (2, 1971), 319–357: see 346.

10. Moritz Csáky writes in relation to the quote from Magda: "In spite of such warnings, the situation after the Ausgleich of 1867, was characterized by limitation, assimilation, and rigorous Magyarization measures, and the final result was the disintegration of the multicultural kingdom;" see Moritz Csáky and Elena Mannová, *Collective Identities in Central Europe in Modern Times* (Bratislava: Institute of History of the Slovak Academy, 1999), 13.

11. George Barany, "Hoping against Hope: The Enlightened Age in Hungary," 339.

12. Ibid., 339; see György Bessenyei, *Magyarság*, [Magyardom] (Vienna, 1779).

13. Pukánszky, *Német polgárság magyar földön*, 12.

14. Ibid., 76.

15. Iibid., 143.

16. This diary is in my personal possession.

17. Béla Pukánszky, *Német polgárság magyar földön*, 143.

18. Ambrus Miskolczy, "A szászok német nemzeti ébredese," [The awakening of the Saxons' German nationalism] in Zoltán Szász ed., *Erdély története* [History of Transylvania] 3 vols. (Budapest: Akadémiai Kiadó 1986), 3: 1329.

19. Kálmán Benda, "A magyar nemesi mozgalom 1790–1792,"[The magyar noble movement 1790–1792]. In *Magyarország története 1790–1848* [History of Hungary 1790–1848], edited by Gyula Mérei and Károly Vörös, 29–117 (Budapest: Akadémiai Kiadó, 1980), 79; see also Sámuel Décsy, *Pannóniai féniksz avagy a hamvából feltámadott Magyar nyelv* [Pannonian Phoenix or the rise of the Magyar language from the ashes] (Vienna, 1790).

20. George Barany, "Hoping against Hope," 348.

21. Béla G. Németh, "Az úri középosztály történetének egy dokumentuma: Herczeg Ferenc emlékezései," [A document in the history of the gentleman middle class: Ferenc Herczeg's memoirs], in Ferenc Herczeg ed., *Emlékezések* (Memoirs), (Budapest: Szépirodalmi Könyvkiado, 1985), 5–32; see 11–12.

22. S. Münnich, *Igló királyi korona és bányaváros története* [The history of the royal and mining town of Spišska Nová Ves] (Iglo, 1895], 468–69.

23. *Zipser Anzieger*, 1863 no. 1, January 3.

24. *Zipser Anzieger*, 1863 no. 16, April 18.

25. Elek Fényes, *A magyar birodalom nemzetiségei* [The nationalities of the Hungarian Kingdom] (Pest: Eggenberger és Társai, 1867), 35.

26. Mihály Horváth, *Polgárosodás, liberalizmus, függetlenségi harc. Válogatott írások* [Embourgeoisement, liberalism, struggle for independence. Selected works of Mihály Horváth] (Budapest: Gondolat, 1985), 35.

27. Endre Arató, "A nemzeti ellentétek kiéleződése a polgári forradalom előtt 1840–1848," [The intensification of the nationalities conflict before the outbreak of the bourgeois revolution 1840–1848], in Gyula Mérei and Károly Vörös eds., *Magyarország története 1790–1848* [History of Hungary 1790–1848] 2 vols. (Budapest: Akadémiai Kiadó, 1980), 985.

28. Pukánszky, *Német polgárság magyar földön,* 77.

29. Domokos Kosáry, *Kossuth és a védegylet,* [Kossuth and the protection association] (Budapest: Atheneum, 1942), 25.

30. Gyula Mérei, "Magyarország gazdasága (1790–1848)," [The Hungarian economy 1790–1848] in Gyula Mérei and Károly Vörös eds., *Magyarország története 1790–1848* [History of Hungary 1790–1848] 2 vols. (Budapest: Akadémiai Kiadó, 1980), 1: 213–323; Péter Hanák, "The Bourgeoisification of the Hungarian Nobility—Reality and Utopia in the 19th Century," in Domokos Kosáry ed., *Etudes historiques hongroises 1985* (Budapest: Akadémiai Kiadó, 1985), 403–421.

31. Domokos Kosáry, *Kossuth Lajos a reformkorban* [Louis Kossuth in the Reform Period] (Budapest: Antiqua, 1946), 229–230; Hanák, "The Bourgeoisification of the Hungarian Nobility," 407.

32. Hanák, "The Bourgeoisification of the Hungarian Nobility," 407.

33. Ibid., 2: 1194–1195.

34. Németh, "Az úri középosztály," 18.

35. A. C. Janos, *The Politics of Backwardness in Hungary, 1825–1945* (Princeton, N.J.: Princeton University Press, 1982), 94.

36. Kálmán Mikszáth, *A Noszty fiú esete Tóth Marival,* [The Young Noszti's Affair with Mária Tóth] (Budapest: Szépirodalmi Könyvkiadó, 1968), 432.

37. Mikszáth, *A Noszty fiú esete Tóth Marival,* 325.

38. Katus, "A népesedés és a társadalmiszerkezet változásai," 1140.

39. Lajos Nagy, "Budapest története 1790–1848," in Lajos Nagy eds., *Budapest története III* [History of Budapest III] (Budapest: Akadémiai Kiadó, 1975), 398–399.

40. Károly Vörös, "A fővárostól a székesfővárosig 1873–1896," [From Capital to Royal Capital] in Károly Vörös ed., *Budapest története IV* [History of Budapest IV] (Budapest: Akadémiai Kiadó, 1978), 452–453.

41. Katus, "A népesedés és a társadalmiszerkezet változásai," 1157.

42. Viktor Karády, "Zsidóság és modernizáció a történelmi Magyarországon" [Jews and Modernization in Historic Hungary], in Viktor Karády ed., *Zsidóság és társadalmi egyenlőtlenség (1867–1945)* [Jews and Social Inequality 1867–1945] (Budapest: Replika, 2000), 7–41: see 24.

43. Viktor Karády, "Az asszimiláció Szegeden: szociológiai kérdésvázlat," [Assimilation in Szeged: A sociological inquiry], in Viktor Karády ed., *Zsidóság és társadalmi egyenlőtlenség (1867–1945),* 77–78.

44. Ibid.

45. John Lukacs, *The Historical Portrait of Budapest 1900* (New York: Grove Weidenfeld, 1988), 126.

46. Ibid., 127.
47. Pukánszky, *Német polgárság magyar földön*, 110–112.
48. *Szepesi Hírnök*, May 27, 1882.

7   Conclusion: The Failed Bourgeoisie?

1. Lothar Gall, *Bürgertum in Deutschland* (Berlin: Siedler Verlag, 1989), 17. Mommsen wrote: "I have never had political influence, nor aimed at it. But in my innermost self, and I believe with what is best in me, I have always been an *animal politicum*, and wished to be a citizen. That is not possible in our nation; even the best among us never rises above doing his duty in the ranks and treating political authority like a fetish (*politischen Fetischismus*). This rift between my inner self and the people to whom I belong has firmly and consistently determined me to appear as little as possible as a person before the German public, for which I have no respect." Theodore Mommsen, "Last Wishes, 1899," *Past and Present*, no. 1 (February 1952): 71.
2. Translated and quoted in Karin Kaudelka-Hanisch: "The Titled Businessman: Prussian Commercial Councilors in the Rhineland and Westphalia during the Nineteenth Century," in David Blackbourn and Richard J. Evans, *The German Bourgeoisie* (London; New York: Routledge, 1991), 87–114: see 87.
3. Quoted in Ralph Dahrendorf, *Society and Democracy in Germany* (New York: Norton, 1967), 50. As Don Martindale noted: "[For Weber] Prussia's policies were determined by the attempt to keep the city and its bourgeoisie under political control while political dominance—in the state, the administration, and the highest ranks of the army—was in the hands of the rural aristocrats (the Junkers). Thus he thought that while in other western European lands and the United States urban types had the major voice in the affairs of the nation, in Germany the city man was peculiarly deprived of political responsibility." (Don Martindale, "Prefatory Remarks: The Theory of the City," in Max Weber, *The City*, Don Martindale and Gertrud Neuwirth translation (New York: Free Press, 1966), 36. Or as Reinhard Bendix noted: "[As] a member of the middle class [Weber] inquired into the sources of the collectivism and rationality that prompted English and Hanseatic stockbrokers to impose an ethic of trade upon themselves—a practice that stood in marked contrast to the aping of aristocratic ways among his compatriots." Bendix, *Max Weber: An Intellectual Portrait* (Berkeley: University of California Press, 1977), 48.
4. Geoff Eley, "Liberalism, Europe, and the Bourgeoisie 1860–1914," in Blackbourn and Evans, *The German Bourgeoisie*, 293–317: see 293.
5. François Furet, *Marx and the French Revolution*, Deborah Kan Furet translation (Chicago: University of Chicago Press, 1988), 8.
6. Friedrich Meinecke, *Cosmopolitanism and the National State*, Robert B. Kimber translation (Princeton, NJ: Princeton University Press, 1970), 376.
7. Georg G. Iggers, *New Directions in European Historiography* (Middletown, CT: Wesleyan University Press; Scranton, PA: Distributed by Harper & Row, 1984), 87.

8. Ibid., 97.

9. Friedrich Meinecke, *The German Catastrophe*, Sidney B. Fay translation (Cambridge: Harvard University Press, 1950), 12.

10. Francis L. Carsten, "Medieval Democracy in the Brandenburg Towns and its Defeat in the Fifteenth Century," 90; see also Francis L. Carsten, *The Origins of Prussia* (Oxford: Clarendon Press, 1954), 276.

11. Carsten, *The Origins of Prussia*, 276. Carsten understood his theory to apply to all of Eastern Europe, including Hungary. He wrote: "In spite of wide differences of historical development between Mecklenburg, Pomerania, Brandenburg, Prussia, Poland, Bohemia, Moravia, Hungary, Russia, and the Baltic states, one basic fact applied to all of them: the nobility remained the ruling class, and an urban middle class did not come into being until the later nineteenth century."

12. Kálmán Demkó, *Lőcse története* [History of Levoča] (Lőcse: Reiss Nyomda, 1897), 269.

13. György Granasztói, *A középkori magyar város* [The medieval Hungarian town] (Budapest: Gondolat 1980), 158–159.

14. Jenő Szűcs, "Vázlatok Európa három történeti régiójáról" [Outline of the three historical regions of Europe], in Éva Ring ed., *Helyünk Európában* [Our Place in Europe] 2 vols. (Budapest: Magvető, 1986), 2: 541.

15. Geoff Eley, *From Unification to Nazism* (New York: Routledge, 1992), 12.

16. Ibid., 276.

17. Robert Brenner, "Agrarian Class Structure and Economic Development in Pre-industrial Europe," *Past and Present*, no. 70 (February, 1976).

18. Jenő Szűcs, "Vázlatok Európa három történeti régiójáról," 541.

19. Gyula Szekfű, *Három nemzedék* [Three Generations] (Budapest: Királyi Magyar Egyetemi Nyomda, 1922), 95.

20. Thomas Bender, "Strategies of Narrative Synthesis in American History," *American Historical Review* 107, (February, 2002): 129.

21. István Deák, "Historiography of the Countries of Eastern Europe: Hungary," *American Historical Review* 97 (October, 1992), 1041–1063: see 1042.

22. Ralf Dahrendorf, *Society and Democracy in Germany* (New York: Norton, 1967), 49.

23. As Trevor-Roper put it: "Deserted by the king from whom they had once hoped so much; deserted by their aristocratic patrons; kept from lucrative employment by the rising prices and growing heredity of the offices they coveted; crushed beneath increased burdens of feudal taxation to sustain a lavish and enlarged court from which they were themselves excluded; threatened by the revival of economic gains by the church; debarred by the outbreak of peace, from other opportunities of investment to which they had become accustomed; no wonder if the mere gentry felt themselves betrayed under James I. Naturally they became radical in their politics. Their spokesmen began to speak violently about the aristocracy who had abandoned them." Trevor-Roper, *The Gentry 1540–1640* (London: Published for the Economic History Society by Cambridge University Press, 1953), 38. Important contributions to the English question have been published by Geoff Eley and William Hunt eds., *Reviving the English Revolution*, (London; New York: Verso, 1988), which are reflections on the work of Christopher Hill.

24. Perry Anderson, "The Notion of Bourgeois Revolution," in Perry Anderson ed., *English Questions* (London: Verso, 1992), 105–118: see 109.

25. See the very insightful edited book on the contribution of Christopher Hill, by Geoff Eley and William Hunt, *Reviving the English Revolution* (London; New York: Verso, 1988).

26. David Blackbourn, *Populists and Patricians: Essays in Modern German History* (London; Boston: Allen & Unwin, 1987), 74.

27. Jürgen Kocka, "The European Pattern and the German Case," in: Jürgen Kocka and Allen Mitchell eds., *Bourgeois Society in Nineteenth-Century Europe* (Oxford; Providence: Berg, 1993), 3–40: see 25–26.

28. Ibid., 32.

29. For the Hungarian literature on the bourgeoisie in English look to: Ivan Berend, *History Derailed* (Berkeley: University of California Press, 2003); Ferenc Erdei, *Selected Writings* (Budapest: Akadémiai Kiadó, 1988); András Gerő, *Modern Hungarian Society in the Making*, (Budapest: Central European University Press, 1995); Péter Hanák, *The Garden and the Workshop* (Princeton, NJ: Princeton University Press, 1998); Viktor Karády, *The Jews of Europe in the Modern Era* (Budapest: Central European University, 2004); Mária Kovács, *Liberal Professions and Illiberal Politics* (Washington, DC: Woodrow Wilson Center Press; New York: Oxford University Press, 1994).

30. A. C. Janos, *The Politics of Backwardness, 1825–1945* (Princeton, NJ: Princeton University Press, 1982), 112.

31. Mária Kovács, *Liberal Professions* (1994), 19. Kovács also noted on page 17: "By the turn of the century, an astonishing 56 percent of medical students, nearly half of the engineers, and a third of all private lawyers came from Jewish families. Jews constituted the single largest ethnic component of both the medical and the engineering professions."

32. Gábor Gyáni and György Kövér, *Magyarország társadalomtörténete a második világháborúig* [History of Hungarian Society up to World War Two] (Budapest: Osiris, 1998).

33. The new view of dueling was developed by Ute Frevert. Look to Frevert, "Bourgeois Honour: Middle-Class Duelists in Germany from the Late Eighteenth to the Early Twentieth Century," in Blackbourn and Evans eds., *The German Bourgeoisie*, 255–292.

34. Hanák, "The Bourgeoisification of the Hungarian Nobility."

35. Hanák, "*The Garden and the Workshop*; Berend, *History Derailed*; Kovács, *Liberal Professions and Illiberal Politics*; Viktor Karády, *The Jews of Europe in the Modern Era*.

36. Janos, *The Politics of Backwardness*, 111.

37. William O. McCagg, *Jewish Nobles and Geniuses in Modern Hungary*, (Boulder, CO: East European Quarterly; distributed by Columbia University Press, New York, 1972).

38. Karády, "Zsidóság és modernizáció a történelmi Magyarországon" [Jews and Modernization in Historic Hungary], in Viktor Karády, *Zsidóság és társadalmi egyenlőtlenség (1867–1945)*, 7–41.

39. Paul Nathan, *Der Prozess von Tisza–Eszlár* (Berlin, F. Fontane & co., 1892); Andrew Handler, *Blood Libel at Tiszaeszlar* (Boulder, CO: East European Monographs; New York: distributed by Columbia University Press, 1980).

40. Attila Pók, "Germans, Hungarians, and the Destruction of the Hungarian Jewry," in Randolph L. Braham with Scott Miller, *The Nazis' Last Victims* (Detroit: Wayne State University Press, ca.1998), 45–47.

41. Janos, *The Politics of Backwardness*, 227.

Bibliography

Anderson, Benedict. *Imagined Communities: Reflections on the Origin and Spread of Nationalism*. London: Verso, 1983.

Anderson, Perry. *Lineages of the Absolutist State*. London: New Left Books, 1974.

———. "The Notion of Bourgeois Revolution." In *English Questions*, 105–118. London: Verso, 1992.

Angyal, Dávid. *Késmárki Thököly Imre, 1657–1705* (Emmerich Thököly 1657–1705, from Kežmarok). 2 vols. Budapest: Mühner V., 1888–1889.

Arató, Endre. "A nemzeti ellentétek kiéleződése a polgári forradalom előtt 1840–1848" [The intensification of the nationalities conflict before the outbreak of the bourgeois revolution 1840–1848]. In *Magyarország története 1790–1848* [History of Hungary 1790–1848], edited by Gyula Mérei and Károly Vörös, 977–1054. Budapest: Akadémiai Kiadó, 1980.

Bácskai, Vera. *Magyar mezővárosok a XV. században* [Magyar agrarian towns in the fifteenth century]. Budapest: Akadémiai Kiadó, 1965.

———. *A vállalkozók előfutárai* [Early entrepreneurs]. Budapest: Magvető, 1989.

Balázs, Éva H. *Berzeviczy Gergely. A reformpolitikus 1763–1795* [Gergely Berzeviczy, the reform politician]. Budapest: Akadémiai Kiadó, 1967.

———. *Hungary and the Habsburgs 1765–1800*. Translated by Tim Wilkinson. Budapest: CEU Press, 1997.

Barany George. "Hoping against Hope: The Enlightenment Age in Hungary." *American Historical Review*, 2 (1971): 319–357.

Baráthová, Nora. *Kezmarský hrad*. Martin: Osveta, 1989.

Barta, Gábor ed. *Miért halt meg Zrínyi Péter? A Wesselényi-összeesküvés története* [Why did Péter Zrínyi die? The history of the Wesselényi conspiracy]. Budapest: Móra, 1986.

———. *Két tárgyalás Sztambulban: Hyeronimus Łaski tárgyalása a töröknél János király nevében, Habardanecz János jelentése 1528. nyári sztambuli tárgyalásairól* [Two conferences in Istanbul: Hyeronimus Łaski's meeting with the Turks in the name of King János; and János Habardanecz's report of his Istanbul conference in the summer of 1528]. Budapest: Balassi, 1996.

Benczédi, László. "Rendi szervezkedés és a kuruc mozgalom" [Feudal conspiracy and the Kuruc movement]. In *Magyarország története 1526–1686* [History of Hungary, 1526–1686], edited by Pál Zsigmond Pach and Ágnes R. Várkonyi, 1155–1272. Budapest: Akadémiai Kiadó, 1987.

Benda, Kálmán. "A magyar Jakobinus mozgalom," [The Hungarian Jacobin Movement]. In *Magyarország története 1790–1848* [History of Hungary 1790–1848], edited by Gyula Mérei and Károly Vörös, 159–212. Budapest: Akadémiai Kiadó, 1980.

——. *A Magyar Jakobinusok iratai* [The writings of the Hungarian Jacobins]. 3 vols. Budapest: Akadémiai Kiadó, 1952.

——. "A magyar nemesi mozgalom 1790–1792" [The Magyar noble movement 1790–1792]. In *Magyarország története 1790–1848* [History of Hungary 1790–1848], edited by Gyula Mérei and Károly Vörös, 29–117. Budapest: Akadémiai Kiadó, 1980.

——. "Az udvar és uralkodó osztály szövetsége a forradalom ellen 1795–1812" [The Court and the ruling classes' alliance against the revolution 1795–1812]. In *Magyarország története 1790–1848* [History of Hungary 1790–1848], edited by Gyula Mérei and Károly Vörös, 425–472. Budapest: Akadémiai Kiadó, 1980.

Bender, Thomas. "Strategies of Narrative Synthesis in American History." *American Historical Review* 107 (February, 2002): 129–153.

Bendix, Reinhard. *Max Weber: An Intellectual Portrait.* Berkeley: University of California Press, 1977.

Berend, Ivan T. "The Historical Evolution of Eastern Europe as a Region." In *Power, Purpose, and Collective Choice*, edited by Ellen Comisso and Laura D'Andrea Tyson, 153–170. Ithaca, NY: Cornell University Press, 1986.

——. *History Derailed.* Berkeley: University of California Press, 2003.

Bérenger, Jean. *The History of the Habsburg Empire.* Translated by C.A. Simpson. London: New York: Longman, 1994.

Bernard, Paul P. *From Enlightenment to the Police State: The Public Life of Johann Anton Pergen.* Chicago: University of Illinois Press, 1991.

Bessenyei, György. "Magyar Országnak Törvényes Állása" [The legal-administrative position of Hungary (1804)]. In *Bessenyei György: Prózai Munkák.* Budapest: Akadémiai Kiadó, 1986.

Blackbourn, David. *Populists and Patricians: Essays in Modern German History.* London; Boston, MA: Allen & Unwin, 1987.

Blackbourn, David and Richard J. Evans. *The German Bourgeoisie.* London; New York: Routledge, 1991.

Blum, Jerome. "The Rise of Serfdom in Eastern Europe." *American Historical Review* 62 (July, 1957): 807–836.

Bogucka, Maria. *Baltic Commerce and Urban Society, 1500–1700: Gdansk/Danzig and its Polish Context.* Aldershot: Ashgate Pub. Co., 2003.

——. *The Lost World of the Sarmatians.* Warszawa: Polish Academy of Sciences, Institute of History, 1996.

——. *Nicholas Copernicus.* Leon Szwajcer translation, Wrocław: Ossolínski State Publishing House, 1973.

Bramsted, Ernest Kohn. *Aristocracy and the Middle-Classes in Germany.* London: P. S. King & Sons, 1937.

Braudel, Fernand. *Civilization and Capitalism 15th–18th century: The Wheels of Commerce.* Translated by Siân Reynolds. London: Fontana Press, 1985.

Brenner, Robert. "Agrarian Class Structure and Economic Development in Pre-Industrial Europe." *Past and Present* no. 70 (February, 1976): 30–74.

Bruckner, György. *A reformáció és ellenreformáció története a Szepességben. 1520–1745* [The history of the reformation and counter-reformation in Scepius County 1520–1745]. Budapest: Szepességi Szövetség, 1922.

——. "Késmárk és a Thököly család" [Kežmarok and the Thököly family]. *Közlemények Szepes Vármegye Múltjából* (1909): 23–76.

Carsten, Francis L. "The Origins of the Junkers." *The English Historical Review* 62, no. 243 (April, 1947): 145–178.

——. "Medieval Democracy in the Brandenburg Towns and Its Defeat in the Fifteenth Century." *Transaction of the Royal Historical Society*, 4th ser. (London, 1943): 73–92.

——. *Origins of Prussia.* Oxford: Clarendon Press, 1954.

Chalupecký, Ivan. *Kežmarok.* Košice: Východoslov. vydav., 1968.

Cowan, Alexander. *The Urban Patriciate: Lübeck and Venice, 1580–1700.* Köln: Böhlau, 1986.

Csáky, Moritz. *Von der Aufklärung zum Liberalismus: Studien zum Frühliberalismus in Ungarn.* Wien: Verlag der Österreichischen Akademie der Wissenschaften, 1981.

Csáky, Moritz and Elena Mannová. *Collective Identities in Central Europe in Modern Times.* Translated by Martin Styan. Bratislava: Institute of History of the Slovak Academy, 1999.

Dahrendorf, Ralph. *Society and Democracy in Germany.* New York: Norton, 1967.

Daniel, David P. "Calvinism in Hungary: the Theological and Ecclesiastic Transition to the Reformed Faith." In *Calvinism in Europe*, edited by Andrew Pettegree, Alastair Duke and Gillian Lewis, 205– 231. Cambridge; New York: Cambridge University Press, 1994.

——. "Hungary." In *The Early Reformation in Europe*, edited by Andrew Pettegree, 49–69. Cambridge [England]; New York: Cambridge University Press, 1992.

De Vries, Jan. *European Urbanization, 1500–1800.* Cambridge, MA: Harvard University Press, 1984.

Deák, István. "Historiography of the Countries of Eastern Europe: Hungary." *American Historical Review* 97 (October, 1992): 1041–1063.

Dee, John. *A True and Faithful Relation of What Passed for Many Years Between Dr. John Dee and Some Spirits.* London: Printed by D. Maxwell for T. Garthwait, 1659.

Demkó, Kálmán. *Lőcse története* [History of Levoča]. Lőcse: Reiss Nyomda, 1897.

Divéky, Adorján. *A Lengyelországnak elzálogosított XVI szepesi város vissza-csatolása 1770-ben* [The 1770 reunification of the XVI Scepius towns mortgaged previously to Poland]. Budapest: Szepesi Szövetség, 1929.

Dobb, Maurice. "A Reply." In *The Transition from Feudalism to Capitalism*, edited by Rodney Hilton, 57–67. London: New Left Books, 1976.

Domanovszky, Sándor. *A szepesi városok árumegállító joga: Lőcse és Késmárk küzdelme az árumegállításért, 1358–1570* [The staple rights of the Zipser towns: The conflict between Levoča and Kežmarok to stop merchandise, 1358–1570]. Budapest: Magyar Tudományos Akadémia, 1922.

Edmonds, Albert Sydney. "The Henkels, Early Printers in New Market, Virginia, with a Bibliography." *William and Mary College Quarterly Historical Magazine*, 2nd Ser., vol. 18, no.2 (April, 1938): 174–195.

Eley, Geoff. *From Unification to Nazism*. New York: Routledge, 1992.

——. "Liberalism, Europe, and the Bourgeoisie 1860–1914." In *The German Bourgeoisie* edited by Blackbourn and Evans, 293–317. London; New York: Routledge, 1991.

Eley, Geoff and William Hunt ed. *Reviving the English Revolution*. London; New York: Verso, 1988.

Elias, Norbert. *The Civilizing Process*. Translated by Edmund Jephcott. Oxford: Cambridge, MA: Blackwell, ca.1994.

Engel, Pál. *Királyi hatalom és arisztokrácia viszonya a Zsigmond-korban: 1387–1437* [The relationship of royal authority to the aristocracy during the reign of Sigismund: 1387–1437]. Budapest: Akadémiai Kiadó, 1977.

Erdei, Ferenc. "A Magyar társadalom a két világháború között" [Hungarian society in the interwar period]. *Valóság*, no. 4 (1976): 23–53; and no. 5 (1976): 36–58.

Evans, R. J. W. *The Making of the Habsburg Monarchy 1550–1700*. Oxford: Clarendon Press; New York: Oxford University Press, 1979.

——. *Rudolph and his World*. Oxford: Clarendon Press; New York: Oxford University Press, 1984, ca.1973.

Femée, Martin. *The Historie of the Trovbles of Hvngarie*. London: F. Kyngston, 1600.

Fényes, Elek. *A magyar birodalom nemzetiségei* [The nationalities of the Hungarian Kingdom]. Pest: Eggenberger és Társai, 1867.

Fraknói, Vilmos. *Martinovics Élete* [The life of Martinovics]. Budapest: Athenaeum, 1921.

Freifeld, Alice. *Nationalism and the Crowd in Liberal Hungary, 1848–1914*. Washington DC: Woodrow Wilson Press; Baltimore, MD: John Hopkins University Press, 2000.

Friedrichs, Christopher R. *The Early Modern City, 1450–1750*. London: Longman, 1995.

Fügedi, Erik. *Kolduló barátok, polgárok, nemesek* [Begging friars, burghers, nobles]. Budapest: Magvető, 1981.

Furet, François. *Marx and the French Revolution*. Translated by Deborah Kan Furet. Chicago, IL: University of Chicago Press, 1988.

Gall, Lothar. *Bürgertum in Deutschland*. Berlin: Siedler Verlag, 1989.

Gellner, Ernest. *Nations and Nationalism*. Ithaca, NY: Cornell University Press, 1983.

Genersich, Christian. *Merkwürdigkeit der königlichen Freystadt Käisermarkt*. Kaschau: Franz Lederer, 1804.

Gerő, András. *Modern Hungarian Society in the Making*. Translated by James Patterson and Enikő Koncz. Budapest: Central European University Press, 1995.

Granasztói, György. *A középkori magyar város* [The medieval Hungarian town]. Budapest: Gondolat, 1980.

Greschik, V. "Die Belagerung Käsmarkt durch Emmericus Thököly" [The siege of Kežmarok by Thököly]. *Közlemények Szepes Vármegye Múltjából* (1923): 123–140.

Gyáni, Gábor. *Történészdiskurzusok* [Historical Discourses]. Budapest: L'Harmattan, 2002.

Gyáni, Gábor and György Kövér. *Magyarország társadalomtörténete a második világháborúig* [History of Hungarian society up to World War Two]. Budapest: Osiris, 1998.

Gyimesi, Sándor. "Frühkapitalistische Entwicklung und Spätfeudalismus in 16. und 17 Jh. in Ungarn." *Jahrbuch für Wirtschaftgeschichte* 2 (1987): 51–64.

——. *A városok a feudalizmusból a kapitalizmusba való átmenet időszakában* [Towns during the transition from feudalism to capitalism]. Budapest: Akadémiai Kiadó, 1975.

Hagen, William. "Crisis of the Seventeenth Century in Brandenburg: The Thirty Years' War, the Destabilization of Serfdom and the Rise of Absolutism." *American Historical Review* 94 (April, 1989): 302–35.

——. "How Mighty the Junkers? Peasant Rents and Seigniorial Profits in Sixteenth Century Brandenburg." *Past and Present*, no. 108 (1985): 80–116.

——. *Ordinary Prussians*. New York: Cambridge University Press, 2002.

Hanák, Péter. "The Bourgeoisification of the Hungarian Nobility—Reality and Utopia in the Nineteenth Century." In *Etudes historiques hongroises 1985*, edited by Domokos Kosáry, 403– 421. Budapest: Akadémiai Kiadó 1985.

——. *The Garden and the Workshop*. Princeton, NJ: Princeton University Press, 1998.

——. "Magyarország társadalma a századforduló idején" [Hungarian society at the turn of the century]. In *Magyarország története 1890–1918* [History of Hungary 1890–1918], edited by Péter Hanák and Ferenc Mucsi. Budapest: Akadémiai Kiadó, 1988.

Handler, Andrew. *Blood Libel at Tiszaeszlar*. Boulder, CO: distributed by Columbia University Press, 1980.

Harkess, Deborah E. "Shows in the Showstone: A Theater of Alchemy and Apocalypse in the Angel Conversations of John Dee (1527–1608/9)." *Renaissance Quarterly*, vol. 49, no. 4 (Winter, 1996): 707–737.

Herlihy, David. *Pisa in the Early Renaissance: A Study of Urban Growth*. New Haven, CT: Yale University Press, 1958.

Hibbert, A. B. "The Origins of the Medieval Town Patriciate." *Past and Present*, no. 3 (February 1953): 15–27.

Hillar, Marian with Claire S. Allen. *Michael Servetus: Intellectual Giant, Humanist, and Martyr*. Lanham, MD: University Press of America, 2002.

Hilton, Rodney H. "Capitalism—What's in a Name?" *Past and Present* no. 1 (February, 1952): 32–43.

Hobsbawm, Eric. "The General Crisis of the European Economy in the 17th Century: *I*." *Past and Present* 5 (May, 1954), 33–53; and "*The Crisis of the 17th Century: II*" 6 (November, 1954), 44–65.

Hohenberg, Paul M. and Lynn Hollen Lees. *The Making of Urban Europe, 1000–1950*. Cambridge, MA: Harvard University Press, 1985.

Hóman, Bálint and Gyula Szekfű. *Magyar történet* [History of Hungary]. 5 vols. Budapest: Királyi Magyar Egyetemi Nyomda, 1935–36.

Horváth, Mihály. *Polgárosodás, liberalizmus, függetlenségi harc. Válogatott írások* [Embourgeoisement, liberalism, struggle for independence. Selected works of Mihály Horváth]. Budapest: Gondolat, 1985.

Iggers, Georg G. *New Directions in European Historiography*. Middletown, CT: Wesleyan University Press; Scranton, PA: Distributed by Harper & Row, 1984.

Iványi, Béla. "Késmárkt város lakói és azoknak vagyoni viszonyai 1541-ben" [The social composition and wealth of the population of Kežmarok in 1541]. *Közlemények Szepes Vármegye Múltjából* (1916): 68–86.

Ives, Margaret. *Enlightenment and National Revival*. Ann Arbor, University Microfilms International, 1979.

Janos, A. C. *The Politics of Backwardness in Hungary, 1825–1945*. Princeton, N.J.: Princeton University Press, 1982.

Kann, Robert. *A Study in Austrian Intellectual History*. New York: Frederick A. Praeger, 1960.

Karády, Viktor. "Az asszimiláció Szegeden: szociológiai kérdésvázlat" [Assimilation in Szeged: A sociological inquiry]. In *Zsidóság és társadalmi egyenlőtlenség (1867–1945)* [Jews and Social Inequality 1867–1945]. Budapest: Replika, 2000.

———. *The Jews of Europe in the Modern Era*. Translated by Tim Wilkinson. Budapest: Central European University, 2004.

———. "Zsidóság és modernizáció a történelmi Magyarországon" [Jews and Modernization in Historic Hungary]. In *Zsidóság és társadalmi egyenlőtlenség (1867–1945)* [Jews and Social Inequality 1867–1945], 7–41. Budapest: Replika, 2000.

Katus, László. "A népesedés és a társadalmiszerkezet változásai" [Population and social structural transformation]. In *Magyarország története 1848–1890* [History of Hungary 1848–1890], edited by Endre Kovács and László Katus, 1119–1164. Budapest: Akadémiai Kiadó, 1987.

Kaudelka-Hanisch, Karin: "The Titled Businessman: Prussian Commercial Councilors in the Rhineland and Westphalia during the Nineteenth Century." In *The German Bourgeoisie*, edited by David Blackbourn and Richard J. Evans, 87–114. London; New York: Routledge, 1991.

Kerekes, György. *A kassai kereskedők életéről 1687–1913* [The life of the Košice merchants]. Budapest: Felsőmagyarországi Nyomda, 1913.

———. *Bepillantás Kassa régi céhéletébe 1597–1647* [A look at the history of the early Merchant's Guild of Košice, 1597–1647]. Budapest: Lampel Franklin, 1912.

Kertész, Andrei. *Hermannstadt in Siebenbürgen*. Sibiu: Verlag Terra Incognita, 1999.

Knapp, G. F. *Die Bauernbefreiung und der Ursprung der Landarbeiter in den älteren Theilen Preussens*. München: Duncker & Humblot, 1927.

Kocka, Jürgen. "The European Pattern and the German Case." In *Bourgeois Society in Nineteenth-Century Europe*, edited by Jürgen Kocka and Allen Mitchell, Oxford; Providence, RI: Berg, 1993.

Konrád, George and Ivan Szelényi. *The Intellectuals on the Road to Class Power*. Translated by Andrew Arato and Richard E. Allen. New York: Hardcourt Brace and Jovanovich, 1979.

Köpeczi, Bela. *Függetlenség és haladás: politikai gondolkodás a régi magyar függetlenségiharcok századaiban* [Battle for independence and progress: the political thoughts of the old Magyar independence wars]. Budapest: Szépirodalmi Kiadó, 1977.

——. *II. Rákóczi Ferenc az államférfi és az író* [Ferenc Rákóczi, the statesman and writer]. Budapest: Magvető, 1976.

Kosáry, Domokos. *Művelődés a XVIII. századi Magyarországon* [Culture and society in eighteenth century Hungary]. Budapest: Akadémiai Kiadó, 1996.

——. *Kossuth és a Védegylet* [Kossuth and the protection association]. Budapest: Atheneum, 1942.

——. *Kossuth Lajos a reformkorban* [Louis Kossuth in the Reform Period]. Budapest: Antiqua, 1946.

Kovács, Mária. *Liberal Professions and Illiberal Politics: Hungary from the Habsburgs to the Holocaust.* Washington, DC: Woodrow Wilson Center Press; New York: Oxford University Press, 1994.

Kowalská, Eva. "Das volkschulwesen und die Gestaltung der Bildung in den Städten der Slowakei im 18. Jahrhundert." *Studia Historica Slovaca* XVII (1990): 125–152.

Kriedt, Peter. *Peasants, Landlords and Merchants: Europe and the World Economy 1500–1800.* Cambridge; New York: Cambridge University Press, 1983.

Kubinyi, András. "Budapest története a későbbi középkorban Buda elestéig 1541-ben" [The history of Budapest from the late medieval period to Buda's fall in 1541] In *Budapest története a későbbi középkorban és a török hódoltság idején,* [History of Budapest in the late medieval period and the Turkish occupation), edited by László Gerevich and Domokos Kosáry, 7–240. Budapest: Budapest Főváros Tanácsa, 1973.

Kürti, László. "The Ungaresca and Heyduck Music and Dance Tradition of Renaissance Europe." *Sixteenth Century Journal* 14, no. 1 (1983): 63–104.

Langsam, Walter Consuelo. "Emperor Francis II and the Austrian Jacobins, 1792–1796." *American History Review* 50 (April, 1945): 471–490.

Liechty, Daniel. *Andreas Fischer and the Sabbatarian Anabaptists.* Scottdale, PA: Herald Press, 1988.

Lipták, Johann. *Alchimisten, Gottsucher, und Schatzgräber in der Zips.* Kesmark: P. Sauter, 1938.

——. *Geschichte des evangelische Lyceum in Käsmarkt.* Käsmarkt: Lyzealpatronat, 1933.

Lukacs, John. *The Historical Portrait of Budapest 1900.* New York: Grove Weidenfeld, 1988.

Makkai, László. *A magyar városfejlődés és városépítés történeti vázlata* [A historical outline of Hungarian town development and town building]. Budapest: Tankönyvkiadó, 1963.

Mályusz, Elemér. *A mezővárosi fejlődés* [The Development of Agrarian Towns]. Budapest, 1953.

Mannheim, Karl. *Ideologie und Utopie.* Bonn: F. Cohen, 1929.

Marczali, Henrik. *Magyarország története II. József korában* [The history of Hungary in the age of Joseph II] 3 vols. Budapest: Magyar Tudományos Akadémia Könyvkiadó-Hivatal, 1882–1888.

Marczali, Henrik. *Az 1790/1 országgyűlés* [National Diet of 1790/91]. Budapest: Magyar Tudományos Akadémia, 1907.

McCagg, William O., *Jewish Nobles and Geniuses in Modern Hungary*. Boulder, CO: distributed by Columbia University Press, New York, 1972.

Meinecke, Friedrich. *Cosmopolitanism and the National State*. Translated by Robert B. Kimber. Princeton, NJ: Princeton University Press, 1970.

——. *The German Catastrophe*. Translated by Sidney B. Fay. Cambridge: Harvard University Press, 1950.

Melton, Edgar. "Gutsherrschaft in East Elbian Germany and Livonia, 1500–1800: A Critique of the Model." *Central European History* 21(December, 1988): 315–349.

Mérei, Gyula. "Magyarország gazdasága (1790–1848)" [The Hungarian Economy 1790–1848]. In *Magyarország története 1790–1848* [History of Hungary 1790–1848], edited by Gyula Mérei and Károly Vörös, 213–323. Budapest: Akadémiai Kiadó, 1980.

Merrington, John. "Town and Country in the Transition to Capitalism." In *The Transition from Feudalism to Capitalism*, edited by Rodney Hilton, 170–195. London: New Left Books, 1976.

Mikszáth, Kálmán. *A Fekete Város* [The Black City]. Budapest, Franklin, 1910.

——. *A Noszty fiú esete Tóth Marival* [The Young Noszti's Affair with Mária Tóth]. Budapest: Szépirodalmi Könyvkiadó, 1968.

Miskolczy, Ambrus. "A szászok német nemzeti ébredése" [The awakening of the Saxons' German nationalism]. In *Erdély története* [History of Transylvania], edited by Zoltán Szász, 1346–1424. 3 vols. Budapest: Akadémiai Kiadó, 1986.

Molnár, Erik. *A Magyar társadalom története az Árpádkortól Mohácsig* [The history of Hungarian society from the rule of the Árpáds to Mohács]. Budapest: Szikra Kiadas, 1949.

Mommsen, Theodore. "Last Wishes, 1899." *Past and Present*, no. 1 (February 1952): 71.

Münnich, Sándor. *Igló királyi korona és bányaváros története* [The history of the royal and mining town of Spišska Nová Ves]. Igló, 1895.

Műnster, Sebastian. *Cosmographey oder beschreibung aller länder herschaftenn vnd fürnemesten stetten des gantzen erdbodens*. Getruckt zu Basel, 1588.

Nagy, Iván. *Magyarország családai* [Encyclopedia of Hungarian families]. 12 vols. Pest: Kiadja I. Friebeisz, 1857–1865.

Nagy, Lajos. "Budapest története 1790–1848." In *Budapest története III* [History of Budapest III], edited by Domokos Kosáry, 255–555. Budapest: Akadémiai Kiadó, 1975.

Nathan, Paul. *Der Prozess von Tisza-Eszlár*. Berlin: F. Fontane & co., 1892.

Némedi, Lajos. "Bessenyei György és a magyar művelődés" [György Bessenyei and Hungarian culture]. *Valóság* (1958): 80–78.

Nemes, Robert. *The Once and Future Budapest*. DeKalb: Northern Illinois University Press, 2005.

Németh, Béla G. "Az úri középosztály történetének egy dokumentuma: Herczeg Ferenc emlékezései" [A document in the history of the gentleman middle class: Ferenc Herczeg's memoirs]. In *Emlékezések* (Memoirs), by Ferenc Herczeg, 5–32. Budapest: Szépirodalmi Könyvkiadó, 1985.

Németh, István H. "Végvárak, városok, hadseregszállítók, 1526–1593" [Border castles, towns, and the transporters of troops, 1526–1593]. *Történelmi Szemle* 3–4 (2000): 203–244.

Nussbächer, Gernot. *Johannes Benkner*. Buçuresti: Kriterion, 1988.

———. *Johannes Honterus: sein Leben und Werk im Bild*. Bukarest: Kriterion, 1978.

Ogilvie, Sheilagh. "Communities and the Second Serfdom in Early Modern Bohemia." *Past and Present*, 187 (May, 2005): 69–119.

Ozment, Steven E. *The Bürgermeister's Daughter*. New York: Harper Perennial, 1997.

Pach, Zsigmond Pál. *Die ungarische Agrarentwicklung im 16–17. Jahrhundert: Abbiegung vom westeuropäischen Entwicklungsgang*. Budapest: Akadémiai Kiadó, 1964.

———. *Hungary and the European Economy in the Early Modern Times*. Aldershot, Hampshire; Brookfield, VT.: Variorum, 1994.

———. "Sixteenth-Century Hungary: Commercial Activity and Market Production by the Nobles." In *Economy and Society in Early Modern Europe: Essays from Annales*, edited by Peter Burke, 113–133. New York: Harper & Row, 1972.

Palcsó, István. *A késmárki ágostai hitvallású evangélikus kerületi Lyceum története* [History of the Lutheran Lyceum in Kežmarok]. Késmárk: Sauter Nyomda, 1898.

Pauler, Gyula. *Wesselényi Ferencz Nádor és társainak összeesküvése, 1664–1671* [Palatine Ferencz Wesselényi and his co-conspirators 1664–1671]. Budapest: Magyar Tudományos Akadémia Könyvkiadó-Hivatalában, 1876.

Paulinyi, Oszkár. *A középkori magyar réztermelés gazdasági jelentősége* [The economic significance of medieval Hungarian copper production]. Budapest: Sárkány Nyomda, 1933.

Peter, Katalin. "Hungary." In *The Reformation in National Context*, edited by Bob Scribner, Roy Porter and Mikuláš Teich, 155–169. Cambridge, NY: Cambridge University Press, 1994.

Peters, Jan eds. *Konflikt und Kontrolle in Gutsherrschaftsgesellschaften*. Göttingen: Vandenhoeck & Ruprecht, 1995.

Philippi, Maja. *Kronstadt: historische Betrachtungen über eine Stadt in Siebenbürgen*. Bukarest: Kriterion-Verlag; Heidelberg: Arbeitskreis für Siebenbürgische Landeskunde Heidelberg, 1996.

Pirenne, Henri. *Belgian Democracy, Its Early History*. Translated by J. V. Saunders. Manchester: The University Press; London, New York [etc.] Longmans, Green & Co., 1915.

———. *Early Democracies in the Low Countries; Urban Society and Political Conflict in the Middle Ages and the Renaissance*. Translated by J. V. Saunders. New York: Harper & Row, 1963.

———. *A History of Europe from the Invasions to the XVI Century*. Translated by Bernard Miall. New York: University Books, 1956.

———. *Medieval Cities: Their Origins and the Revival of Trade*. Translated by Frank D. Halsey. Princeton, NJ: Princeton University Press, 1925.

———. "The Stages in the Social History of Capitalism." *The American Historical Review*, vol. 19, no. 3 (April, 1914): 494–515.

———. *Die Fugger*. Frankfurt am Main: H. Scheffler, 1960.

Pólya, Jakab. *A pesti polgári kereskedelmi testület* [The Pest burgher commercial association]. Budapest: Athenaeum, 1896.

Probszt-Ohstorff, Günther V. *Die alten 7 niederungarischen Bergstädte im Slowakischen Erzgebirge.* Wien: Montan-Verlag, 1960.

Pukánszky, Béla. *Német polgárság magyar földön* [German Burghers on Hungarian Land]. Budapest: Franklin-Társulat, 1940.

Rácz, István. *Városlakó nemesek az Alföldön 1541–1848 között* [Urbanized nobles of the plains between 1541–1848]. Budapest: Akadémiai Kiadó, 1988.

———. *A debreceni civisvagyon* (An Inventory of the Debrecen Civics). Budapest: Akadémiai Kiadó, 1989.

Rady, Martyn C. *Medieval Buda: A Study of Municipal Government and Jurisdiction in the Kingdom of Hungary.* Boulder, CO: distributed by Columbia University Press, 1985.

Rév, István. "Local Autonomy or Centralism: When was the Original Sin Committed?" *International Journal of Urban and Regional Research,* 8 (1984): 38–63.

Rosenberg, Hans. *Bureaucracy, Aristocracy and Autocracy: The Prussian Experience, 1660–1815.* Cambridge, MA: Harvard University Press, 1958.

Roth, Harald. *Historische Stätten Siebenbürgen.* Stuttgart: Alfred Kröner Verlag, 2003.

Schneider, Johann. *Definitiones propositiones Wolffinae.* Lomnicz: 1769.

Schwartner, Martin. *Statistik des Königreichs Ungarn.* Pest: Gedruckt bey M. Trattner, 1798.

Scott, Tom. *Freiburg and the Breisgau.* Oxford; New York: Clarendon Press, 1986.

———. *Society and Economy in Germany, 1300–1600.* New York: Palgrave, 2002.

Sinkovics, István. "Útkeresés Mohács után: Az ország három részre szakadása 1526–1541" [The search for order after Mohács: The partition of the kingdom into three parts 1526–1541]. In *Magyarország története 1526–1686,* [History of Hungary 1526–1686], edited by Pál Zsigmond Pach and Ágnes R. Várkonyi, 147–222. Budapest: Akadémiai Kiadó, 1987.

Spengler, Oswald. *Decline of the West.* Translated by Charles F. Atkinson. 2 vols. in 1. New York: A.A. Knopf, 1934.

Szakály, Ferenc. *Magyar adóztatás a török hódoltságban* [Hungarian taxation during the Ottoman occupation]. Budapest: Akadémiai Kiadó, 1981.

Szekfű, Gyula. *Három nemzedék* [Three generations]. Budapest: Királyi Magyar Nyomda, 1922.

Szelényi, Balázs A. "The Dynamics of Urban Development: Towns in Sixteenth and Seventeenth-Century Hungary." *American Historical Review,* 109 (April, 2004): 360–386.

———. "Enlightenment from Below: German-Hungarian Patriots in Eighteenth-Century Hungary." *Austrian History Yearbook,* 34 (2003): 111–143.

Szelényi, Iván. "The City in the Transition to Socialism." *International Journal of Urban and Regional Research,* 8 (1984): 90–107.

Szelényi, Ödön. "Johann Genersich 1761–1823. Egy szepesi pedagógus" [Johann Genersich 1761–1823. A Zipser pedagogue]. *Közlemények Szepes Vármegye Múltjából* (1914): 1–74; and 113–140.

Szontágh, Daniel. *Iglói és Zabari Szontágh nemzetség származási története és oklevelei* [The history and documentation of the Spišska Nová Ves and Zabar Sonntag family]. Budapest: Emich Nyomda, 1864.

Szűcs, Jenő. *Városok és kézművesség a XV. századi Magyarországon* [Towns and handicraft production in sixteenth century Hungary]. Budapest: Tudományos és Ismeretterjesztő Kiadó, 1955.

——. *Vázlat Európa három történeti régiójáról* [The three regions of Europe]. Budapest: Magvető, 1983.

Teutsch, Friedrich. *Die Siebenbürger Sachsen in vergangenheit und gegenwart*. Leipzig: K. F. Koehler, 1916.

Tocqueville Alexis de. *The Old Régime and the French Revolution*. Translated by Stuart Gilbert. New York: Doubleday, 1983.

Topolski, Jerzy. *The Manorial Economy in Early Modern East-Central Europe: Origins, Development and Consequences*. Aldershot: Ashgate, 1994.

Trattner, Walter I. "God and Expansion in Elizabethan England: John Dee, 1527–1583." *Journal of the History of Ideas*, vol. 25, no.1 (Jan-Mar., 1964): 17–34.

Trevor-Roper, H. R. *The Gentry 1540–1640*. London: Published for the Economic History Society by Cambridge University Press, 1953.

Turóczi-Trostler, József ed. *Magyar Simplicissimus*. Budapest: Tudományos Ismeretterjesztő Kőnyvkiadó, 1956.

Várkonyi, Ágnes R. *Erdélyi változások: az erdélyi fejedelemség a török kiűzésének korában, 1660–1711* [Changes in Transylvania: Transylvania during the expulsion of the Ottomans, 1660–1711]. Budapest: Magvető, 1984.

——. "Gazdaság és társadalom a 17. század második felében (1648–1686)" [Economy and society during the second half of the seventeenth century] In *Magyarország története 1526–1686* [The history of Hungary, 1526–1686], edited by Zsigmond Pál Pach and Ágnes R. Várkonyi, 1273–1424. Budapest: Akadémiai Kiadó, 1987.

Verhulst, Adriaan. "The Origins of Towns in the Low Countries." *Past and Present* 122 (February 1989): 3–36.

Vörös, Károly. "A fővárostól a székesfővárosig 1873–1896" [From Capital to Royal Capital]. In *Budapest története IV* [History of Budapest IV], 321–524. Budapest: Akadémiai Kiadó, 1978.

——. "A magyaroszági társadalom 1790–1848" [Hungarian society 1790–1848]. In *Magyarország története 1790–1848* [History of Hungary 1790–1848], edited by Gyula Mérei and Károly Vörös, 473–600. Budapest: Akadémiai Kiadó, 1980.

Walker, Mack. *German Home Towns: Community, State, and General Estate, 1648–1871*. Ithaca, NY: Cornell University Press, 1971.

Wangermann, Ernst. *From Joseph II to the Jacobin Trials*. London: Oxford University Press, 1969.

Weber, Eugen Joseph. *Peasants into Frenchmen: The Modernization of Rural France, 1870–1914*. Stanford, CA: Stanford University Press, 1976.

Weber, Max. *The City*. Translated by Don Martindale and Gertrud Neuwirth. New York: Free Press, 1966.

Williams, George Hunston. *Radical Reformation*. Philadelphia, PA: Westminster Press, 1962.

Wittstock, Oskar. *Johannes Honterus, der Siebenbürger Humanist und Reformator. Der Mann, das Werk, die Zeit.* Göttingen: Vandenhoeck u. Ruprecht, 1970.

Wunder, Heidi. "Serfdom in Later Medieval and Early Modern Germany." In *Social Relations and Ideas*, edited by T. S. Aston, 273–294. Cambridge; New York: Cambridge University Press, 1983.

Index